A Certain Share of Low Cu

A Certain Share of Low Cunning

A history of the Bow Street Runners, 1792–1839

David J. Cox

 Routledge
Taylor & Francis Group

LONDON AND NEW YORK

First published by Willan Publishing 2004
This edition published by Routledge 2012
2 Park Square, Milton Park, Abingdon, Oxon OX14 4RN
711 Third Avenue, New York, NY 10017

Routledge is an imprint of the Taylor & Francis Group, an informa business

ISBN   978-1-84392-773-0 hardback
ISBN   978-0-415-62751-1 paperback

British Library Cataloguing-in-Publication Data

A catalogue record for this book is available from the British Library

Project managed by Deer Park Productions, Tavistock, Devon
Typeset by GCS, Leighton Buzzard, Bedfordshire

*Dedicated to the memory of Benjamin Robins (c.1755–1812)
whose unfortunate demise led indirectly to the writing
of this book, and in loving memory of my mother,
May Cox (1929–2009), who was an inspiration to me
throughout her life.*

Contents

List of tables

List of abbreviations

BL   British Library
CUP   Cambridge University Press
IUP   Irish University Press
OBP   Old Bailey Proceedings Online
OU   Open University
OUP   Oxford University Press
PP   Parliamentary Papers
TNA   The National Archives

Acknowledgements

This book has its genesis in a serendipitous discovery in Dudley Archives and Local History Service back in 1999, when I came across a reference to Bow Street 'Runners' being utilised in a local murder investigation. This mention caught my attention as I mused on whether or not this use of a London-based body of men was unusual. Little did I realise that it was to be the start of ten years of research.

During that decade I received help, advice and encouragement from a great many people. I would firstly like to thank all of the staff of the many archives and record offices (unfortunately too numerous to mention individually) that I consulted during the researching of this book – all of whom gave me a great deal of help and often pointed me in the right direction. I especially extend my gratitude to the archivists and staff at Stafford Record Office and the William Salt Library, who were without exception courteous and helpful. Much of the original research was carried out at the British Library and the National Archives, and I would like to thank the staff at both venerable institutions for their unfailing help and advice. I also paid several visits to the Metropolitan Police Museum in Charlton, and would like to express my gratitude to Steve Earl and Ray Seal for their unrivalled enthusiasm and extensive knowledge of their collection.

I was greatly encouraged in my Masters research by Dr Edwina Newman and in my PhD research by my two supervisors, Dr John Archer and Dr Laurie Feehan, whose comments and advice were much appreciated.

My thanks also go to the numerous leading experts in the fields of policing history and criminal justice history who gave me invaluable advice and help; particular thanks must go to Professor John Beattie and Professor Clive Emsley, both of whom have encouraged me to continue in my research over many years. Professor Beattie in particular has been extremely generous both with his time and with his interest in my research. Dr Robert M. Morris was a fount of knowledge regarding aspects of the early Metropolitan Police and the functioning of the Home Department, while my friend and colleague, Professor Barry Godfrey, has been an invaluable source of knowledge with his expertise in the historiography of criminal justice history.

The Internet has proved invaluable in my research, and I would like to extend a note of appreciation for all those who worked on the Old Bailey Proceedings Online project (especially Professor Robert Shoemaker and Professor Tim Hitchcock) and the staff of the British Library Nineteenth-Century Newspapers Online project. Without either of these wonderful websites, this book would have been considerably more difficult to research.

I would also like to thank the many friends who have expressed interest and encouragement in this project (especially my unofficial proofreader), together with those individuals who helped me with particular aspects of my research; my especial gratitude to Frances Bevan for information on her ancestor, George Thomas Joseph Ruthven.

Finally, and most importantly, I would like to acknowledge the unfailing help and encouragement that I received from my father, Frank, and my late mother, May, throughout the writing of this book.

Chapter 1

Introduction: revealing an 'Eleusinian mystery'

Introduction

The study of policing history has undergone a sea-change in recent years; no longer do we simply have 'traditional' teleological or linear accounts such as those offered by Reith or Howard, which largely ignored the centuries of policing history prior to the creation of the Metropolitan Police in 1829.[1] The subject has benefited from the attention of historians who hold a wide spectrum of views ranging from traditional and revisionist to pluralist.[2] This has led to a much wider understanding of the often complex issues involved in such research. Both macro- and micro-historical studies have been published, ranging from general overviews to histories of individual police forces, and while there has been an inevitable concentration on the situation within the metropolis, an increasing amount of research is now being focused on provincial policing.[3]

Within this panoply of studies, however, there is one aspect of pre-Metropolitan Police historiography that continues to be under-represented: the history of the small group of men stationed at Bow Street Police Office in the period 1748–1839.[4] These men headed the force that is better known today as the Bow Street 'Runners'. This term is somewhat misleading, as it is often used to refer indiscriminately to all of the ranks based at Bow Street Police Office.[5] The general term 'runner' as used when describing a messenger or minor member of an organisation dates back to at least the seventeenth century, but the first unambiguous reference to employees at Bow Street Police Office as such was in 1755, when a defendant in a trial at the Old Bailey was described as 'a runner of Mr Fielding's office to carry persons backward and forward'.[6]

One of the first printed uses of the term 'runner' being specifically applied to Bow Street is credited to the Reverend Henry Bate, in the form of a poem printed 5 March 1785 in the *Morning Herald*, in which he penned the following lines after the artist Nathaniel Hone (who had coincidentally recently painted a portrait of Sir John Fielding) accused Sir Joshua Reynolds of plagiarism:

What's Raphael, Guido and the rest?
Poor dogs, Sir Joshua, at the best!
If no idea bright
They lose – without Hone's demi-devil
Like Bow Street runner – most uncivil
Bringing the theft to light.

Senior Bow Street personnel never referred to themselves as 'runners', considering the term to be derogatory and demeaning. Throughout this book the term 'runner' is therefore used only when it appears in quotations, with senior Bow Street personnel always being referred to as Principal Officers in order to avoid confusion with other ranks.

There has been very little published research into this small body of men, especially with regard to their activities outside the metropolis.[7] Consequently, although the various other Bow Street forces are mentioned in passing, and the functioning of the Police Office from 1748 is examined in some detail, this book concentrates on the Principal Officers and especially on their work in the provinces of Britain in the period 1792–1839. A certain degree of comparison is also made with regard to their metropolitan employment during the same period. It provides a fresh insight into a previously under-researched area of policing history and will also hopefully help stimulate further research into pre-metropolitan policing, both in the capital and the provinces.

Much of the little that has been written on the subject of Bow Street Police Office has often relied on inaccurate interpretation of secondary sources, with little or no investigation of primary sources. This has resulted in a great deal of contradictory and often ill-informed opinion, illustrated by the coupled contradictory quotes below:

The Bow Street establishment originated from a number of shadowy figures, some of whom had criminal backgrounds and

who used their connections within the criminal underworld to act as semi-official officers of law-enforcement.[8]
They were men of unblemished character, proven fidelity and consummate bravery.[9]

The Bow Street 'Runners' […] were the tiny seed out of which the Metropolitan Police was to grow.[10]
In essence, the Runners themselves were perhaps closer to being a private police force than the noble precursors to the Metropolitan Police.[11]

In 1811 […] Britain had no police force.[12]
The Bow Street 'Runners' were a kind of national CID long before anyone thought of a metropolitan police force.[13]

Known to history as Bow Street Runners, they quickly proved their worth.[14]
We are not by any means devout believers in the old Bow Street Police. To say the truth, we think there was a vast amount of humbug about those worthies.[15]

The Bow Street 'Runners' more nearly resembled a disreputable private detective agency than a branch of a modern police force.[16]
The demeanour of the Bow-street officers was, without exception, such as might be expected from men who knew their duty, and had the full power to perform it.[17]

It is clear from the above examples that a great variety of opinion has been aired about the formation, use and effectiveness of the Principal Officers; indeed, it has been remarked that 'writing about them is almost as fantastic a task as writing about the Eleusinian mysteries'.[18]

This book aims to remove much of the mystery from this area of policing history. It separates myth from reality and fact from fiction with regard to many aspects of the history of the Principal Officers, and is especially concerned with their involvement in provincially originated crime, with a considerable degree of comparison being made between their activities in London and the provinces. Previous accounts concerning the activities of Bow Street have concentrated almost exclusively on events within the metropolis, the corollary of this being the misleading impression that the main, if not sole, focus of the Principal Officers' work was within the capital.

In an attempt to give a more balanced and less London-centric view of the work of the Bow Street Police Office, the book provides a detailed analytical account of the various roles and activities of the Principal Officers with specific regard to cases originating in the provinces in the years 1792–1839, thereby placing the Principal Officers firmly within the wider context of provincial law enforcement of the period. It also demonstrates the differences between the Principal Officers and the less senior personnel employed by Bow Street Police Office, and discusses their particular roles within the organisation.

Through detailed analysis of both qualitative and quantitative research data, it argues that the use of Bow Street personnel in provincially instigated cases was much more common than has been assumed by many historians. It also demonstrates that the range of activities carried out by Bow Street personnel while employed on such cases was far more complex than may be gleaned from the majority of books and articles concerning early-nineteenth-century provincial policing, which often do little more than touch on the subject.

The Principal Officers, memorably (though somewhat inaccurately) described by Leon Radzinowicz as 'a closely knit caste of speculators in the detection of crime', are throughout the course of the book clearly differentiated from the various other forces based at Bow Street, while many previously unknown aspects of their careers are investigated through a selective survey of provincially instigated cases in which they were employed.[19]

The book examines a wide range of primary documents in order to extrapolate contemporary views on Bow Street from a variety of sources. It also debates, through the use of contemporary sources that reflected 'popular' and private opinions of Bow Street Police Office, the changing nature of their reputation with both the general public and those in positions of authority, and discusses what effect such changes had with regard to their employment on provincially instigated cases.

It also provides a clear distinction between the Principal Officers and their less senior colleagues, clearly and precisely delineating who the Principal Officers were during any given year in the period 1792–1839 by providing a unique and accurate service record (see Appendix 1) of all Principal Officers between 1792 and 1839, with their respective years of employment and length of service as Principal Officers. Previous accounts of the activities of the Bow Street forces have invariably conflated or confused Principal Officers with other less senior Bow Street personnel such as Patrol Constables, and this has led to considerable misinformation being promulgated about their respective roles.[20] The confusion over the term 'Runner' has also meant that the Principal Officers have been accused of being involved in several corruption scandals that in fact should be laid at the door of less senior personnel.[21] The specific nature of the work of the Principal Officers has been ignored or underrated by many police historians, through a combination of confusion with the work of the various less senior Bow Street patrols and an often surprisingly unchallenging acceptance of several contemporary and later critics' viewpoints.[22]

It also places the provincial operations of the Bow Street Office and its senior personnel within in the wider context of pre-Metropolitan Police history. The research on which this book is based, although by no means a comprehensive survey of all provincially originated cases, goes some way to filling the lacuna, with over 600 cases involving Principal Officers being recorded and analysed with regard to the types of case in which they were involved; who employed them and why; how the Officers operated, including their interaction with local law-enforcement bodies; and how they were perceived by those who utilised their services.

The book concludes with a discussion on the legacy of the Principal Officers with regard to subsequent developments within policing. Bow Street Police Office and its personnel have long been regarded by many historians as little more than a discrete and often inconsequential footnote to the history of policing, leading to a partial and incomplete understanding of their work. This viewpoint is challenged in the book, which argues that in several ways the utilisation of Principal Officers in provincially instigated cases paved the way for important subsequent developments in policing, especially with regard to detective practices.

Geographical boundaries

The book treats mainland Britain, together with its small outlying islands such as the Shetlands, as one geographical entity (although England, Scotland and Wales are often referred to individually). Ireland (including what is now Northern Ireland) is for practical purposes treated as a separate country. Although Ireland became part of the United Kingdom of Great Britain following the Act of Union in 1801, in many ways it continued to be administered in a discrete manner – in particular its policing was uniquely complex and militaristic in nature, in many ways following a continental model, and consequently this aspect of its history is considerably different from that of mainland Britain.[23] The scope of this history is beyond the boundaries of this book, and consequently any cases that emanated from Ireland are listed as originating abroad.

The geographical area of the metropolis is defined for the purposes of this book as a radius of seven miles from Charing Cross, thereby corresponding with the area placed under the jurisdiction of the Metropolitan Police at the creation of the force in 1829. The boundaries of metropolitan London obviously expanded considerably during the period under discussion, but cases from the period 1792–1839 that occurred within the above boundary are not specifically discussed with regard to provincial cases. It is recognised that this boundary is perforce somewhat arbitrary in nature, but a reasonable and coherent limit needed to be created. The City of London is also excluded from the geographical area under discussion, as it had its own law-enforcement agencies. Throughout the period under discussion (and beyond) the City was regarded in this respect as separate from the rest of the metropolis, and as such lies outside the remit of the book.[24]

Sources

A comprehensive range of primary and secondary material has been referred to in order to gain an understanding of the types and location of cases originating in the provinces in which Principal Officers were involved (see the Bibliography for a complete listing of primary and secondary sources). The primary sources in particular are widely scattered and fragmentary, with many of the records apparently being destroyed both during the Gordon Riots in 1780 and in the move to the new Bow Street building in 1881.[25] This research is therefore based primarily (but by no means exclusively) on provincial and metropolitan newspaper reports of cases involving Principal Officers. These reports provided a framework from which to undertake further quantitative and qualitative discussions.

The role of newspapers in the reporting of crime

Both provincial and metropolitan newspapers of the late eighteenth and early nineteenth centuries devoted a considerable amount of their typeface to criminal matters. In London, metropolitan newspapers regularly reported on the proceedings of the Old Bailey and the other courts within the metropolis, while provincial papers often devoted several columns in each issue to important national or local trials. Provincial papers were not above unshamefacedly 'lifting' accounts of interesting criminal cases directly from the London weeklies, often not even crediting the source. Similarly, *The Times* was quite happy to reprint verbatim accounts of criminal activity from numerous provincial papers, usually, but not always, acknowledging the source. Then, as now, as Jeremy Black remarks, 'crime was a major draw in the press'.[26] Provincial papers in particular also carried numerous advertisements of rewards offered by victims or relatives of victims after a crime had been perpetrated, and these contained often quite detailed descriptions of the suspected offender(s).[27]

Despite the continuing growth of publication of newspapers, it must be borne in mind that due to their relatively high cost they were not readily available to the majority of the public. Many newspapers including *The Times* and provincial papers such as the *Staffordshire Advertiser* cost between 4d and 7d in the period under discussion, and were consequently too expensive for general consumption. Recent studies into newspaper circulation in a slightly earlier period (1771) suggest that 'well-established papers may normally have sold between one thousand and two thousand copies'.[28] The *Manchester Guardian* in its edition of 2 May 1823 proudly stated that it averaged certified weekly sales of 1,865. The extent to which provincial newspapers were circulated among the local populace is still not known precisely, but research by Ivan Asquith suggests that between 1.6 and 1.8 per cent of the adult population bought or read a weekly newspaper, daily newspapers being at this time almost unknown due to the limitations of transport and printing methods.[29] Current research suggests that around two-thirds of the English population were literate to varying degrees by the 1840s. This accords with one of the few statistical sources available from the period – see Table 1.1 overleaf:

Reasons for reporting cases

Those cases that were reported reflected the perceived interests of the various publications' readerships; as Jeremy Black states: 'the press was largely read by upper and middle-class consumers', and consequently 'the press reflected the interests and views of the

Table 1.1 Convicts' literacy rates, 1838

Convicts unable to read or write	35.85%
Read and write imperfectly	52.08%
Read and write well	9.46%
Received superior instruction	0.43%
Unknown standard	2.18%

Source: *Manchester Guardian*, 25 April 1838

middling orders.'[30] Cases that were considered of limited interest to the readership of the various publications may well therefore have been unreported in either national or local newspapers or journals. Conversely, cases involving high-profile and prominent people such as the aristocracy or well-known political figures often merited a considerable degree of attention. Sir Nathaniel Conant in his evidence to the 1816 Select Committee was of the opinion that serious offences, 'where they are of any importance, are universally known through the newspapers'.[31]

Then as now, sensational or particularly horrific cases often made headlines. Esther Snell's recent research into the crime reporting of the *Kentish Post* in the eighteenth century has suggested a high degree of editorial selectivity in the crimes reported, with particular emphasis placed on violent crime, which accounted for 67 per cent of such reports, and murder being the third most frequently reported crime.[32] Such research suggests that even in local cases, newspapers only reported crimes that it was thought would interest their readerships. Cases occurring in other parts of the country would have had even less appeal to provincial readers (or newspaper editors), thus making it unlikely that local publications would report such instances.[33]

Levels of under-reporting

The various newspapers consulted as primary sources for this book undoubtedly only contain references to a relatively small percentage of cases in which the Officers were involved.[34] Out of the fifty or more main newspaper sources consulted, *The Times* emerges as the most consistent chronicler of provincial Bow Street investigations, recording almost 200 of the 601 cases – just under one-third of the total number of recorded cases. Despite the recent availability of searchable online nineteenth-century newspapers, which will undoubtedly transform research into this field, the role of newspapers in the publicising and detection of crime currently remains under-researched; this is especially the case with regard to provincial newspapers.[35] It is to be expected that many more future research publications will take full advantage of this technological advance. The exact degree of under-reporting of the activities of Principal Officers is impossible to ascertain, as the definitive total number of cases involving these individuals remains unknown.

However, some idea of the level of under-reporting of Bow Street's provincial activities can be demonstrated with regard to the specific crime of poaching, as some evidence survives to provide a very tentative projection.[36]

Only nine such cases involving Principal Officers are reported in the utilised sources during the 48 year period.[37] By contrast, John Stafford, Chief Clerk at Bow Street, in his evidence to the 1823 Select Committee on Laws relating to Game, was specifically asked: 'In the course of your practice are many informations lodged in the office at Bow Street, for offences against the Game Laws?' He replied:

All the offences against the Game Laws, which are of an atrocious description, I think are generally reported to the public office in Bow Street, more especially in cases where the keepers have either been killed or dangerously wounded, and the assistance of an officer from Bow Street is required; the gentleman whose keeper has been assaulted, or some of the magistrates in the neighbourhood, generally send a report of the circumstances of the case where they require assistance from the office, and from such reports it is that I derive any knowledge I may possess with respect to these offences. I should think, [...] that perhaps the number of applications within the last two or three years, may have amounted to nearly twenty; they have been much more numerous of late years than they were formerly.[38]

This statement, when compared to the recorded levels of provincial poaching cases, suggests that there was a considerable degree of under-reporting of criminal cases in general, as there is no reason to suppose that this low level was unique to poaching – especially as such a crime was seen as a particular threat to the stability and power of the ruling classes who constituted the majority of the readership of newspapers.[39]

Development of *Hue & Cry*

From the time of the creation of the Principal Officers, the Fieldings were keen to publicise the Officers' existence in an attempt to increase the reporting and solving of crime (although, for obvious reasons, the Officers' individual identities were not widely circulated). Henry Fielding began the process with the short-lived *Covent Garden Journal*, which ran from 1752 to 1756, and his half-brother, John, continued with the publication of the *Public Advertiser* from late 1754, followed by the *Quarterly* and *Weekly Pursuit* in 1772.[40] On 3 December 1773 John published the first edition of *Fielding's General Preventive Plan or Public Hue & Cry*. The first edition claimed:

> the front page of this newspaper is stuck up in the Market Place of every Corporate Town from Cornwall to Edinburgh, by order of the mayors and chief officers of such corporations and also in some conspicuous place of the Public Road, by the Magistrates of the counties at large to which it is sent.[41]

Promotion of Bow Street Police Office through the publication of *Hue & Cry*

Even Bow Street's own publication, *Hue & Cry*, contains a total of only 136 provincial cases (an average of *c*.3.5 cases per year of available publication).[42] This relatively low level of cases seems at first to be somewhat surprising given the stated aims and objectives of the publication which are discussed below, but it must be remembered that for the majority of the period, the publication was simply a single sheet of paper folded once to provide four pages; only a limited amount of information could therefore be included within each issue.

The vast majority of *Hue & Cry* was given over to the advertisement of rewards for missing valuables and detailed descriptions of both goods and suspects rather than to accounts of the activities of the Principal Officers. Neither was *Hue & Cry* exclusively concerned with the provinces – much of the publication concerned itself with metropolitan crime, while the rear page was usually exclusively devoted to listing the names of Army and Navy deserters.[43] The publication also occasionally provided details of cases being investigated by the other London Police Offices.

The publication was often flagrant in the self-promotion of the Bow Street system of policing; for example, in 1809 it carried details of the robbery of the Whitehaven Bank, in which some £15,000 was stolen, remarking that the particular nature of the case 'renders it extremely difficult for any other than the Bow Street police to discover, explore and trace'.[44] The other constituents of the Bow Street police were also often praised for their effectiveness; in 1816 it referred to a case involving the Horse Patrol, 'whom scarcely any robber can escape', while in 1822 it reported that 'the Day Patrol lately established at Bow Street has already been of great service in clearing the streets of pick-pockets; the most experienced men of the Night Patrol having been appointed to this service'.[45]

It is difficult to establish to what degree this self-promotion affected the choice of cases referred to in the publication. The other London Police Offices are occasionally represented in the newspaper, but to a much lesser extent than the activities of Bow Street, and there is, perhaps unsurprisingly, no mention of failures or investigations into corruption involving Bow Street personnel.

There was increasing uncertainty among commentators on policing matters as to the practical effectiveness of *Hue & Cry* with regard to its use in crime detection. In 1825 *The Times* reported that during a case in which £500 was stolen, one of the barristers made reference to *Hue & Cry*, stating that:

> The *Hue & Cry* is not sold like other newspapers. It is sent by order of the Home Office or Chief Police Office [...] – to the men of law in town or country it was scarcely known more than by name.[46]

In a similar vein, Edwin Chadwick, no supporter of Bow Street, suggested in 1829 that the amount of cases referred to in each edition of the publication was a mere drop in the ocean of crime – he is quoted as saying that *Hue & Cry* 'served no other purpose than setting a man with a wooden leg to pursue a fox', and he was quite certain of the reason why:

> It was perhaps from some vague conception of the utility of publicity in all matters of police, that the *Hue & Cry Gazette* [sic] was instituted chiefly for the purpose of advertising property stolen, and the escape of offenders for whose apprehension rewards were offered. [...] It is never seen by the public, nor can we learn that it is ever regularly seen by the officers of the several police establishments.[47]

These views clearly contradict the advertised intent of the publication and, as it has been calculated that by the end of the period under discussion there was a total of over 3,000 magistrates in England and Wales who could all theoretically have received a copy of *Hue & Cry*, there appears to be a huge discrepancy between its stated aims and its practical impact.[48]

However, Chadwick may deliberately have been somewhat overcritical of the publication in order to further his own objectives (which implicitly included the disbanding of the Bow Street policing system). Henry Goddard, one of the best-known Principal Officers, certainly mentions *Hue & Cry* as being of use in his *Memoirs*; he refers to it on several occasions when checking lists of stolen property (the publication often carried comprehensive and exhaustive details of such goods). The 1818 Select Committee *Report* also mentions it favourably in the context of dissemination of information, at least with regard to more serious offences:

> Your Committee are of opinion that [...] the more enormous offences are at present rapidly published and circulated, by the diurnal press, the correspondence of magistrates, and the *Hue And Cry and Police Gazette*.[49]

That the publication of serious crimes in *Hue & Cry* was still seen as a common strategy of provincial law-enforcement bodies in 1839 is exemplified in the evidence of Mr Sadler, High Constable of Stockport, to the 1839 Select Committee on the Constabulary Force in England and Wales. He was asked what measures he usually adopted when he received notice of a serious felony and replied that he instructed local searches and investigations to be carried out, including interviewing all known local fences and suspects, but, if these investigations were unforthcoming, he stated that 'it may be requisite to send to the *Hue & Cry* in London, and advertise and adopt any measures that may be expedient'.[50] Sadler's evidence suggests that even at the end of the period under discussion, advertising details of provincial felonies in *Hue & Cry* was still considered to be a worthwhile activity.

Whatever the perceived efficacy of *Hue & Cry*, it has certainly been under-utilised in the subsequent study of policing history. It is of significant interest not just for the activities of the various London Police Offices, but for the considerable amount of detail that it carries about the formative years of the Metropolitan Police, and the interaction between existing law-enforcement agencies and the newly created force.[51]

Limitations of sources

Although the book does provide a certain amount of quantitative analysis of the number and location of provincial and metropolitan investigations carried out by Principal Officers, at no times does it claim to be a comprehensive or definitive account of all such cases that involved Bow Street – rather it has been deliberately selective in its choice of sources. Quite apart from self-imposed selectivity due to practical reasons, there are also several inescapable limitations to the primary source material.[52] There are, for example, very few extant copies of *Hue & Cry* available for the period between 1792 and 1801, and two of the main provincial papers consulted for the research, the *Manchester Guardian* and the *Staffordshire Advertiser*, do not cover the whole chronological period.[53] Many of the printed primary sources consulted are predominantly London-centric, although several of the online newspaper titles available through the British Library Newspapers Online website were provincially produced. Similarly, the use of the Old Bailey Proceedings Online (OBP) as the main source for metropolitan cases has limitations in that it does not provide comprehensive coverage of the Principal Officers' activities within London, and has the further limitation that only investigations that led to a trial are included, as opposed to the sources utilised for provincial cases, which may have not proceeded to trial.[54]

Consequently, the book demonstrates an awareness that an unequal bias exists within such sources in regard to the reporting of both provincially originating cases and metropolitan cases. Although this inevitably somewhat limits the degree of statistical evidence that can be gathered from the sources, it is demonstrated below that this does not negate their usefulness in providing numerous comparisons when studying the activities of the Principal Officers. Although extremely detailed in many respects, the OBP only deal with indictable cases that were thought too serious or complicated to be dealt with by magistrates. However, it will be seen below that the majority of the provincial cases involving Principal Officers did fall into this category in that they were felonies rather than misdemeanours, and that the *OBP* therefore provide (to a certain extent) a valid comparison with regard to types of offence and victim.

Origination of primary sources

The majority of the consulted primary sources other than newspapers were written or created by the ruling local or national elite, with only a relatively few accounts surviving from other levels of society. These accounts include the aforementioned autobiography of one of the later Principal Officers (not written until the 1870s, although often surprisingly accurate with regard to dates and incidental detail), and a fictionalised 'memoir' from 1827, purporting to be written by one of the Principal Officers but most probably written by either one of the more minor personnel at Bow Street or a Fleet Street 'hack'.[55] A few much shorter first-hand accounts of particular cases written by Principal Officers also survive, and these provide rare insights into how the Officers themselves saw their role and their duties.[56]

The potential bias of such evidence clearly has to be borne in mind when utilising such sources; for example, *Hue & Cry*, being the official 'mouthpiece' of Bow Street, was unlikely to contain much criticism of Bow Street personnel or their methods. Similarly, the various newspapers were published and edited with a specific readership in mind – one that was overwhelmingly middle- or upper-class – and this could have affected the selection of cases that were reported.

Secondary sources

Although the research for the book is predominantly based on a comprehensive analysis of selected primary source material, a considerable amount of secondary source material exists with regard to wider policing issues of the late eighteenth and early nineteenth centuries. Many such sources were consulted in order to examine how the provincial activities of Principal Officers related to and influenced (or were influenced by) other aspects of contemporary law enforcement, including developments within the metropolis.[57] Only comparatively few secondary sources deal specifically with Bow Street, with little of significance being published on the subject since 1982.[58] Less than a handful of these concern themselves directly with Bow Street and its personnel. Rather the majority are concerned with other aspects of policing or criminal justice history – and consequently do little more than mention Bow Street in passing (often inaccurately). Frequently, these sources were consulted as much for what they omit as for what they include.

Of such limited sources, the most useful in regard to recording a number of the provincial activities of the Principal Officers is also the earliest: the two-volume *Chronicle of Bow Street Police Office: with an account of the Magistrates, 'Runners', and Police*, written by Percy Fitzgerald in 1888.[59] These two volumes cover the entire period of

Bow Street Magistrates Court's history up to the year of publication, and include a considerable amount of detail about the key personnel, with several references to provincial cases. However, Fitzgerald's work was not written as an academic treatise, more as a series of anecdotal and sometimes confusing tales interspersed with the occasional personal comment. There is no bibliography, and references to Fitzgerald's source material are few and far between. He clearly draws on sources that have been subsequently lost, and this is often extremely frustrating as many of his assertions and observations cannot be verified through other sources.[60]

Neither does Fitzgerald satisfactorily separate the activities of the Principal Officers from those of the less senior personnel, although he does provide brief details of the various forces available to the Bow Street magistrates in a chapter entitled 'The Bow Street Forces'.[61] No chronology is included, and there is no list of Principal Officers provided. The book does, however, prove useful in providing supplementary details for several of the provincial cases mentioned briefly in other primary sources, and does give, as Anthony Babington states in his introductory essay to the 1972 reprint of Fitzgerald's work, 'a most valuable assortment of anecdotes and reports connected with the most famous magistrates' office in the world'.[62]

The next account of Bow Street Police Office was not published until 1932, when Gilbert Armitage wrote *The History of the Bow Street Runners 1729–1829*.[63] This book proved to be of very limited use as it is largely an abridgement of Fitzgerald's pioneering account, with little additional or new information added. It was not until 1956 when Patrick Pringle published his groundbreaking study, *Hue & Cry: The Birth of the British Police*, that any new research on the subject was forthcoming.[64] This book was the first to discuss and analyse in any detail how the Bow Street Office functioned during its existence, and although now somewhat dated in its approach, containing few references and an extremely limited bibliography, it remains one of the best general studies of the subject available, especially for placing Bow Street in the wider context of policing history. In the same year, Pringle edited a one-volume publication of Henry Goddard's four-volume unpublished manuscript and thus brought the only known extant autobiography of a Principal Officer to the attention of a wider public.

Unfortunately, although Goddard's *Memoirs* are extremely useful for their first-hand account of numerous provincial cases and for giving a flavour of the life of a Principal Officer, he only became a Principal Officer in 1834, having previously been employed at Bow

Street as a Patrol Constable from 1824 to 1827, then at Marlborough Street as a Principal Officer until he subsequently rejoined Bow Street, and therefore the book does not cover the earlier years of the period under discussion in any depth (although Goddard does make the occasional allusion to earlier cases not investigated by him).[65]

In 1969 Anthony Babington, a circuit court judge and an author of several books on aspects of legal history, wrote *A House in Bow Street: Crime and the Magistracy, London 1740–1881*. This was the first new account of the activities of Bow Street personnel published since Pringle's work (a second edition was produced in 1999, but is in fact a virtually unaltered reprint).[66] However, much of the book concentrates on the Fieldings' tenure at Bow Street together with the architectural history of the building, with little attention being paid to the provincial activities of its personnel. It contains little new research, drawing heavily on previously published secondary sources, and as such has little to offer in the way of insights or revelations as to the provincial activities of the Principal Officers. A short article appeared in *Police Review* in 1973, and at the time of writing the most recent book primarily concerned with Bow Street Office remains *Tales from Bow Street*, published in 1982. The book is written by an ex-Metropolitan Police officer in a very anecdotal and non-academic style; it simply retells a relatively small number of metropolitan cases, and spends much of its time discussing the post-1839 period.[67]

The above handful of books comprise the complete known canon of works dealing primarily with Bow Street in the period up to 1839; a considerable gap therefore remains in disseminated knowledge about the activities of Bow Street's personnel, especially with regard to the provincial activities of the Principal Officers.

With regard to secondary literature dealing with the wider issues of early nineteenth-century policing history, the state of research is much healthier; as Clive Emsley (who himself has done a great deal to improve the situation) states, 'the study of nineteenth-century policing is now fairly well developed'.[68] However, most writers on policing history, be they traditionally orthodox and Whiggish, revisionist or pluralist, have so far failed to pay much attention either to the specific conditions occurring at Bow Street throughout the period under discussion, or to the employment of the Principal Officers outside London, and consequently little research into this topic has been published in the past two decades. Earlier historians such as Leon Radzinowicz barely refer to the situation outside London, while many later historians, as John Rule states, 'purport to cover the period before 1829, but rarely give it much space and so end up presenting it as the *hors d'oeuvre* before Peel's main course'.[69]

Of those accounts that do deal at all with the period under discussion, the majority concentrate (as did many contemporary politicians) almost exclusively on the system in use within the metropolis: see, for example, Rawlings' *Policing: A Short History* and Critchley's *A History of Police in England & Wales*.[70] Admittedly, Critchley does go some way towards implicitly acknowledging this omission in his short chapter 'Self-help outside London', in which he remarks that 'throughout the whole of this period the Government not only remained indifferent to local affairs, but, as the Webbs put it "deliberately abstained from any consideration of them"'.[71] However, he then reflects the lack of attention generally paid to the provinces by devoting less than five pages to the subject.

Research such as John Styles' investigation into Sir John Fielding's attempts to improve the methods of criminal investigation and detection outside London and his account of the activities of a particularly diligent magistrate remain very much honourable exceptions to the rule.[72] However, there are signs that in recent years increasing emphasis is being placed on research into provincial policing matters. This has often taken the form of non-critical chronological histories of provincial police forces, but occasionally a more analytical approach has been taken, leading to greater academic focus on the subject.[73]

This introductory chapter has delineated the rationale, aims and objectives of the book. That there is a real need for a fresh and in-depth look at the functioning of Bow Street and its personnel, especially with regard to the Principal Officers' investigation of provincial cases, has been demonstrated by the brief analysis of the available primary and secondary sources.

The story of Bow Street and especially that of its Principal Officers is a complex and intriguing one, and contains many examples of courage, intelligence, duplicity and occasionally humour. The book is interspersed with numerous case studies that serve to bring the subjects of the book to life – many of the Principal Officers took part in exciting, dangerous investigations, calling upon their ingenuity, perspicacity and cunning. It is hoped that some of these elements are reflected within the remaining pages of this book.

The next chapter focuses briefly on the history of Bow Street Office, outlining its formation and development, before exploring in detail the role of the Principal Officers within the organisation, with especial emphasis on their provincial activities. It also deals with the numerous accusations of corruption within the Bow Street system, arguing that the Principal Officers have been somewhat unfairly vilified by many historians.

Notes

1 Charles Reith, *A Short History of the British Police* (Oxford: OUP, 1948), and George Howard, *Guardians of the Queen's Peace: The Development and Work of Britain's Police* (London: Odhams, 1953). Such publications concentrated heavily on the development of the Metropolitan Police as a logical progression from chaos into order, expressing the broad view that policing before the advent of the Metropolitan Police was universally bad and inefficient and that 1829 marked a distinct watershed in the creation of a professional and efficient police.

2 A concise and incisive comparison of traditional versus revisionist views on policing history can be found in Robert Reiner, *The Politics of the Police*, 3rd edn (Oxford: OUP, 2000), in which he summarises the respective views (referred to as 'cop-sided' and 'lop-sided' respectively) of traditionalists and revisionists with regard to the creation of the Metropolitan Police. The historical viewpoint has more recently swung to a pluralist one, in which certain aspects of both orthodox and traditional histories have been syncretised into a more balanced account of policing history.

3 For examples of fundamentally pluralist overviews of English policing, see Clive Emsley, *The Great British Bobby: A History of British Policing from 1829 to the Present* (London: Quercus, 2009), Clive Emsley, *The English Police: A Political and Social History*, 2nd edn (London: Longman, 1996) or Philip Rawlings, *Policing: A Short History* (Cullompton: Willan, 2002). Non-academic and semi-academic histories of individual forces abound; see John W. Reilly, *Policing Birmingham: An Account of 150 Years of Police in Birmingham* (Birmingham: West Midlands Police, 1990) or Maurice Morson, *A Force Remembered: The Illustrated History of the Norwich City Police 1836–1967* (Derby: Breedon Books, 2000) for typical examples.

4 Throughout the period under discussion the terms Police Office and Public Office were used interchangeably. To avoid any confusion, the term Police Office is used throughout this book, except for quotations where the term Public Office was originally used.

5 See the Glossary for a more detailed explanation of the complex structure of Bow Street's various forces.

6 Old Bailey Proceedings Online (OBP at: http://www.oldbaileyonline.org), September 1755, trial of Francis Pryer, John West, Edward Wright, Winifred Farrel, t17550409-25.

7 Professor Beattie has recently been carrying out research into the metropolitan work of the Bow Street Office. A book based on his research and provisionally entitled *The First English Detectives: The Bow Street Runners and the Policing of London, 1750–1840* is due in the near future and it is hoped that our respective books will together give a comprehensive picture of the Bow Street Office's metropolitan and provincial work throughout the period of its existence (J. Beattie, personal communication, November 2009).

8 R. C. Sopenoff, 'The Police of London: The Early History of the Metropolitan Police 1829–1856' (unpublished PhD, Temple University, 1978), p. 14.

9 F. Holmes Dudden, *Henry Fielding, His Life, Works, and Times*, two vols (Oxford: Clarendon Press, 1952), vol. 2, p. 768.

10 David Ascoli, *The Queen's Peace: The Origins and Development of the Metropolitan Police 1829–1979* (London: Hamish Hamilton, 1979), p. 38.

11 Clifford D. Shearing and Philip C. Stenning (eds), *Private Policing* (London: Sage, 1987), p. 81.

12 P. D. James and T. Critchley, *The Maul and the Pear Tree: The Ratcliff Highway Murders 1811* (London: Faber & Faber, 2000), p. xvi.

13 Editorial comment in Henry Goddard, *Memoirs of a Bow Street Runner*, ed. Patrick Pringle (London: Museum Press, 1956), p. 73. Henry Goddard served as a Principal Officer from 1834 to 1839 and is the only Officer to have had his memoirs published as a book. Originally written in the mid-to-late 1870s, the four-volume manuscript is held at the Metropolitan Police Museum Archives.

14 David Bentley, *English Criminal Justice in the Nineteenth Century* (London: Hambledon Press, 1998), pp. 4–5.

15 Charles Dickens, *Household Words*, vol. 1, no. 18 (Saturday, 27 July 1850).

16 Francis Sheppard, *London 1808–1870: The Infernal Wen* (London: Secker & Warburg, 1971), p. 37.

17 Samuel Bamford, *Passages in the Life of a Radical* (Oxford: OUP, 1964), p. 81.

18 E. F. Bleiler in his introduction to Anon., *Richmond – Scenes from the Life of a Bow Street Runner* (New York: Dover, 1976 [reprint of 1827 original]), p. vii. The Eleusinian mysteries were a series of highly secretive religious initiation rites carried out by a classical Greek cult in honour of Demeter and Persephone and have never been satisfactorily explained.

19 Sir Leon Radzinowicz, *A History of English Criminal Law and Its Administration from 1750*, vol. 2 (London: Stevens & Sons, 1956), p. 263.

20 Les Waters, a former police officer and member of the Police History Society, has carried out a limited amount of research in this field, but to date has not published the results of his findings. His unpublished material is deposited at the Metropolitan Police Archives; 'The Bow Street Runners: A Handbook of Police in London working for Bow Street and the other Middlesex Justices Act Offices 1750–1839' (Huntingdon: unpublished work for Police History Society, undated c.1992) has proved invaluable in researching this book.

21 Examples of this confusion include David Eastwood, *Government and Community in the English Provinces 1700–1870* (Basingstoke: Macmillan, 1997), p. 68, which states that at Cheltenham 'in the 1820s the Commission began to employ a regular police force of beadles and a night watch and, from 1823, the force was led by a former Bow Street "Runner"'. In fact the individual referred to was a former Conductor of the Night Patrol

rather than a Principal Officer (which in itself suggests that some of the less senior personnel at Bow Street were highly regarded by provincial law-enforcement agencies). Similarly, T. Critchley, in *A History of Police in England and Wales* (London: Constable, 1978), p. 43 confusingly refers to both Horse Patrol personnel and Principal Officers as Bow Street 'Runners'.

22 'Traditional' historians such as Reith and Ascoli were often scathing in their contempt for Bow Street's operations, considering that the Police Office and its officials were a byword for corruption and inefficiency. More recently, many revisionist and pluralist historians, while occasionally challenging some of these assumptions, have rarely seen fit to give Bow Street more than a passing mention in their respective histories of policing.

23 For a detailed and thoroughly researched investigation into Ireland's eighteenth- and nineteenth-century policing history, see Stanley H. Palmer, *Police and Protest in England and Ireland 1780–1850* (London: Longman, 1992).

24 Recent research has been carried out on the pre-Metropolitan Policing situation in the City of London by Drew Gray (University College, Northampton), summarised in his paper '*A Well-Constructed and Efficient System of Police'? Constables, Substitutes and the Watching Systems in the City of London c.1750–1839*, presented at the European Centre for Policing Studies Seminar, Open University, 1 July 2002, and further examined in his article 'The Regulation of Violence in the Metropolis: The Prosecution of Assault in the Summary Courts, *c.*1780–1820', *The London Journal*, vol. 32, no. 1 (March 2007), pp. 75–87. A doctoral thesis on the subject was also written in 1997 by Andrew Todd Harris: 'Policing the City, 1785–1838: Local Knowledge and Central Authority in the City of London (England)' (unpublished, Stanford University), while Donald Rumbelow's book, *I Spy Blue: The Police and Crime in the City of London from Elizabeth I to Victoria* (London and Basingstoke: St. Martin's Press, 1971) deals with a similar theme. One of the most comprehensive surveys of pre-Metropolitan Police law enforcement remains Elaine A. Reynolds, *Before the Bobbies: The Night Watch and Police Reform in Metropolitan London: 1720–1830* (Basingstoke: Macmillan, 1998), while Ruth Paley has provided a useful synthesis of her research into early metropolitan policing in her article '"An Imperfect, Inadequate and Wretched System"?: Policing London Before Peel', *Criminal Justice History*, vol. X (1989), pp. 95–130.

25 See Patrick Pringle, *Hue & Cry: The Birth of the British Police* (London: Museum Press, 1956), p. 201 and Anthony Babington, *A House in Bow Street: Crime and the Magistracy, London 1740–1881*, pp. 152–63 for details of the Riots. Regarding the destruction of records following the demise of the old Bow Street Office, see Babington, *A House in Bow Street*, p. 240. For a fascinating account of unruly crowds in the capital, see Robert Shoemaker, *The London Mob: Violence and Disorder in Eighteenth-Century England* (London: Hambledon & London, 2004), and for a specific analysis

of moral panics and public street violence, see Peter King, 'Moral Panics and Violent Street Crime 1750–2000: A Comparative Analysis', in B. Godfrey, C. Emsley and G. Dunstall (eds), *Comparative Histories of Crime* (Cullompton: Willan, 2003), pp. 53–71.

26 Jeremy Black, *The English Press 1621–1861* (Stroud: Sutton, 2001), p. 54.

27 The period under discussion was one of great expansion with regard to the publication of newspapers; the *Staffordshire Advertiser* of 18 April 1795 provides the following account of the number of newspapers printed in 1795: 'There are at this time one hundred and fifty-eight newspapers published in Great Britain and Ireland viz. 38 in London, 72 in the county towns of England; 14 published daily in London, 10 three times a week, 2 twice a week and 12 weekly.'

28 John Golby, 'Newspapers', in *Sources and Methods for Family and Community History: A Handbook*, vol. 4, eds Michael Drake, Ruth Finegan and Jacqueline Eustace (Cambridge: CUP/OU, 1997), pp. 98–102, at p.99.

29 Ivan Asquith, 'The Structure, Ownership and Control of Press, 1780–1855', in *Newspaper History from the Seventeenth Century to the Present Day*, eds George Boyce, James Curran and Pauline Wingate (London: Constable, 1978), pp. 98–116, at p. 100.

30 Black, *The English Press 1621–1861*, pp. 19 and 106.

31 PP 1816, p. 11.

32 Esther Snell, *Representations of Crime in the Eighteenth-Century Newspaper: The Construction of Crime Reportage in the Kentish Post*, paper delivered at the European Centre for Policing Studies, Open University, Milton Keynes, March 2005. Her research was part of a PhD thesis: 'Attitudes to Violent Crime in Post-Restoration England' (unpublished, Canterbury, 2005). See also her article 'Changing Discourses of Crime: Representations of Criminality in the Eighteenth-Century Newspaper Press', *Continuity and Change,* vol. 22, no. 1 (2007), pp. 13–47.

33 However, misdemeanours of extremely limited local interest were often published in local newspapers in the form of formal apologies or letters disputing another correspondent's viewpoint. Shane Sullivan has recently completed a PhD thesis on the subject of informal justice ('Law and Informal Order: Informal Mechanisms of Justice in Kent, 1700–1880', Canterbury, 2005) and his paper 'The Newspaper Apology as a Secular Penance 1768–1820', given at the European Centre for Policing Studies, Open University, in October 2005, discusses the use of newspapers for the informal settling of mainly petty disputes, suggesting that on occasion such a method could also be used as an alternative to a court appearance in quite serious cases such as assault.

34 For a full list of the various newspapers consulted, see the Bibliography.

35 John Styles provided a notable exception by concentrating on the advantages of detection gained through the advertising of crimes in provincial newspapers in his chapter 'Print and Policing – Crime

Advertising in Eighteenth-Century Provincial England', in D. Hay and F. Snyder (eds), *Policy and Prosecution in Britain, 1750–1850* (Oxford: OUP, 1989), pp. 55–112, and both Esther Snell's and Peter King's recent respective research have helped to reduce this paucity.

36 For an introduction to the history and influence of newspapers in this period, see Hannah Barker, *Newspapers, Politics and Public Opinion in Late Eighteenth-Century England* (Oxford: Clarendon Press, 1998), while a more general overview can be found in Hannah Barker, *Newspapers, Politics and English Society 1695–1855* (Harlow: Pearson Educational, 2000). Newspapers were not above creating interest in crime through the instigation of 'moral panics'; see Peter King's contention that newspapers could play a significant part in influencing public perceptions of crime (Peter King, 'Newspaper Reporting, Prosecution Practice and Perceptions of Urban Crime: The Colchester Crime Wave of 1765', *Continuity and Change*, vol. 2, no. 3 (1987), pp. 423–54) or Jennifer Davis's research into the newspaper-driven reaction to the garrotting and robbery of Hugh Pilkington MP in 1862 (Jennifer Davis, 'The London Garotting Panic of 1862: A Moral Panic and the Creation of a Criminal Class in Mid-Victorian England', in V. A. C. Gatrell, B. Lenman and G. Parker (eds), *Crime and the Law: The Social History of Crime in Western Europe since 1500* (London: Europa Publications, 1980), pp. 190–213).

37 It has to be noted, however, that a further nine cases also involved attacks on gamekeepers and that these cases are recorded under the more serious category of murder/attempted murder.

38 *Report from the Select Committee on the laws relating to Game*, PP 1823 (107) IV 260, p. 37.

39 The figures quoted by Stafford are of course the numbers of applications for assistance and may therefore be somewhat higher than the number of cases upon which Principal Officers were actually employed after receiving the approbation of the Bow Street magistrates.

40 The *Covent Garden Journal* was first published in January 1752 and ran until Henry's death. In October 1754 the *Public Advertiser* was introduced, continuing in various guises until 1794. The *Quarterly* and *Weekly Pursuit* were sent out free to justices of the peace on request.

41 *Hue & Cry*, 3 December 1773, Shropshire Archives QS 20/1.

42 For the majority of the period under discussion *Hue & Cry* was published on a weekly basis, but from the mid-1830s it became a thrice-weekly publication and eventually metamorphosed into the *Police Gazette*.

43 Despite this inclusion of a weekly list of deserters, Bow Street officers were never employed in the search for such deserters, and indeed were specifically dissuaded from doing so by the Bow Street magistrates.

44 *Hue & Cry*, 1 April 1809. In this instance, *Hue & Cry's* peroration on behalf of the superiority of Principal Officers proved justified – the perpetrators were successfully captured and tried.

45 *Hue & Cry*, 14 December 1816 and 16 November 1822.

46 *The Times*, 17 December 1825.

47 Quoted in Radzinowicz, *A History of English Criminal Law*, vol. 2, p. 461, and E. Chadwick, 'Preventive Police', *London Review*, vol. 1 (1829), pp. 276 and 280.

48 Carl H. E. Zangerl, 'The Social Composition of the County Magistracy in England and Wales, 1831–1887', *Journal of British Studies*, vol. XI (1971), pp. 113–25, Table 5, p. 93, and see Chapter 3, this volume, Table 3.4.

49 Goddard, *Memoirs*, vol. 1, pp. 12 and 33, and PP 1818, p. 23.

50 *Crime and Punishment Police vol. VIII* (IUP Reprints Series): *First Report on the Constabulary Force in England and Wales*, PP 1839 (169) vol. XIX, p. 109.

51 A concise history of the development of *Hue & Cry* can be found in Les Waters, 'Paper Pursuit: A Brief Account of the History of the *Police Gazette*', *Journal of the Police History Society*, vol. 1 (1986), pp. 30–41. This remains the only study of the newspaper yet published.

52 See the Bibliography for a full list of the various Home Department (HO), Metropolitan Police (MEPO) and Treasury (T) records consulted during the course of this research.

53 The *Manchester Guardian* was first published in May 1821, while the *Staffordshire Advertiser* began in January 1795.

54 In particular, the OBP only dealt in general with cases that originated north of the River Thames, cases that originated south of the river being dealt with at other courts including Southwark. However, at the time of the period under discussion, much of the South Bank and environs remained relatively undeveloped and sparsely populated when compared to the area to the north of the river. Consequently, the Old Bailey dealt with the majority of indictable crimes brought to trial in the capital.

55 Henry Goddard, *Memoirs* (four-volume manuscript, 1875–79), and Anon., *Richmond – Scenes from the Life of a Bow Street Runner*. The *Preface* to the latter work insists that there is no connection between the pseudonymic 'Richmond' and former Bow Street clerk, Mr John Richmond. This individual was sacked from his position as clerk at Bow Street Police Office in late 1825 because he did not 'suffer a sense of duty or propriety to restrain the gratification of his lust, or his avarice' (HO 60/1, letter dispensing with Richmond's services, pp. 208–10). This statement may of course be a deliberate attempt to further muddy the water as to authorship.

56 See Anon. (Samuel Hercules Taunton), 'A Reminiscence of a Bow Street Officer', *Harpers New Monthly Magazine*, vol. 5, no. 28 (September 1852), pp. 483–94, and HO 64/6 ff. 9–13, letter dated 13 December 1836 to Home Department from Richard Gardner, Principal Officer, as examples. Taunton's anonymously published article may well have formed part of a more comprehensive autobiographical work that has unfortunately never seen the light of day, and it may also have been the source of

rumours which have persisted concerning the existence of a further autobiographical work by another Principal Officer – unfortunately such a journal has not yet been found. For further information and suggestions as to the supposed author of these unfound memoirs, see Les Waters, 'The Bow Street Runners'.

57 For a list of the main primary and secondary sources consulted see the Bibliography.

58 There have been passing mentions in other sources since, including Elaine A. Reynolds, *Before the Bobbies: The Night Watch and Police Reform in Metropolitan London: 1720–1830*, and important journal articles such as Ruth Paley, '"An Imperfect, Inadequate and Wretched System"?: Policing London Before Peel', but these have all concentrated on other aspects of policing, and have not dealt specifically with the provincial activities of Bow Street Police Office.

59 Fitzgerald, *Chronicle of Bow Street Police Office*.

60 An example of this can be found at pp. 107–10, vol. 2, where Fitzgerald provides a long passage concerning a Principal Officer's reminiscence of a murder case of 1812–13; he is clearly quoting from a then extant source which I have been subsequently unable to locate.

61 Ibid., vol. 1, pp. 88–120.

62 Fitzgerald, *Chronicle of Bow Street Public Office*, Introduction, p. xxiv, reprint edition.

63 Armitage, *The History of the Bow Street Runners 1729–1829*.

64 Pringle, *Hue & Cry: The Birth of the British Police*.

65 Pringle's Introduction and editorial comments are also extremely useful in their own right – he was one of the first historians to attempt to place Bow Street Office and its personnel in a wider historical context.

66 Babington, *A House in Bow Street*.

67 Ronald Pearsall, 'The first Metropolitan Detectives: The Beginnings of the Bow Street "Runners" and Their Place in the History of the British Police', *Police Review*, no. 4208 (7 September 1973), pp. 1238–40; Joan Lock, *Tales from Bow Street* (London: Hale, 1982).

68 Clive Emsley, 'A Typology of Nineteenth-Century Police', *Crime, Histoire et Sociétés*, vol. 3 no. 1 (1999), pp. 29–44, at p. 42. For further research by Emsley on this subject, see *Policing and Its Context 1750–1870* (London: Macmillan Press, 1983), *Crime and Society in England 1750–1900*, 3rd edn (London: Longman, 2004), and *The English Police: A Political and Social History*, 2nd edn (London: Longman, 1996).

69 Radzinowicz, *A History of English Criminal Law and Its Administration*, and John Rule, *Albion's People: English Society, 1714–1815* (London: Macmillan, 1992), p. 30.

70 Rawlings, *Policing: A Short History*, and Critchley, *A History of Police in England and Wales*.

71 Critchley, *A History of Police in England and Wales*, p. 25.

72 John Styles, 'Sir John Fielding and the problem of criminal investigation

in eighteenth-century England', *Transactions of the Royal Historical Society*, vol. 33, Fifth Series (1983), pp. 127–49, and John Styles, 'An Eighteenth-Century Magistrate as Detective: Samuel Lister of Little Horton', *Bradford Antiquary*, New Series, Part XLVII (October 1982), pp. 98–117.

73 Analytical approaches to provincial policing include David Eastwood, *Government and Community in the English Provinces 1700–1870*, and John Rule and Roger Wells, *Crime, Protest and Popular Politics in Southern England 1740–1850* (London: Hambledon Press, 1997).

Chapter 2

'Men of known and approved fidelity': the development of the Bow Street system

Introduction

Although this book is primarily concerned with the provincial activities of the Principal Officers, it is necessary to contextualise the background within which the Principal Officers operated. This chapter therefore discusses how Bow Street Police Office functioned and the operation of Principal Officers within this framework. It details the ways in which they differed from other Bow Street personnel and also investigates the accusations of widespread corruption within Bow Street that were levelled by both contemporary and later commentators.

Formation and development

Henry Fielding is now chiefly remembered as the author of rollicking picaresque novels such as *Tom Jones* (published in 1749), but just a few months prior to the publication of his best-seller he had been appointed as a Justice of the Peace for Westminster, moving into his predecessor Thomas De Veil's former house at No. 4 Bow Street, Covent Garden, in order to carry out the duties of his new post. Magistrates at this time received no official stipend; theirs was fundamentally a voluntary post (although limited expenses were paid). Indeed, the prospective incumbent had to meet certain financial criteria in order to prove that they could carry out the duties of the post without having to profit from the imposition of dubious fines on those found guilty of numerous petty offences. By 1744 a magistrate had to have a financial qualification of holding land worth a minimum of £100 per year in the county on whose Commission of Peace the magistrate wanted to be recorded.[1] However, despite such theoretical safeguards, with almost innumerable opportunities available to unscrupulous individuals, many were still regarded as corrupt; contemptuously nicknamed 'trading justices', they were often seen as eager to line their own pockets at the expense of justice. On 3 July 1793, W. Upton, clerk at Hatton Garden Police Office, memorably wrote to the Home Department stating that, prior to the introduction of stipendiary magistrates at the Police Offices, 'Had a canine animal brought a shilling in his mouth with a label for specifying his complaint, a warrant was readily granted.' He was perhaps unsurprisingly at pains to point out that this was no longer the case: 'Magistrates now [...] are men of ability, strict integrity and distinguished humanity.[2]

Fielding seems to have gone to considerable effort to rectify the public's dim view of the Westminster magistracy in particular.[3] He claimed to have abolished many of the venal practices of the 'trading justices', bringing a sense of judicial authority and fair-mindedness to his magisterial decisions. In his *Journal of a Voyage to Lisbon*, he states that:

> By composing, instead of inflaming, the quarrels of porters and beggars (which I blush to say hath not been universally practised), and by refusing to take a shilling from a man who most undoubtedly would not have had another left, I had reduced an income of £500 a year of the dirtiest money upon earth to little more than £300, a considerable portion of which remained with my clerk.[4]

This claim may of course be little more than self-aggrandisement, but Pringle, one of the few historians to have investigated the early development of Bow Street Police Office in any depth, lends at least a degree of reinforcement to the validity of Fielding's claim, stating that 'after a thorough search I have been unable to discover the slightest evidence that Fielding ever took a bribe or any other illegal payment.'[5]

Whatever the exact degree of honesty employed by Fielding, he was unquestionably the prime mover in creating the force that was soon to be colloquially known as the Bow Street 'Runners'.

Six ex-constables of Westminster (together with a servant of Saunders Welch, the High Constable of Holborn) comprised the original force based at Bow Street, created in the winter of 1748/9. These men were again sworn in as constables for Westminster and their remit was to act as a professional detective body, investigating crimes in and around the capital under Fielding's direction.

Fielding was keen to have his embryonic force put on an official footing, and in August 1753, after a series of daring highway robberies had generated widespread fear throughout the populace of the capital, he successfully petitioned the Duke of Newcastle, First Lord of the Treasury, for £600 of government money to fund the continuation of the force, thus achieving at least semi-official recognition of his body of men.[6] From this moment on, the Home Department held the purse-strings and thereby assumed overall financial control of the operating of Bow Street, but the day-to-day functioning of the office was largely left in the hands of the respective Chief Magistrates (see Table 2.1 for details of names and tenure in office).[7]

Efforts to distance and differentiate Principal Officers from thieftakers

Thieftakers were individuals who operated privately without any official status or power – they attempted to capture suspected criminals in order to claim any reward money on offer from either

Table 2.1 Chief Magistrates of Bow Street, 1739–1839

Name of Chief Magistrate	Years in which office held
Thomas De Veil	1739–1748
Henry Fielding	1748–1754
Sir John Fielding	1754–1780
Sir Sampson Wright	1780–1793
Sir William Addington	1793–1800
Sir Richard Ford	1800–1806
James Read (refused to accept the knighthood that was normally conferred with the post)	1806–1813
Sir Nathaniel Conant	1813–1820
Sir Robert Baker	1820–1821
Sir Richard Birnie	1821–1832
Sir Frederick Roe	1832–1839

the state or private individuals. It was widely believed that many of them operated illegally by framing innocent people or enticing gullible persons to commit crimes for which they were then arrested, with the thieftaker claiming any reward that was offered.

Beattie remarks that 'the term thieftaker dates back to at least 1609 – John Pulman was labelled a thieftaker by a magistrate drawing up a recognizance', while Paley states that such thieftakers 'straddled the margins of the conventional and criminal worlds and formed, in effect, a sort of entrepreneurial police force'.[8] The majority of such individuals were London-based and did not travel throughout Britain in their employment.[9] They possessed no constabulary powers and those who operated in the provinces were confined to large towns and cities – for example, the *Staffordshire Advertiser* reported that in January 1801 the famous entrepreneurial industrialist, Matthew Boulton, after a series of robberies at his Soho Manufactory, 'procured some of the constables and thieftakers from Birmingham, to the number of twenty in the whole, who were well-armed, and concealed in the Manufactory' in order to arrest the offenders – but such thieftakers appear to have been localised in their operations.[10]

From the beginning, it is clear that Fielding regarded his force as more than mere thieftakers. While he may have referred to them as such in a convenient shorthand description in his *Journey of Voyage to Lisbon*: 'a set of thieftakers, whom I had enlisted into the service, all men of known and approved fidelity and intrepidity', both he and his immediate successor, Sir John Fielding (Henry's blind younger half-brother), viewed the Bow Street men as having a much wider remit than the infamous 'professional' thieftakers such as Jonathan Wild or Stephen McDaniel.[11] They were acutely aware of the public's extremely low opinion of such individuals, often forcibly expressed by contemporary commentators such as Edward Sayer, who, in his *Observations on the Police or Civil Government of Westminster with a proposal for reform* (1784), was concerned about

employing mostly thieves to take thieves, thus turning their own arts against themselves. In the present situation of the Westminster government this measure may be both prudent and necessary; but at no time, and in no situation, can it be either honourable or effectual; for surely the employment of professed and generally unrepentant offenders can reflect little lustre upon the administration of justice.[12]

The Fieldings went to considerable lengths to explain the difference between such individuals and their new force. Henry Fielding, in his 1751 treatise, *An Enquiry into the Causes of the Late Increase of Robberies*, answered criticism in the form of a series of rhetorical questions:

> I will venture to say, that if to do Good to Society be laudable, so is the Office of a Thief-catcher; and if to do this Good at the extreme Hazard of your Life be honourable, then is this Office honourable. True, it may be said; but he doth this with a View to a Reward. And doth not the Soldier and the Sailor venture his Life with the same View? For who, as a Great Man lately says, serves the Public for nothing? [...]. If to bring Thieves to Justice be a scandalous Office, what becomes of all those who are conven'd in this Business, some of whom are rightly thought to be among the most honourable Officers in Government? If on the contrary they be, as it surely is, why should the Post of Danger in this Warfare alone be excluded from all Share of Honour?[13]

Sir John Fielding, in his *Plan for preventing robberies within twenty miles of London, with an account of the rise and establishment of the real thieftakers*, published in October 1754, was equally at pains to correct any public misconceptions as to the honesty and trustworthiness of his 'set of brave fellows'.[14] He faced a difficult challenge, and he 'was forced to conceal the names of his four [*sic*] Bow Street "Runners" from the public for fear of reprisals'.[15]

During Sir John's career as Chief Magistrate at Bow Street (1754–80), he diligently continued Henry's campaign to gain greater acceptance of Bow Street Police Office from both a miserly government and a sceptical public. In *The Public Advertiser* of 17 October 1754, the following advertisement appeared:

> Whereas many thieves and robbers daily escape justice for want of immediate pursuit, it is therefore recommended to all persons, who shall henceforth be robbed on the highway or in the streets, or whose shops or houses shall be broken open, that they give immediate notice thereof, together with as accurate a description of the offenders as possible, to John Fielding, Esq., at his house in Bow Street, Covent Garden [...]. And if they would send a special messenger on these occasions, Mr Fielding would not only pay that messenger for his trouble, but would immediately despatch a set of brave fellows in pursuit [...]. It is to be hoped that the late success of this plan will make all

persons for the future industrious to give the earliest notice possible of all robberies and robbers whatever.

The 'Police Act' of 1792

Bow Street continued with its unique function until 1792, when the Middlesex Justices Act created seven other Police Offices all based largely on the lines of Bow Street Police Office. This Act, known to contemporaries as the 'Police Act', had far-reaching consequences with regard to policing within the metropolis. It fundamentally changed the way in which law enforcement was conducted by establishing a series of Public or Police Offices, with the system of trading justices being swept away throughout the metropolis (excluding the City of London) and replaced by stipendiary magistrates.[16] Each of the new Offices was to have its own contingent of Principal Officers, and these Officers could subsequently also be employed outside the metropolis, usually on notorious cases such as the 1828 murder of Maria Marten – better known as the 'Murder in the Red Barn', which involved James Lea of Lambeth Street Police Office – though to a markedly lesser extent than their colleagues based at Bow Street.[17]

With the passing of the Act, the perceived advantages of the Bow Street system were to some extent officially recognised (though the status of Bow Street was still not formally encapsulated in law).[18] No specific mention of Bow Street Police Office is made in the Act, but it is clear that the other Police Offices were created in Bow Street's mould:

Cap. XV That the justices [...] retain and employ a sufficient number of fit and able men, whom they are hereby authorised and impowered to swear in, to act as constables for preserving the peace and preventing robberies and other felonies, and apprehending offenders against the peace within the said counties of Middlesex and Surrey respectively [...]. That no greater number than six shall at one and the same time be so retained as aforesaid at any one of the said publick offices.

Cap. XVI The Receiver to pay [...] to the constables so appointed as aforesaid, for their trouble and attendance as aforesaid, any sum not exceeding twelve shillings per week, and any extraordinary expenses they shall appear to have been necessarily put to in apprehending offenders, and executing the orders of the justices acting under and by virtue of this act, such extraordinary expenses being first examined and approved of by the justices attending the office in which such constables shall have been respectively appointed.[19]

The functioning of Bow Street Police Office

The Police Office operated on three distinct but related levels. Firstly, it functioned as a judicial centre, being the site of a magistrates' court where people from the City of Westminster could bring or defend summary charges. Secondly, it acted as the hub of an executive law-enforcement system for its section of the metropolis (excluding the City of London), possessing an array of Patrols operating at various levels and in several locations in and around the metropolis.[20] Finally, it acted as the administrative centre where victims from throughout Britain could apply for the services of a Principal Officer. Such applications could be made either directly or through the intervention of a third party such as a local magistrate or the Home Department.

The small force of Principal Officers (never numbering at any given time more than twelve in theory and eleven in practice) was not the only means of law enforcement available to the Fieldings or their successors. Occasional Foot Patrols around the City of Westminster were taking place by the mid-1760s, and on 17 October 1763 an eight-man Horse Patrol took to the streets.[21] This proved short-lived due to the perceived high cost of maintaining it and within a year the experiment had been discontinued.[22] However, a Horse Patrol was re-established in 1805 by Bow Street Chief Magistrate Sir Richard Ford, and this force, which patrolled the areas around the turnpiked roads leading into London and which can be regarded as 'the first uniformed police force in England', continued under the aegis of Bow Street Police Office until finally being placed under the jurisdiction of the Metropolitan Police on 13 August 1836.[23]

Similarly, a more organised and permanent Foot or Night Patrol, operative during the hours of darkness in 16 districts of central London, was established in 1790 by Sir Sampson Wright, Chief Magistrate at Bow Street, and this continued in various guises until the advent of the Metropolitan Police in 1829. In 1821 a Day Patrol, often known by its official title of the Dismounted Horse Patrol, was created; this force operated in the area of the metropolis between the jurisdiction of the Horse Patrol and the Foot Patrol.[24]

To a large extent these forces acted discretely from the other systems of police available to the populace of London and Westminster (although they did cooperate when it was seen as mutually beneficial). This book is not the place to discuss the pre-1829 policing situation in detail, but by the beginning of the nineteenth century, there were just over 3,000 men employed in keeping the peace in the capital; *Jackson's Oxford Journal* of 9 October 1802 provided a detailed breakdown of the fragmented system (see Table 2.2).

Table 2.2 List of police personnel operating in the metropolis, 1802

City of London, Marshalmen, Beadles and Constables	319
City of London Watchmen and Patroles	803
City and Liberty of Westminster, Constables	71
City and Liberty of Westminster Watchmen and Patroles	302
Holborn Division, Constables	79
Holborn Division, Watchmen and Patroles	377
Finsbury Division, Constables	69
Finsbury Division, Watchmen and Patroles	185
Tower Hamlets, Constables	218
Tower Hamlets, Watchmen and Patroles	268
Liberty of Tower of London, Constables	17
Liberty of Tower of London, Watchmen and Patroles	14
Kensington & Chelsea Division, Constables	22
Kensington & Chelsea Division, Watchmen and Patroles	66
Borough of Southwark, Constables	88
Borough of Southwark, Watchmen and Patroles	79
Seven Police Offices, including Bow Street	150
Total	3127*

*It is interesting to note that the total number of police personnel is considerably more than the original complement of 1,011 officers that were walking the beat following the creation of the Metropolitan Police force in 1829. This force consisted of 8 Superintendents, 20 Inspectors, 88 Sergeants and 895 Constables (Martin Fido and Keith Skinner, *The Official Encyclopedia of Scotland Yard*, p. 184). This number had swollen to some 4,400 men by 1842, when the first Metropolitan detectives were employed.

Legal powers of Bow Street personnel

Despite being sworn in as constables for Westminster, all levels of Bow Street personnel, including the Principal Officers, had very limited powers outside the City and Liberty of Westminster, with few rights beyond those of private citizens outside this location for much of the period under discussion.[25] This situation changed only slowly and gradually throughout the first decades of the nineteenth century.

The *Twenty-eighth Report from the Select Committee on Finance: Police, including Convict Establishments* of June 1798 proposed that 'the Commissions of the Magistrates of the [...] eight offices of police should extend [...] over the whole metropolis, and the four above-mentioned counties [Middlesex, Surrey, Kent and Essex]'.[26] However, this proposal was not accepted, and by 1802 the Act of 42 Geo. III c.76 still only allowed jurisdiction within Middlesex and Surrey, with constables also prohibited from voting in parish elections.[27] This situation continued until 1814, when the Act of 54 Geo. III c.37 was the first to differentiate between Bow Street and the other London Police Offices, cap. XXIII stating:

> It is expected that the officers and patrol belonging to the said public office in Bow Street, should be sworn in as constables, and be empowered to act within the limits of the several counties of Middlesex, Surrey, Essex, Kent, the City and Liberty of Westminster and the liberty of the Tower of London.

This anomaly, which implicitly suggests that it envisaged that the majority of Bow Street's activities would occur in the immediate environs of the capital, continued until the Act of 2 Geo. IV 1821, c.118, whereby officers from all London Police Offices were given jurisdiction in all four counties surrounding the metropolis. However, in 1825 Bow Street was again singled out by the Act of 6 Geo. IV c.21 in which Bow Street Officers and Patrols were given the exclusive additional powers of a constable at royal palaces and a ten-mile radius around such residences.

With regard to their legal status outside the metropolis and surrounding four counties, Principal Officers were regarded as ordinary citizens. If directed by the magistrates at Westminster to investigate within the provinces, they had to apply to the respective local magistrates for a warrant to enable them to arrest suspects, and these warrants had to be served in person by the parish constable, as 'warrants were usually directed by the justice to be executed by a constable'.[28] To further complicate matters, if the investigation crossed county boundaries, the warrant had to be renewed or endorsed by magistrates in each such county.[29]

This long-winded and impractical requirement was still in force in 1829, when Edwin Chadwick referred to the business as 'an iniquitous practice'.[30] Principal Officer John Vickery was equally unhappy with the situation; in his evidence to the 1816 Select Committee he complained that:

> I have been obliged to wait and call in the assistance of a constable to execute a warrant. In felonies we are not constables to execute a warrant out of the county; and I have been put to great expense, where it would have been avoided, if we could have seized the party without waiting to apply for the assistance of a constable of the district.[31]

Similarly, Henry Goddard (the only Principal Officer whose written memoirs are known to survive) records in his *Memoirs* that in 1834 he had to engage the services of the local constable in an arson case in Oare, Wiltshire: 'The Colonel [a local Justice of the Peace] was of my opinion, and without a moment's hesitation gave me the warrant. Being thus armed I found out the Parish Constable, who accompanied me.'[32]

However, some warrants seem to have been issued directly by the Home Department, and as such appear to have been of sufficient legal standing to be served directly by a Principal Officer. In the Turner-Wakefield case of 1826 in which Edward Gibbon Wakefield had eloped to the continent with the young and impressionable daughter of a wealthy Manchester gentleman, the solicitor acting on behalf of the young lady's distraught father had obtained an English warrant for Wakefield's arrest in Calais, after the Secretary of State for the Home Department had been in touch with the relevant French authorities. There is also circumstantial evidence that on certain occasions Bow Street personnel did not allow lack of legal authority to stand in their way of making an arrest. Francis Place, a leading figure in the London Corresponding Society (LCS), remarks in his *Autobiography* that on 19 April 1798, 'the whole committee of the LCS were seized by a general warrant, or by no warrant at all, by some Principal Officers and King's Messengers [...] in Wych Street'.[33]

The situation regarding the obtaining and serving of warrants was clearly unsatisfactory and necessitated considerable cooperation and liaison between Bow Street personnel and the local parish constabulary and magistracy. If these institutions were ineffective, the efficiency of the Bow Street personnel could in turn be compromised and the investigation hampered. However, the situation was allowed to continue without modification, and this undoubtedly increased contemporary perception of an ill-organised and disparate policing situation, both within London and the provinces. An example of the often ludicrously complex nature of warrants can be seen in the report of a trial of 1801 held at the Old Bailey. Principal Officer John Sayer conducted a search of premises for stolen goods, but due to the location of the house had to be accompanied by Thomas Lawrence, a Marshalman of the City of London, who reported that 'I was with Sayer; I went in consequence of a warrant from Bow Street, backed in the City, to Haye's [*the suspect's*] house; the back part of the house is in the City, the other part is in Middlesex'.[34]

Differences between Principal Officers and other forces based at Bow Street

The various other forces based at Bow Street had one crucial and major difference from Principal Officers: they did not operate as a matter of course outside the metropolis; rather they were primarily employed to carry out their duties within the area of the metropolis, ranging from the inner City of Westminster to the turnpiked roads on the outskirts of London. The patrols were never intended to be anything more than a preventive force for the metropolitan area, and dealt primarily with the more mundane and less glamorous policing duties such as patrolling their 'beat' and discouraging and disturbing the activities of petty thieves and prostitutes, whereas the role of the Principal Officers was from the outset considered to be fundamentally detective in nature. Members of the patrols did, however, assist Principal Officers in several of the more high-profile investigations within London, such as the Cato Street Conspiracy in 1820, or similar cases in which a large amount of manpower was required.[35] Several of the Principal Officers began their careers as Patrol Constables and served a long apprenticeship – Stephen Lavender was a Patrol Constable as early as 1793 but did not become a Principal Officer until 1807.[36]

On a few occasions Patrol Conductors or (even more rarely) Patrol Constables were similarly utilised by Bow Street Police Office in provincially instigated cases. John Townsend stated in his evidence to the 1816 Select Committee that on occasion the magistrates were 'obliged to refer to minor officers – some of the patrol, and send them rather than the Public should be injured', and Sir Richard Birnie similarly informed the 1822 Select Committee on the Police of the metropolis that 'we can resort, on extraordinary occasions, to the patrol'.[37]

Even the gaoler at Bow Street (until 1836 usually a former Patrol Constable) was pressed into service on a couple of occasions. In November 1830, following the burglary of a pawnbroker's in Bristol, in which over £2,000 was stolen, Thomas Ford, Bow Street's gaoler, was despatched to investigate, being 'the only officer whose services were at the time available', while in 1838, Goddard records in his *Memoirs* that 'finding all my brother officers were engaged [...], I obtained Tyrol our gaoler'.[38]

Such distinctions between Principal Officers and members of the various Patrols seem at first sight to have often escaped the attention of the contemporary media, many of the consulted newspapers using the terms 'officer' and 'constable' interchangeably (often in the same article) when referring to the Bow Street forces. Similarly, various members of the Office were often collectively and indiscriminately referred to as 'Runners' in both the national and local press.

However, this appears to be more the adoption of a convenient and memorable generic term than a deliberate attempt to conflate the activities of the Principal Officers with the lesser members of the Bow Street force. In *The Times* reporting of the 'Blood-Money Scandal' of 1816, in which four Patrol members were found guilty of compounding felonies and illegally profiting from their employment, the newspaper went to considerable lengths to separate the perpetrators of the scandal from the reputation of the Principal Officers. The report states categorically that the accused Patrol members 'must not be confused with the Bow Street Officers, who are respectable persons; their names are Townsend, Sayer, Pearkes, Lavender, Vickery, Adkins, Taunton and Bishop'.[39]

The scandal revolved around the illegal activities of George Vaughan, a member of the Horse Patrol, who was convicted in September 1816 of conspiring with other members of the Patrol to compound felonies in order to claim the rewards on offer. Over a period of several weeks, Vaughan arranged for a number of burglaries to be carried out by unwitting dupes, who were then arrested by the Bow Street Patrol members who were lying in wait. That this illegal action was carried out with the connivance of several of the Bow Street personnel is not in question, but none of those implicated was a Principal Officer.

Vaughan himself appears to have been a Patrol Constable rather than a more senior Conductor of Patrol: a list exists of the names of Conductors of Patrol as at April 1815 and Vaughan is not among them.[40]

Relationship between Bow Street and the other Police Offices

The various other Police Offices enjoyed an often uneasy relationship with the Bow Street Office, employees of the latter considering themselves *primus inter pares* with regard to their colleagues in the more recent establishments. When John Stafford, Chief Clerk at Bow Street, was interviewed during the course of the 1816 Select Committee inquiry into the Police of the metropolis, he confidently stated that 'I beg to say that I consider our Officers a very superior class of men to some of those who are employed at the other Offices'.[41] When asked 'To what is it owing, that the Police Officers at Bow Street are of a higher class than at the other Offices?' he replied:

Owing to the carefulness observed in selecting and appointing them, and to their having a better school for instruction, and to their being brought up to regular habits. When a man solicits employment at Bow Street, he is placed at first upon the Patrol; and after having been there for some time, and his conduct being approved of, he may succeed to the appointment of Conductor, or perhaps be selected for an Officer, and that gives them those habits which are not to be acquired elsewhere, and operates as a stimulus to their exertions.[42]

This superiority, perceived or actual, undoubtedly caused a degree of friction between Bow Street and the Police Offices created in 1792. John Nelson Lavender, a Principal Officer at Queen Square (and possibly related to Stephen Lavender, a Principal Officer and Edward Lavender, a Bow Street clerk), had been a Bow Street Patrol Constable, leaving following a quarrel with Mr Bond, a Bow Street magistrate. He gave the following evidence at the 1816 Select Committee:

At the Bow Street Office I believe they are paid for every thing (with regard to expenses), and that very liberally; but they are under a different establishment from the other police offices [...]. I do not think, since I have been at Queen's Square Office, which is six years, that my payment for extra services has amounted to seven pounds.[43]

There appears to be some remnant of implicit ill-feeling in Lavender's reply, but his superior at Queen's Square, Chief Magistrate Robert Rainsford, in his evidence to the 1822 Select Committee gave a more dispassionate and generous view:

> The officers sent into the country from Bow street are officers of superior trust; there are four or five who do not attend at all to the regular business of the office; there is Vickery, and three or four more who are very experienced men; they are the principal persons sent into the country.[44]

Despite the rivalry and occasional display of bad feeling between Bow Street Police Office and the other Police Offices, there was a degree of correspondence between the organisations; although often regarded by both contemporaries and later commentators as existing almost in splendid isolation, Bow Street could not, and did not, operate in a vacuum. Consequently, Bow Street personnel, including the Principal Officers, did interact and cooperate to an extent with the other Police Offices.

Indeed, many of Bow Street's personnel began their careers at one or other of the Police Offices created in 1792. John Vickery served for a number of years at Worship Street Police Office before transferring (along with the Worship Street Chief Magistrate, John Nares) to Bow Street in 1807, while Henry Goddard, who started his policing career at Bow Street in 1824, was promoted to Principal Officer at Marlborough Street, and then returned to Bow Street in 1834 as Principal Officer in a move clearly considered to be a further promotion.[45]

The limited cooperation between Bow Street and the other Police Offices did occasionally extend beyond the various offices providing a career path for future Bow Street officials; there are a few documented cases where Principal Officers from Bow Street collaborated on investigations with Principal Officers from other Police Offices, but generally this was inhibited by an apparent mutual distaste for sharing information and personnel. The 1818 Select Committee had previously specifically commented upon this lack of cooperation: 'It appears evident to Your Committee [...] that little or no communication takes place between the different police offices, upon any regular system.'[46]

Sir Richard Birnie, Bow Street Chief Magistrate, made this lack of communication clear in his evidence to the 1822 Select Committee. When asked, 'Do the other offices dispatch their officers into the country in the same way in which the officers at Bow Street are dispatched?' he replied: 'I believe not; they sometimes do, but I think very rarely, send them.'[47] He then stated that he was fundamentally opposed to this practice for two main reasons: namely that firstly the other offices did not consult with Bow Street and that secondly the policing of London may have suffered if all the officers were absent from the other offices.

Social status and contemporary perceptions of Principal Officers

Only two known portraits of Principal Officers survive (not including a photograph of Henry Goddard taken much later in life). The first (in a private collection) is of George Thomas Joseph Ruthven, Bow Street Principal Officer from 1818 to 1839.[48] The anonymous painting dates from *c*.1830 and shows Ruthven posing in front of the Bow Street Police Office. He is elegantly and expensively dressed, with the look of a confident and successful self-made man-about-town, and is depicted holding his badge of office, a gilt-topped tipstaff. Ruthven's portrait corresponds closely to George Dilnot's later description of the Principal Officer – he is described as being 'a middle-aged, powerfully built man, with red face, sandy hair, and small expressive eyes, who invariably wore a blue coat and a black cravat'.[49]

Ruthven's great-great-great-granddaughter has stated that his descendants were made aware of his vocation by Ruthven and that he was very proud of his position as a Principal Officer.[50] It is impossible for an exact comparison between the Principal Officers and a modern detective police officer, but their rank would most likely equate to either Detective Chief Inspector or Detective Superintendent. Ruthven was one of the more active Principal Officers, and achieved a certain amount of contemporaneous fame for his part in the arrest of Arthur Thistlewood and his colleagues in the Cato Street Conspiracy of 1820.

The other is a portrait of John Townsend towards the latter part of his career as a Principal Officer and at the height of his fame. The portrait corresponds closely to two contemporary descriptions of the Principal Officer: Captain Gronow recalled Townsend as 'a little fat man with a flaxen wig, kerseymere breeches, a blue straight-cut coat, and a broad-brimmed white hat', while Reverend Richardson described him as being 'generally encased in a light-colour suit, knee-breeches, and short gaiters, a white hat of the breadth of brim and Stuart-shaped crown'.[51] It shows a Principal Officer as self-confident and sure of his abilities (if a little eccentrically dressed). Townsend was in some ways atypical of the Principal Officers; he was a personal friend of the Prince Regent and spent much of his time as part of the Royal entourage, as well as being employed by the Bank of England for ten days per quarter, for which he was paid a guinea per day.[52] He had served for many years at Bow Street as a Patrol Officer before rising to the rank of Principal Officer in 1800, and served for a further 32 years.

These images can be seen as representative of the self-perception of many of the Principal Officers; they were confident and sure of their ability, conscious that they occupied a position of considerable authority and celebrity, both within the metropolis and the provinces. They were very defensive of their elevated status within Bow Street – invariably referring to themselves as Principal or Senior Officers when defining their status in the press or as witnesses in criminal trials.[53] Several, despite having originated from working-class backgrounds, moved in 'high-society' circles, with Principal Officers being the only form of police allowed within the threshold of Buckingham Palace until 1838.[54] John Townsend is probably the best example of this rise in status – he appears to have begun his working life as a costermonger and coal-dealer, and ended as a personal friend of the Prince Regent.[55]

Several of the Officers appear to have felt the need to write their memoirs in order to record their deeds for posterity, although only one complete such document is known to have survived. Apart from Goddard, several other Officers including Ruthven and Taunton wrote about their lives and employment, but only Goddard's *Memoirs* and one short (anonymous) article by Taunton remains in the public sphere.[56] This suggests that they thought their work and lives worthy of recording, and was fairly unusual among working-class people.[57] Bow Street Officers also appear in numerous works of literature ranging from Dickens to Byron, and play a prominent role in at least one contemporary work of detective fiction.[58] In *Delaware: or the Ruined Family* by the prolific novelist G. P. R. James, not only is one of the characters a fictional Bow Street Officer, but the aforementioned George Ruthven also makes a 'cameo' appearance and is even given dialogue.[59]

Following the 'Blood-Money Scandal' the *Staffordshire Advertiser* remarked in an editorial that 'if we consider the classes and the habits of life from which police-officers are taken, it is absurd to expect in them a degree of integrity which we may safely trust with temptation'.[60] The advent of the Metropolitan Police did not necessarily change this view of the morals of police officers overnight; on 2 July 1836 the *Manchester Guardian* published extracts from a *Report* by Mr G. Samouelle of the Natural History Department of the British Museum, in which he unwittingly demonstrated middle-class prejudice, stating with surprise that visitors to the Museum included 'common policemen, soldiers, sailors, artillery men, livery servants, and of course, occasional mechanics, but their good conduct I was very much pleased to see'. Peel himself was concerned that the Metropolitan Police were seen as respectable individuals, and was congratulated by Wellington in having succeeded in this aim in a letter dated 3 November 1829: 'I congratulate you upon the entire success of the Police in London. It is impossible to see anything more respectable than they are'.[61] However, Peel was equally certain that he did not want the working class to permeate into the upper echelons of the force; he wrote in his reply to Wellington on 5 November 1829 that 'the chief danger of the function of the new system will be, if it is made a job, if gentlemen's servants and so forth are placed in the higher offices. I must frame regulations to guard against this as effectually as I can.'

Although the Principal Officers were not involved with the 'Blood-Money' scandal, they were often drawn from the ranks of the working class that were so denigrated by the *Staffordshire Advertiser* or Peel. Several of the Principal Officers originated from working-class backgrounds: Goddard, Leadbitter and Gardner are respectively recorded as being a fishmonger, a gardener and a servant to the Duke of Bedford before joining Bow Street's ranks as Patrol Constables, but such men later moved regularly and easily among members of both the gentry and the aristocracy.[62]

The *Staffordshire Advertiser's* comments are clearly more a reflection on the prevailing attitude to the working classes than an objective viewpoint, but such general condemnation did not make it easy for the senior personnel at Bow Street to regain the public's trust, and did little to enhance Bow Street's reputation in the eyes of the respective Select Committees that investigated the policing situation within London.

Numerous contemporary and later commentators have been quick to point out the shortcomings of both the Bow Street system and individual Officers, especially the opportunities available for corrupt officials to line their own pockets. Several contemporaneous censorial terms for Bow Street officials existed, ranging from 'runners' to 'myrmidons', while Francis Grose's *Lexicon Balatronicum*, originally published in 1785, records the use of the word 'pig' to specifically describe a Bow Street Officer.[63] They were known as myrmidons from as early as 1754, when a letter from a clerk of the Privy Council contained the following: 'Mr Justice Fielding sent for me yesterday, and put into my hands the enclosed petition, to himself, from his six myrmidons.'[64]

However, the majority of this disapprobation appears to have been reserved for the system rather than being directed at individual Officers employed by Bow Street. That their collective reputation was severely (if unfairly) damaged by both the 1816 'Blood-Money' scandal and the findings of the 1828 Select Committee *Report* is undeniable, but what is perhaps surprising, given the unfavourable nature of much later commentary about the Officers, is that by the beginning of the nineteenth century, the Principal Officers seem to have carved a generally favourable reputation for themselves among at least some of their contemporaries (admittedly usually those who benefited from their services or presence), with several sources such as those detailed below illustrating that many of the Officers were held in high regard by those who had dealings with them.

There are numerous references to the good character and standing of Officers throughout the period under discussion, the following being just a sample of such testimonials. In 1796 William Anthony is referred to in a Home Department missive as 'a person of a sober and steady behaviour'.[65] In January 1812, the *Leeds Mercury* reported Mr Sheridan MP as stating that 'the Bow Street officers were an honest and meritorious class of men', while *The Times* reported in 1818, following the successful prosecution of a burglary suspect in Middleton, Northamptonshire that 'the county magistrates, in admiration of the zeal, intelligence, and courage of Lavender, have resolved to give him a very handsome reward', after he arrested five people 'with extraordinary celerity and resolution'.[66] On 24 January 1832 Henry Fall was appointed as Bow Street Officer, being a former Metropolitan Police officer and described in an official memo as 'a man of respectable connexions and high character'.[67]

In 1834 a letter from the employer of an attacked gamekeeper praised the efforts of Ballard: 'William Ballard conducted himself very well and has been as active as he could', while on 25 April 1836 a testimonial letter concerning James John Smith, who was retiring through ill-health, stated that he conducted himself throughout his career 'with great zeal and intelligence [...] a most efficient and useful officer'.[68] Provincial magistrates also occasionally wrote to Bow Street to commend the Police Office on the behaviour of its staff; such a letter is recorded by Goddard in his *Memoirs*.[69] Such glowing reports do not fit easily with many later historians' viewpoint of Bow Street being a byword for corruption and inefficiency.

Further circumstantial evidence in the form of the Officers' post-Bow Street careers points to certain Officers being held in high regard by their contemporaries in the provinces. Goddard became Chief Constable of Northamptonshire upon his leaving Bow Street in late 1839, while Lavender was appointed Deputy Constable of Manchester Police in 1821, indicating that these two Officers were considered efficient and able.[70] Both John Vickery and Harry Adkins became Governor of Cold Bath Fields House of Correction upon their retirement, while Harry Adkins' elder brother William became Governor of Warwick Gaol. Vickery was certainly a favourite with John Nares, magistrate of Worship Street Police Office, and followed him from Worship Street when Nares was appointed magistrate at Bow Street. He was described by John Stafford, Chief Clerk and magistrate at Bow Street, in his evidence to the 1823 Select Committee on Game Laws, as 'a very intelligent Officer'.[71]

Similarly, Robert Rainsford, magistrate at Queen's Square, in his evidence to the 1822 Select Committee remarked that 'there is Vickery, and three or four more, who are very experienced men; they are the principal persons sent into the country'.[72] Daniel Bishop, despite the furore over the Warwick Bank incident toward the end of his career, seems to have been a clever and resourceful Officer; regarded as an expert on poaching matters, he was selected to give evidence on the subject to the 1823 Select Committee, while George Ruthven was one of the handful of Officers whose death was deemed worthy of an obituary in the *Gentleman's Magazine*.[73] The radical Samuel Bamford, not an individual to be easily impressed by authority, recorded favourable impressions of his dealings with Bow Street, in stark contrast to his treatment at the hands of the Manchester Police:

> The demeanour of the Bow Street officers was, without exception, such as might be expected from men who knew their duty, and had the full power to perform it. It presented a striking contrast to the conduct which was at that time generally practised by men of the same station at Manchester.[74]

The post of Principal Officer was also viewed with some awe and fear by those who had dealings with them; this is exemplified by Mr E. Brown, a surgeon charged with conspiring to engrave false bank notes, who was arrested by Samuel Taunton who told him that 'you must come with me. I am a Bow Street Officer'. The suspect is reported to have stated somewhat melodramatically, 'Then I am a dead man'.[75] This level of notoriety was undoubtedly used by provincial employers of the Principal Officers in order to impress upon the local populace that a matter was being taken extremely seriously. In 1804, Lord Hawkesbury wrote to Bow Street, requesting the services of two of the 'most knowing and most known officers from your office' in order to attend the election hustings in Brentford, and his use of the phrase 'most known officers' indicates that one of the purposes of their employment was that they should be seen around Brentford and their presence remarked upon.[76] Similarly, in a request for Bow Street officers in order to quell prospective rioting in Buckinghamshire by the 'Northamptonshire Nutters', the Warden of New College, Oxford stated that 'one or two officers from Bow Street would be quite sufficient: it is not the number but the name; the circumstances of an officer from Bow Street being on the spot will inspire the rioters with terror'.[77]

The fact that there were only 35 Principal Officers in service in total over the period of 48 years covered by this book also suggests that the Officers were regarded as efficient in their work by their employers.[78] It is also significant that no Principal Officer was ever sacked from his post (with the temporary exception of Daniel Bishop, as discussed below), and although isolated cases where Officers were reprimanded for minor lapses of behaviour are recorded, such reprimands remained very much the exception.[79] The lack of recorded disciplinary measures against Principal Officers is not of course conclusive evidence of either their efficacy or probity, but with the numerous changes of both Chief Magistrate and Secretary of State for the Home Department over the period, it does suggest that both the magistrates and the government were on the whole happy with the standard of Principal Officers.

The Warwick Bank incident

However, there were occasional scandals that threatened to undermine this generally favourable view of the Principal Officers. The 'Blood-Money Scandal' of 1816 undoubtedly adversely affected public opinion, despite no Principal Officer being involved, while the only case in which a Principal Officer (as opposed to other Bow Street personnel) was found guilty of either complicity or corruption generated considerable contemporary interest.[80] In December 1827, a large amount of money was stolen from the Warwick Bank. An arrest was soon made and much of the money was recovered after a series of negotiations between the Bank and the thieves. The case aroused considerable attention from the national press, and on 8 December 1827 the following comments appeared in *The Times*:

> The name of the negotiator is not concealed; he holds some character for activity and intelligence; but when the present transaction is compared with one of a similar description that took place not a hundred miles from Ludgate Hill, some years ago, and in which his name was involved in a very unofficer-like manner, something more than a doubting credence is attached to it. [...] The above are the facts most positively circulated, and, should the noble secretary of the head of the Home Department wish to know who this honest officer is; he can easily obtain the information by asking any of his corps.[81]

The Home Office circulated a letter on 4 December 1827 to the Mayor of Whitehall, which resulted in the following circular being sent by Samuel March Phillips (Under-Secretary of State at the Home Department) to each of the head magistrates at the various Police Offices:

> Gentlemen, a statement, as you are aware, has been for some days past generally and confidently made, that after a robbery of great magnitude of property belonging to the Warwick bank, the property so lost has been recovered through the agency of a police officer, who is charged with being guilty of compounding a felony [...]. His Lordship [Lord Lansdowne, Secretary of State for the Home Department] desires you will immediately make a strict inquiry into the conduct of your officers with reference to such imputation, and that you will report the results of your inquiry to me for his Lordship's information.[82]

The Principal Officer involved, Daniel Bishop, was accused of acting in complicity with the thieves and the Bank in order to recover the bulk of the stolen money. Bishop had already been the subject of allegations of corruption; a damning letter purporting to be from an alleged burglar, John Ingram, was published in *The Times* of 7 April 1825: 'Mr Bishop of Bow Street, is very learnt, and if you don't understand this, he will explain. He takes a fee for his opinion, like all others connected with the law.'

A letter dated 10 April 1828 details the results of the inquiry into Bishop's conduct, and found him guilty of giving money to Ikey Solomons (a notorious fence with criminal connections):

> As Mr Peel considers Bishop to be unworthy of trust and as he deems it absolutely necessary that a public example should be made which may operate as a warning to other officers, he desires that you will forthwith dismiss Bishop from his situation as a police officer.[83]

The letter is also extremely critical of magistrates at Bow Street, with G. R. Minshull being particularly roundly criticised, the letter rhetorically asking 'what control can there be on the part of the magistrates over their subordinate officers, or what knowledge can the magistrates have of the real state of crime in the metropolis?'.[84] Bishop petitioned for his reinstatement, but in a letter dated 15 April, Peel stated that he could not consider reinstating him because:

> Mr Peel strongly suspects that he so acted, and on reviewing the whole of the case, thinks there was such gross negligence in his conduct, as shows him to be very unfit for his office. Mr Peel considers an example, of this kind, more especially necessary, in the present state of the police.[85]

The Warwick Bank incident sparked a major inquiry into the past behaviour of Principal Officers and magistrates with regard to the recovery of large sums of stolen money. Stephen Lavender was contacted and he gave evidence 'respecting every instance in which officers of police either with or without the concurrence of the magistrates were concerned in the recovery of stolen property on the payment of a certain sum of money'.[86]

Another letter followed dated 18 April 1828 and addressed to Sir Richard Birnie regarding the conduct of Lavender in a transaction 'which is represented to have taken place about Christmas of the year 1819 or 1820'.[87] Lavender admitted to receiving £400 with which he paid for the return of stolen goods, but he claimed that he had the full support of Mr Stafford, Principal Clerk, and Sir Richard Birnie, Chief Magistrate, and 'that what took place was with his [Birnie's] concurrence and approbation'.[88] Lavender denied keeping any part of the money but admitted to claiming expenses for his trouble. He also stated that 'instances of this kind were at that time by no means infrequent at Bow Street and that every person, connected with the office was perfectly connivant of the fact'.[89]

In a letter dated 10 July 1828, Peel demands to know the truth of this statement from Birnie, stating that 'many police officers appear to have been implicated in transactions similar to that proved against Bishop'.[90] Sir Richard Birnie's reply is not known, but a letter to Daniel Bishop from Peel dated 19 July 1828 survives, stating that Bishop was to be reinstated as Peel had reluctantly decided that he should not be singled out for opprobrium, due to the 'great laxity of practice which he is sorry to observe, has been allowed to pass unchecked, and indeed unnoticed by the superiors of the police'.[91]

Evidence of the 1828 Select Committee

The Warwick Bank affair clearly influenced contemporary public and private opinion as to the honesty of the Bow Street personnel, and this opinion in turn has coloured many historians' and commentators' perceptions. The 1828 Select Committee *Report* in particular is often quoted as providing indisputable evidence of the widespread corruption of the Principal Officers. In a recent example Stephen Inwood claims, without citing any substantive evidence, that:

> The 1828 Committee [...] found an organised system, connived at by the magistrates, in which City and Bow Street Public Officers helped banks recover stolen money from robbers, and shared large rewards with criminals and fences. It is certainly true that several Bow Street and City detectives retired with large and unexplained fortunes, and it is clear that the business of crime investigation, which was Bow Street Public Office's special strength, involved corrupting contact with the criminal world.[92]

Financial standing of Principal Officers

In stating that some of the Bow Street Officers amassed 'large and unexplained fortunes' Inwood is simply echoing persistent but apocryphal stories that Townsend retired with £20,000 while Sayer left £30,000 at the time of his death.[93] In his evidence to the 1837 Select Committee, E. G. Wakefield referred to fences such as Ikey Solomons and thieftakers as leaving fortunes amounting to £20–30,000, and there may have been some subsequent confusion over the individuals concerned.

The surviving wills of the Principal Officers, together with what is known from other sources of evidence such as their obituaries and their post-Bow Street lives, do not immediately suggest that the majority retired with huge fortunes. However, it is conceded that if an Officer had amassed considerable ill-gotten wealth, it is unlikely that such a fortune would have been acknowledged in a formal document such as a will. The will of perhaps the most famous of all the Principal Officers, John Townsend, was proved on 31 July 1832, but unfortunately it is a very brief document which does not mention any monetary amounts, leaving all his worldly goods to his wife, Ann.[94]

John Vickery, a long-serving Principal Officer, died in 1840 and in his will, proved 11 July 1840, left two dwelling houses and lands in Odiham, Hampshire (his birthplace), together with a total of £80 of bequests, together with unspecified stocks and annuities in public accounts. He left his estate in trust to his son, John Vickery Junior, and his daughter, Phoebe Vickery, and also left provision for his three other children.[95] Vickery had been badly injured in 1822 during the course of his work at Bow Street and retired through ill-health, though he subsequently became Governor of Cold Bath Fields House of Correction in 1823, serving until 1829.[96]

Perhaps the most interesting surviving will is that of a John Sayer of Bridge Row, Pimlico, who wrote the document on 9 September 1832.[97] The will was proved on 15 May 1833, but it does not make clear when Sayer died or what his occupation had been. Fitzgerald states that John Sayer, the Principal Officer, died in his house in 'the neighbourhood of Chelsea'.[98] Bridge Row, Pimlico, was located very close to Chelsea Hospital, just south-east of Sloane Square in the district of Chelsea. If this will is that of the Principal Officer implicated in complicity following the Paisley Bank robbery of 1810, it is certainly true that he died a wealthy man – the will lists bequests of many thousands of pounds to his friends, and he also left several properties in Bridge Row to various fortunate beneficiaries.

The other surviving wills of George Ruthven, Henry Edwards and William Adkins, all long-serving Principal Officers, do not mention specific sums of money, but it is known that Ruthven retired in 1839 to become the landlord of the One Tun Tavern in Covent Garden, somewhat surprisingly describing himself in his will as a 'yeoman', while William Adkins left Bow Street in 1810, being subsequently elected as the new Governor of Coldbath Fields on 16 November of that year.[99] His younger brother, Harry, left Bow Street in 1820 to become the Governor of Birmingham Gaol, subsequently leaving this post in 1826 to become Governor of Warwick Gaol, a position he held for many years.[100] It is also known that Francis Keys, a Principal Officer from 1835 to 1839, became the landlord of the Duke of York public house in Barnet, Middlesex, and remained there for many years; he was still described as such in 1846.

It is clear from these surviving records that many of the Officers involved did not feel either able or willing to cease working when they retired from Bow Street. It is obviously impossible to ascertain their financial state at the time of their leaving Bow Street, but such continuance of employment suggests that they may not have been in a position to simply retire to a comfortable life of leisure on the proceeds of any 'ill-gotten' gains.

Individual officers undoubtedly did occasionally profit well out of their employment. In his obituary Ruthven is reported to have received 'a £220 pension from the British Government, and pensions likewise from the Russian and Prussian Governments, for his services in discovering forgeries to an immense extent connected with their countries'.[101] Officers could certainly make a considerable amount from the successful investigation of certain cases; after £35,000 was stolen from Rundell & Bridges, jewellers in Ludgate Hill, London, Vickery was consulted and in the company of one of the jeweller's employees, traced delinquents through France, Holland and Frankfurt. He managed to recover £20,000, with the result that 'the firm made him a very liberal present'.[102] Ruthven, for his part in capturing the ringleaders of the Cato Street Conspiracy in 1820, received a reward, shared with twelve Patrol Constables, of £333.[103] Certain of the officers undoubtedly profited from an assiduously cultivated friendship with generous patrons of their services; Townsend was for many years to be seen in company with the Prince Regent, and together with two other Officers, was allowed £200 per year for attending the Regent while in London, Windsor or Brighton.[104]

Like Inwood, many other commentators, contemporary and later, have accepted without much question that many if not all of the Principal Officers were indeed corrupt. In 1820, John Wade caustically remarked with regard to the payment of parliamentary rewards to the Officers that 'the sums derived from this source, as is well known, are not only in proportion to the turpitude of offenders, but also to the turpitude of the officer'.[105] Towards the end of the nineteenth century Fitzgerald dryly remarked of Bow Street that 'the wheels of the detective car moved but sluggishly, or scarcely at all, if ungreased'.[106] Similarly, in the mid-twentieth century, Radzinowicz stated that 'the bills drawn up by police officers for time, trouble and expenses were virtually limited only by their consciences'.[107]

One of the few historians to defend the Principal Officers' reputation was Pringle, who states in his *Introduction* to Goddard's *Memoirs* that 'not one Bow Street Runner was ever charged with a criminal offence or, so far as I know, dismissed on suspicion of being corrupt'.[108] In point of fact, Pringle was mistaken, for as has been shown above, Daniel Bishop was temporarily dismissed for corruption before being grudgingly reinstated, but at least Pringle had closely studied all the evidence then available to him before reaching his conclusion.

There was undoubtedly a degree of contemporary worry and criticism over the system of payments to Bow Street personnel; an example can be found in the *Morning Chronicle*, 17 March 1830, which carried a Court of Common Council report detailing salaries of non-Metropolitan Police officers. Marshals of City of London received £500 per year, while Mr Charles Pearson remarked that 'at Bow Street, which was the head police-office for vigilance and activity, Bishop and Ruthven were in request; they received only £50 a year each, as retaining fees, from the public, and were the much more active, displaying the truth of the adage that you must not keep a rat-catcher's dog too highly fed.'

The widespread allegations of corruption at Bow Street clearly angered several of the Bow Street magistrates; in one memorable outburst in 1827, Thomas Halls, a magistrate at Bow Street, made the following sarcastic comments after it had emerged in evidence that an unnamed Bow Street Officer had rejected a bribe:

> 'What!', rejoined the Magistrate, 'a Bow Street Public Officer reject a bribe? Wonders will never cease. It is really hardly to be credited, that a member of such a corrupt system of police as that which Bow Street is represented to be, should reject the offer of a sovereign!'[109]

However, despite such denials, heated debate about perceived corruption among Principal Officers continued. In the 1837 Select Committee *Report*, Edward Gibbon Wakefield was questioned and stated that:

> Under the old police, what was called detection was a mockery, except in a few cases where large sums had been lost and grievous crimes committed, and a great stir was made; on those particular occasions the officers of Bow Street exerted

themselves; and very great pains were sometimes taken to detect the criminal, but, except in such cases, there appeared to me to be no means whatever of detection [...] amongst the old police it was very difficult to distinguish the thief from the policeman.[110]

Wakefield may not have been the most impartial of witnesses, having been brought back from France by a Principal Officer some ten years earlier after abducting a 15-year-old heiress, for which he subsequently served a three-year prison sentence at Newgate, but he did reflect a widely held view of the problems surrounding the offering of rewards.

The 1828 Select Committee *Report* is the one to which many commentators and historians refer when citing evidence of widespread corruption among Principal Officers. It was undoubtedly one of the most important and influential reports dealing with the contemporary policing situation, coming as it did just over a year before the creation of the Metropolitan Police. Much of the *Report* was concerned with the routine functioning of the police and the state of prisons within the metropolis, but another of its remits was to investigate allegations of corruption within both Bow Street and the City police.[111]

Unfortunately, much of the evidence relating to these allegations was not published in the *Report* as it was deemed to be of too sensitive a nature for public consumption. However, the Committee reported that it had found that 'property of various sorts, to a value above £200,000, has, within a few years, been the subject of negotiation or compromise.'[112] In essence, the Committee found that such negotiations had been instigated on the behalf of banks or other financial institutions which had been robbed of large sums of money in order to retrieve as much of the stolen property as possible. The Committee's *Report* implicitly suggested that this practice had been known about for some time: 'Enquiries have proved such compromises to have been negotiated with an unchecked frequency and under an organised system, far beyond what had been supposed to exist', but that the scale of such negotiations was far larger than had been previously estimated.[113]

A specific example was cited in the evidence, where a bank which had been robbed of almost £17,000 was offered restitution of £6,000 of this stolen property for £300 in cash. The Committee heard that the bank applied for a free pardon for any informers, but 'declined advertising a reward of £1,000 and giving a bond not to compound, as the conditions of such grant'.[114] The Committee recognised that such activity by banks was understandable, as the banks were desperate to reduce their losses following large robberies, but was extremely critical of such practice as undermining both the legal and policing system. The evidence published suggests that such negotiations were carried out by a handful of solicitors 'whose practice lies chiefly in the defence of culprits, [...] commonly denominated "Thieves Attorneys", or conversely by Principal Officers from Bow Street or the City of London Police Offices'.[115]

This finding is the major piece of evidence by which Principal Officers have stood accused of corruption. While it would be naive not to acknowledge that minor corruption did occasionally occur, this book argues that the case against the Principal Officers is not as clear-cut as it is has often been portrayed. No Principal Officer was permanently dismissed on corruption charges, and subsequent allegations by later historians have been shown to be largely mistaken. Interestingly, the Committee of 1828 does not even refer to the one case in which circumstantial evidence strongly suggests that an Officer did indeed compound a felony with a view to personal gain.

The case in summary suggests that John Sayer, a Principal Officer, was in league with the wife of one of the robbers of the Paisley Bank in 1810.[116] The bank was robbed of over £20,000, and Sayer informed the bank's agent that he could recover the money if the robbers were guaranteed freedom from prosecution over several other offences. The bank agreed, but upon collection of the money found a shortfall of almost £9,000. This shortfall was never satisfactorily explained, but after Sayer's death in the early 1830s, the missing notes were supposedly located in the house in which Sayer lived with the wife of the bank robber (who had died in 1820). Fitzgerald suggests that Sayer was not directly implicated in the fraud, but that he knew of the existence of the money, keeping quiet to protect his lover.

Despite its distaste for the practices revealed in its *Report*, the 1828 Select Committee was careful not to heap disapprobation on individual Officers, stating that in many such cases the Officer was not acting out of greed or a motive for personal profit:

> They seem in some instances to have been induced to it without a corrupt or dishonest motive; and individuals of them have been satisfied with a much less sum for effecting the compromise, than the reward offered for the apprehension of the guilty parties. In no case, however, does it appear in evidence that any one of them stipulated for a reward before hand; nor connived

at the escape of a thief; nor negotiated a compromise, when he possessed any clue that might lead to the detection of the guilty.[117]

This is clearly at odds with the perception of Principal Officers as a corrupt body of men solely out for personal gain, and reinforces the Officers' argument that they were merely continuing a reasonably effective method of recovering large sums of money on behalf of financial institutions; moreover, they were doing so with the full knowledge and connivance of the Bow Street magistrates. It must be remembered that at no time were the magistrates themselves directly accused of such corruption. Sir Richard Birnie's evidence to the 1828 Committee, although undoubtedly occasionally deliberately vague and disingenuous, especially when he lays the blame for such negotiations on a handful of attorneys, makes it clear that he did not regard the compounding of such crimes as a felony; he would only have done so, he stated, had it been proved 'that such action was undertaken with a view to conniving the escape of the guilty parties'.[118]

As the evidence mounted for the number of cases in which such negotiations had occurred, both the Committee and the press became more concerned with the discontinuance of such a system rather than with apportioning blame. *The Times* remarked that 'the practice of compounding felonies appears to be a necessary evil, which must prevail more or less as long as the police is constituted as it is at present', while the Committee stated that it thought 'the abolition of the system for the future, of much greater importance than the punishment of former offenders'.[119]

However, little compelling evidence has emerged to prove definitively that the majority of Officers were regularly corrupt or complicit with criminals. The Officers appear to have been guilty more of complicity rather than of financial corruption – they operated the system of negotiation with criminals with the implicit sanction of the magistrates, who clearly believed that this was the most cost-effective way of restoring or reclaiming at least some of the banks' or other institutions' assets. It is clear that there were problems with the various systems of payment operated throughout the period, and that many people, including both the magistrates and the Principal Officers, were aware of these, but no one seemed able or willing to devise a satisfactory alternative. The very fact that the Bow Street system continued largely unchanged for almost a century suggests that those in a position to change the functioning and operative methods of the Police Office were unwilling to do so, and that therefore they were generally satisfied with the functioning of the Office.

This situation began to change in the first two decades of the nineteenth century, when the various Committees became much more critical of the way in which Bow Street was administered. The 'Blood-Money Scandal' of 1816, although having nothing to do with the Principal Officers, obviously had a detrimental effect on the public's view of Bow Street as a whole, and also undoubtedly influenced subsequent decisions made by those who had the power to change the system. However, even then, with a few exceptions, the Officers themselves were not directly criticised or accused of corruption; even as late as 1838, the Select Committee was keen to point out that they were not dissatisfied with individual Officers, and thus sought to criticise not them, but rather the whole system. It commented with referral to the Police Offices:

> If the Police office department does not merit the same degree of praise [as the Metropolitan Police], that, in the opinion of your committee, is the fault of the system, and not of the individuals concerned in the execution of its duties.[120]

Conclusion

This chapter has briefly outlined the functioning of Bow Street Office from its formation under the Fieldings, and has demonstrated the role that the Principal Officers played within the organisation, together with the ways in which this role differed from that of the less senior personnel. It has indicated that the Principal Officers were unique among Bow Street employees in being regularly engaged in the detection of provincial crimes. It has also sought to defend the Principal Officers from the majority of unfounded and subsequently unchallenged accusations of widespread corruption, while acknowledging that opportunities for personal gain often came the way of the Principal Officers and that it would be unreasonable to suppose that none of the personnel involved ever succumbed to such illegal financial temptations.

The discussion now turns to the employers of the Principal Officers. Chapter 3 analyses the social, economic and political breakdown of their employers, and discusses what these findings reveal about the provincial uses of Principal Officers, comparing the results with findings from their metropolitan activities.

Notes

1 For an overview of the history of the magistracy in England and Wales, see David J. Cox and Barry Godfrey (eds), *Cinderellas and Packhorses: A History of the Shropshire Magistracy* (Almeley: Logaston Press, 2005).

2 HO 42/26, f. 28.

3 Fielding's predecessor, Thomas De Veil, who was magistrate at Bow Street from 1739 to 1746, has been branded as a typically corrupt 'trading justice' (not least by Fielding). However, both Pringle and Babington question this view, arguing that although De Veil was clearly no saint in either his personal or professional life, the available evidence suggests that his period of office was not overly corrupt when compared to the standards of the day (see Anthony Babington, *A House in Bow Street: Crime and Magistracy, London, 1740–1881*, 2nd edn (London: Macdonald, 1999), pp. 41–60 and Patrick Pringle, *Hue & Cry: The Birth of the British Police* (London: Museum Press, 1956), pp. 59–76).

4 Quoted in Pringle, *Hue & Cry*, p. 79. It is notoriously difficult to equate monetary values from different periods, but a crude multiplication of between 100 and 125 can be made to late-eighteenth and early-nineteenth-century figures in order to compare them with present-day values. For a fascinating overview of inflation over the past millennium, see Peter Wilsher, *The Pound in Your Pocket 1870–1970* (London: Cassell, 1970).

5 Pringle, *Hue & Cry*, p. 80.

6 John Beattie's research suggests that stipends were first officially paid to the three Bow Street magistrates (one Chief Magistrate and two subordinates) in 1768 (J. M. Beattie, 'Sir John Fielding and Public Justice: The Bow Street Magistrates' Court, 1754–1780', *Law and History Review*, vol. 25, no. 1 (Spring 2007), pp. 61–100).

7 The Home Department in the form of the Secretary of State possessed ultimate control over the appointment of all Bow Street personnel, including Chief Magistrates, and this control was publicly demonstrated in 1821 when Sir Robert Baker, Chief Magistrate from 1820, was summarily and unjustly dismissed following the furore surrounding the policing of Queen Caroline's funeral.

8 J. M. Beattie, *Policing and Punishment in London 1660–1750: Urban Crime and the Limits of Terror* (Oxford: OUP, 2001), p. 229, and Ruth Paley, quoted ibid., p. 417. For a brief account of various thieftakers and their fate see Alan Brooke and David Brandon, *Tyburn: London's Fatal Tree* (Thrupp: Sutton, 2004).

9 The term 'thieftaker' has since undergone a considerable shift in meaning; in a booklet entitled *Thieves on Wheels – Some Notes on the Law and Techniques of Thief-taking*, written by the then Deputy Assistant Commissioner of New Scotland Yard, the author argues that every alert police officer has it within his grasp to be a good 'thief-taker' – 'one

of the most envied of reputations which the police service can confer upon its members' (quoted in David Steer, *Uncovering Crime – The Police Role*, Royal Commission on Criminal Procedure Research Study No. 7 (London: HMSO, 1980), p. 14).

10 *Staffordshire Advertiser*, 3 January 1801.

11 Quoted in Gilbert Armitage, *The History of the Bow Street Runners 1729–1829* (London: Wishart & Co., 1932), p. 57. Jonathan Wild was born in Wolverhampton in 1683, styled himself as 'thieftaker-general' and was the model for Peachum in John Gay's *Beggar's Opera*. He was finally hanged in 1725 as a receiver of stolen goods. For a brief account of his life, see David J. Cox and Michael Pearson, *Foul Deeds and Suspicious Deaths Around the Black Country* (Barnsley: Wharncliffe, 2006), pp. 34–43. For accounts of the reputation of thieftakers and their influence, including the notorious 'Thieftakers' Trial' of 1756, see Babington, *A House in Bow Street*, pp. 126–30, and Ruth Paley, 'Thief-takers in London in the Age of the McDaniel Gang c.1745–1754', in D. Hay and F. Snyder (eds), *Policing and Prosecution in Britain, 1750–1850* (Oxford: OUP, 1989), pp. 301–41.

12 Edward Sayer, *Observations on the Police or Civil Government of Westminster with a proposal for reform* (London: Debrett, 1784), p. 25.

13 Henry Fielding, *An enquiry into the causes of the late increase of robbers and related writings*, ed. Malvin R. Zirker (Oxford: Clarendon Press, 1988), pp. 153–4.

14 John Fielding, *A plan for preventing robberies within twenty miles of London, with an account of the rise and establishment of the real thieftakers* (London: A. Millar, 1755).

15 Donald Rumbelow, *I Spy Blue: The Police and Crime in the City of London from Elizabeth I to Victoria* (London: St. Martin's Press, 1971), p. 79.

16 No stipendiary magistrates were appointed outside London until 1813 (Manchester) and 1829 (Merthyr Tydfil) – see David Philips, 'The Black Country Magistracy, 1835–1860: A Changing Elite and the Exercise of Its Power', *Midland History*, vol. III, no. 3 (1976), p. 176.

17 The activities of the Principal Officers from the other London Police Offices are at present woefully under-researched, virtually nothing having been written about them. Joan Lock's book, *Marlborough Street: The Story of a London Court* (London: Robert Hale, 1980) is one of the only books to have been published that concerns itself with a London Public or Police Office other than Bow Street, but the book concentrates heavily on events in the twentieth century, and devotes little time to the early history of the Office. It would appear, however, from an admittedly brief perusal of the activities of such Principal Officers in the sources consulted that, unlike their Bow Street counterparts, their use outside the metropolis seems to have been largely confined to the immediately neighbouring counties. For a full account of the 'Murder in the Red Barn', see Lord Birkett, *The New Newgate Calendar* (London: Folio Society, 1960), pp. 136–50.

18 The seven offices were: Great Marlborough Street, Hatton Garden, Lambeth, Queen's Square, Union Hall, Westminster and Worship Street. A special River Thames Police Office was created in 1798 by a separate Act of Parliament, primarily having jurisdiction over maritime policing of the capital.

19 Middlesex Justices Act (32 Geo. III c.53); full title *An Act for the More Effectual Administration of the Office of a Justice of the Peace in Such Parts of the Counties of Middlesex and Surrey as Lie in or Near the metropolis, and for the More Effectual Prevention of Felonies.*

20 The other Police Offices created by the Middlesex Justices Act fulfilled a similar function in this regard.

21 J. M. Beattie, *English Detectives in the Late-Eighteenth Century*, paper delivered at the European Social Science History Conference, The Hague, March 2002.

22 Pringle, *Hue & Cry*, p. 167.

23 Armitage, *The History of the Bow Street Runners 1729–1829*, p. 129. It appears that the Horse Patrol were not absorbed completely into the Metropolitan Police until September 1837; the *Morning Chronicle*, 9 September 1837, carried a report that the Horse Patrol were incorporated into the Metropolitan Police system on 2 September 1837.

24 Until as late as 1819, the less senior positions at Bow Street seem to have been part-time in nature: in a trial of that year Charles Bolton, a member of a Bow Street Patrol, states that 'I am in the East India Company's employ and am a Bow Street Patrol also' (OBP, December 1819, trial of Alexander Macpherson, t18191201-49. In the late eighteenth century, it is clear that some if not all the Principal Officers were also part-time employees of Bow Street: the list of witnesses in the Thomas Hardy treason trial of 1794 gives the other occupations of several Principal Officers (*Howell's State Trials*, vol. 24 (1794), pp. 1385–95), but this situation seems to have changed by the early years of the nineteenth century – certainly by 1816 the Principal Officers were all employed on a full-time basis.

25 The Principal Officers always operated in plain clothes and carried no official identification apart from a small hollow tipstaff, which was about six or seven inches in length, with a crown-shaped top which unscrewed to allow the insertion of a magistrate's warrant. Similar tipstaves were later utilised by Metropolitan Police detectives from 1867 to 1880 for the very same purposes of identification and as a means to carry warrants (Martin Fido and Keith Skinner, *The Official Encyclopedia of Scotland Yard* (London: Virgin, 1999), p. 262). For a somewhat dated but detailed discussion of the history of tipstaves and truncheons, see Erland Fenn Clark, *Truncheons: Their Romance and Reality* (London: Herbert Jenkins, 1935).

26 *Twenty-eighth Report from the Select Committee on Finance: Police, including Convict Establishments*, Proposal 10.

27 This attempt to shield police officers from political influences continued long after the Metropolitan Police Act and subsequent provincial Acts; constables were not allowed to vote in general or local elections until 1887.

28 John Styles, 'An Eighteenth-Century Magistrate as Detective: Samuel Lister of Little Horton', *Bradford Antiquary*, New Series, Part XLVII (October 1982), p. 103.

29 Joseph Ritson, *In the Office of Constable* (London: Whieldon & Butterworth, 1791), p. 5.

30 E. Chadwick, 'Preventive Police', *London Review*, vol. 1 (1829), pp. 252–308, at p. 255.

31 PP 1816, p. 175.

32 Henry Goddard, *Memoirs of a Bow Street Runner*, ed. P. Pringle (London: Museum Press, 1956), p. 91. There had been a widespread debate in the 1760s about warrants following the writing of the 'Dunk Warrant', a general warrant issued in order to detain the radical John Wilkes in 1763. The resulting legal challenges saw such general warrants (in which no specific person or place was given) made illegal. For a more detailed account see: http://www.montaguemillenium.com/familyresearch.h_1771_dunk.htm.

33 Francis Place, *The Autobiography of Francis Place*, ed. Mary Thale (London: CUP, 1972), p. 176.

34 OBP, May 1801, trial of Thomas Collett, Henry Hayes and Mary Hayes, t18010520-48.

35 At least a dozen Patrol constables assisted several Principal Officers in the Cato Street conspiracy and received a share of the £333 reward given by Parliament (T 38/674 Treasury: Departmental Accounts, Public Office, Bow Street 1816–35).

36 The *Morning Chronicle* of 13 September 1816 carried details of the wages of the Bow Street personnel – Officers received 1 guinea per week, Patrol constables were paid 2s 6d per night, Conductors 5s per night – and also quoted Sir Nathaniel Conant that the 'police officers are chosen from the conductors of the patrole, or persons in some other employ in the view of the Magistrates, from long observation of their general character'.

37 PP 1816, p. 138, and PP 1822, p. 22. This use of Patrol Constables in provincial cases seems to have had the additional benefit of being used as a type of further apprenticeship of constables or conductors whom the Bow Street magistrates were considering for promotion; several of the constables utilised in such provincial cases later became Principal Officers, most notably Daniel Bishop and George Leadbitter – see Chapter 3 for a more detailed discussion on the provincial use of Patrol personnel.

38 *The Times*, 2 November 1830, and Henry Goddard, *Memoirs* (four-volume manuscript, 1875–79), vol. 1, p. 49. *The London Despatch* of 27 November

1836 reported that in future all Principal Officers were to take turns at being gaoler; presumably this was due to a shortage of manpower and symptomatic of the government's increasing unease at Bow Street's uneasy relationship with the ever-expanding Metropolitan Police force.

39   *The Times*, 11 July 1816. This is one of only two occasions that all serving Principal Officers are named in a single newspaper article; in 1808 the *Morning Chronicle* of 5 January, reporting on the attendance at Thomas Carpmeal's funeral, had listed the Officers as Lavender (Carpmeal's son-in-law), Macmanus, Townsend, Sayer, Anthony, Pearks and Adkins.

40   William Howe, *The Whole Four Trials of the Thief Takers and their Confederates* (London: William Howe, 1816) lists the names of those tried as G. Vaughan, R. MacKay, G. Brown, S. Dannely, T. Brock, J. Pelham, M. Power and B. Johnson. None of these was either a Principal Officer or a Patrol Conductor.

41   PP 1816, p. 40.

42   PP 1816, p. 42.

43   PP 1816, p. 145.

44   PP 1822, p. 48.

45   For further details of Goddard's career, see Goddard, *Memoirs of a Bow Street Runner*, ed. Pringle.

46   PP 1818, p. 22.

47   PP 1822, p. 15. Birnie was probably being somewhat disingenuous and dismissive about the role of the other London Police Offices; contemporary newspapers give fairly regular accounts of Principal Officers from other Offices being used outside the metropolis (albeit usually in immediately adjacent areas). Philip Thurmond Smith sums up the position with regard to the other Police Offices succinctly: 'When the new police offices were established in London in 1792 each magistrate had a group of detectives assigned to him, so that by the end of the eighteenth century there were fifty or so detectives in eight or nine separate groups. These detectives confined their investigations to their own areas, much like their modern counterparts, investigating crimes in their own divisions' (Phillip Thurmond Smith, *Political Policing, Public Order, and the London Metropolitan Police* (Westport, CT: Greenwood Press, 1985), pp. 64–5).

48   A reproduction of the painting was kindly supplied by George Ruthven's great-great-great-granddaughter, Frances Bevan.

49   George Dilnot, *Triumphs of Detection* (London: Geoffrey Bles, 1929), pp. 34–5.

50   Personal communication, Frances Bevan, September 2003.

51   Christopher Hibbert (ed.), *Captain Gronow: His Reminiscences of Regency and Victorian Life, 1810–60* (London: Kyle Cathy Ltd, 1991), p. 110; and Rev. J. Richardson, *Recollections: Political, Literary, Dramatic, and Miscellaneous of the last half-century*, 2 vols (London: C. Mitchell, undated c.1860), vol. I, p. 59.

52 PP 1816, p. 137. There is some confusion as to when Townsend commenced his royal duties. Townsend's own evidence to the 1816 Select Committee suggests that he was employed in such a capacity from 1792, following an assassination attempt on the King, while Armitage suggests that such duties did not begin until 1814/15 after Margaret Nicholson tried to kill the King (Armitage, *The History of the Bow Street Runners 1729–1829*, p. 264). The use of Principal Officers in such a capacity seems to have been something of a sinecure restricted to those Officers who, either through increasing age or infirmity, were deemed no longer fit enough to fulfil the often arduous duties of their original post.

53 Throughout the 1,400-plus cases involving Bow Street personnel of all ranks recorded in the OBP there are only a handful of references to 'Runners', and of these only one instance is a situation in which a Bow Street official refers to himself as a 'Runner'.

54 Paul Begg and Keith Skinner, *The Scotland Yard Files: 150 Years of the CID* (London: Headline, 1992), p. 8.

55 Rev. J. Richardson, *Recollections*, vol. I, p. 58.

56 Personal communication with Ruthven's great-great-great-granddaughter, Frances Bevan, September 2003 – unfortunately, Ruthven's writings have not survived within his descendants' possession; Goddard, *Memoirs*; Anon. (Samuel Hercules Taunton), 'A Reminiscence of a Bow Street Officer', *Harpers New Monthly Magazine*, vol. 5, no. 28 (September 1852), pp. 483–94.

57 Research by David Vincent has suggested that only just over a hundred autobiographies of working-class men and women have survived which deal with the period 1790–1850, and that this paucity of sources has severely hampered our analysis of working-class aspirations and self-perception (David Vincent, 'Love and Death and the Nineteenth-Century Working Class', *Social History*, vol. 5 (1980), pp. 23–47). A recent article by Mike Savage has re-evaluated several such classic qualitative studies; 'Revisiting Classic Qualitative Studies' is published online in *Forum: Qualitative Social Research*, vol. 6, no. 1 (January 2005), at: http://qualitative-research.net/fqs/fqs-eng.htm.

58 Bow Street 'Runners' are mentioned in Dickens' *Oliver Twist* (1838), while Bow Street's efforts to prevent prizefighting are referred to in Byron's *Don Juan*, canto 11, verse 19, published in 1824.

59 G. P. R. James, *Delaware; or the Ruined Family*, 3 vols (Edinburgh: G. P. R. James, 1833), vol. III, pp. 165–6.

60 *Staffordshire Advertiser*, 27 July 1816.

61 Charles Stuart Parker (ed.), *Sir Robert Peel: from his private correspondence*, 3 vols (London: John Murray, 1891), vol. II, p. 115. For an investigation into the social composition of the Metropolitan Police, see Haia Shpayer-Makov, *The Making of a Policeman: A Social History of a Labour Force in Metropolitan London, 1829–1914* (Aldershot: Ashgate, 2002).

62 Details of previous employment taken from MEPO 4/508 Foot patrol register 1821–29.

63 http://www.gutenberg.org/catalog/world/readfile?pageno=185&fk_files=9510. The exact phrase was 'China Street Pig'. This is the earliest known use of the word 'pig' to describe the police, and disproves the oft-repeated assertion that the word was first used following the creation of the Metropolitan Police – it was originally thought that the opprobrious term referred to Sir Robert Peel's connection with Tamworth, after which a famous breed of pig is named. 'China Street' was a nickname for Covent Garden, close to the site of the Bow Street Police Office.

64 Letter dated 7 January 1754 from William Sharpe, clerk to the Privy Council, to the Duke of Newcastle's Secretary, quoted in A. R. Leslie-Melville, *The Life and Works of Sir John Fielding* (London: Lincoln & Williams, 1935), p. 52. The term 'myrmidon' was widely used in the eighteenth century to describe uncouth ruffians and derives from classical mythology; the original Myrmidons were followers of Achilles.

65 HO 65/1, letter dated 31 March 1796.

66 *Leeds Mercury*, 25 January 1812 and *The Times*, 27 October 1818. Lavender seems to have been a man of considerable intelligence and culture; on 29 January 1837 the *Literary Examiner* reported that Lavender was 'known to have been caught on various occasions reading Racine and on one occasion following the recitation of *Talma* at the door of a room that he was sent to guard'.

67 HO 60/2 Police Court Entry Book 1830–35, letter dated 24 January 1832.

68 HO 64/1 f. 37, letter dated 19 January 1834; MEPO 1/49 Public Office Letter Book Bow Street, letter dated 25 April 1836.

69 The letter resulted from Goddard's successful investigation into the arson of a barn belonging to a local gentleman farmer near Tunbridge Wells in October 1836.

70 As early as 1798 a Principal Officer, John Rivett, was offered the post of Inspector of the Dublin Police at a salary of £300 per year; although in the event, due to a governmental change of plan, he only spent two weeks in post and later returned to Bow Street to resume his duties there (*Observer*, 14 and 28 January 1798).

71 For an account of Vickery's transfer from Worship Street to Bow Street, see P. Fitzgerald, *Chronicle of Bow Street Police Office: with an account of the Magistrates, 'Runners' and Police*, 2 vols (London: Chapman & Hall, 1888), vol. 1, p. 111, and for Stafford's comments, see PP 1823, p. 37.

72 PP 1822, p. 48.

73 *Gentleman's Magazine*, New Series, vol. xxi (May 1844), p. 552. Townsend had previously achieved an obituary in vol. cii (July 1832), p. 91, while the *Morning Chronicle* of 3 February 1818 had carried brief details of John Pearks' untimely death at the age of 48, and Lavender's death in

1833 was the subject of an article in the *Hull Packet*, 21 June 1833.

74 Samuel Bamford, *Passages in the life of a Radical* (Oxford: OUP, 1964), p. 81.

75 *Manchester Guardian*, 5 January 1828. Whether Mr Brown's reported statement referred to the efficiency of the Officer or the thought that he would not receive a fair trial is unclear.

76 HO 65/1, letter dated 26 July 1804.

77 *Jackson's Oxford Journal*, 9 September 1826. The 'Northamptonshire Nutters' was the name coined for a group of itinerant workers employed to gather in the annual harvest of hazelnuts in Oxfordshire.

78 It must also be borne in mind that the Principal Officers had, almost without exception, also served a considerable apprenticeship of many years in the lower ranks of the various Police Offices.

79 In a rare public outburst, reported in the *Morning Chronicle*, 29 May 1828, Chief Magistrate Sir Richard Birnie heavily criticised Samuel Taunton for taking a prisoner into custody without a warrant: 'You had no right to consider; it is for me to consider and for you to act; you appear to set my authority at nought, and I shall take a note of this.'

80 There were a few other instances apart from the 'Blood-Money Scandal' in which other Bow Street personnel were implicated in illegal activities. In 1811 several members of the Bow Street Patrole were reported to have fled following 'allegations of selling the coins of the realm, for extortion, and for conspiracy' (*Caledonian Mercury*, 9 May 1811). Former Bow Street clerk John Richmond was sacked from his position in late 1825, and in 1831 Thomas Ford, the gaoler at Bow Street, was dismissed for receiving unauthorised payment of 12s 6d from two prostitutes to secure their release (HO 59/2, letter dated 31 December 1831). Thomas Halls, a long-serving Bow Street magistrate, was sentenced in the Insolvent Debtors' Court for almost 2½ years for an unpaid debt of £3,400 in the mid-1830s (*Morning Chronicle*, 24 December 1838).

81 The stimulus for the investigation into Bishop's alleged complicity remains unclear; although research suggests that it was Bishop's involvement in the aftermath of the Warwick Bank robbery, John Tobias states that Bishop's suspension arose from his recovery of a large amount of stolen jewellery from a Mr Delafond, a jeweller of Sackville Street (see J. J. Tobias, *Prince of Fences: The Life and Crimes of Ikey Solomons* (London: Valentine Mitchell, 1974), pp. 53–5). This crime does not appear in the OBP.

82 HO 60/1 Police Court Entry Book, pp. 316–17.

83 HO 60/1 Police Court Entry Book, pp. 360–4. For further details of Ikey Solomon's career, see Tobias, *Prince of Fences*. With regard to the system of negotiating rewards to thieves in order to recover the bulk of the stolen amount (often in the form of large denomination notes which would have been very difficult for the thieves to recirculate), this was not confined to Bow Street. The *Manchester Guardian* of 26

April 1823 comments after the robbery of a large amount of banknotes from Liverpool that 'the usual offer of negociation [*sic*], by allowing a certain percentage for their recovery, as a reward to the thieves for their dexterity, is expected to commence immediately'.

84 HO 60/1 Police Court Entry Book, pp. 360–4.

85 Ibid., p. 367.

86 Ibid., p. 366.

87 Ibid., pp. 368–70. This may refer to the embezzlement of the Leipzig Bank, which came to light in March 1821.

88 Ibid., pp. 368–70.

89 Ibid.

90 Ibid., pp. 397–8.

91 Ibid.

92 Stephen Inwood, *A History of London* (London: Macmillan, 1998), p. 596.

93 The *Examiner*, 22 July 1832 reported that Townsend was stated to have left £25,000 in funds, and asked its readers, 'if so, how could he have got it?' However, it has to be borne in mind that Townsend was somewhat atypical, being a friend to the Prince of Wales and well known in aristocratic circles – he may have benefited financially from these acquaintances in a way that other Principal Officers did not.

94 PROB 11/11803, Prerogative Court of Canterbury and related Probate Jurisdictions: Will Registers 1384–1858, image 223/239.

95 PROB 11/1931, Prerogative Court of Canterbury and related Probate Jurisdictions: Will Registers 1384–1858, image 358/317.

96 Hubert Cole, *Things for the Surgeon: A History of the Resurrection Men* (London: Heinemann, 1964), p. 67.

97 PROB 11/1816, Prerogative Court of Canterbury and related Probate Jurisdictions: Will Registers 1384–1858, image 277/241.

98 Fitzgerald, *Chronicle of Bow Street Police Office*, vol. 1, p. 163. Sayer is known to have last served as a Principal Officer on 10 September 1832 (T38/674 Public Office Expenditure 1816–1835), the day after the will was written, which suggests that the will is indeed that of the Officer.

99 *Staffordshire Advertiser*, 24 November 1810.

100 For further details of Harry Adkins' career at Warwick Gaol, see *Crime and Punishment Prisons vol. XI* (IUP Reprints Series): *Report relating to the Petitions of Messrs Lovett and Collins (Warwick Gaol)*, PP 1839 (462) vol. XXXVIII.

101 Fitzgerald, *Chronicle of Bow Street Police Office*, vol. 1, p. 116.

102 Ibid., p.112.

103 T 38/674 Treasury: Departmental Accounts, Public Office, Bow Street 1816–35. *The Times* of 1 July 1820 reported that Ruthven also received an individual payment of £408 from public subscriptions for his part in the capture of the conspirators.

104 John Wade, *The Black Book or Corruption Unmasked* (London: John Fairburn, 1820), p. 97.

105 Ibid.
106 Fitzgerald, *Chronicle of Bow Street Police Office*, vol. 1, p. 122.
107 Sir L. Radzinowicz, *A History of English Criminal Law and Its Administration from 1750*, vol. 2 (London: Stevens & Sons, 1956), p. 249.
108 Goddard, *Memoirs of a Bow Street Runner*, ed. Pringle, p. xx.
109 *The Times*, 4 December 1827.
110 PP 1837, p. 121.
111 The Report makes it clear in its introduction that Bow Street and the City were the only two Police Offices investigated with regard to allegations of corruption (PP 1828, p. 11).
112 PP 1828, p. 10.
113 Ibid., p. 9.
114 Ibid., pp. 9–10.
115 Ibid., p. 11.
116 Fitzgerald, *Chronicle of Bow Street Police Office*, vol. 1, pp. 158–63.
117 PP 1828, p. 12.
118 Ibid., pp. 12–13. At least one of the magistrates had no money worries; in 1834 Sir Fredrick Adair Roe was left a legacy of £100,000 by his uncle, Alexander Adair. Despite this considerable sum, Roe continued as Chief Magistrate until 1839.
119 *The Times*, 14 April 1828, and PP 1828, p. 13.
120 PP 1837–38, p. 136.

Chapter 3

'If the gentleman writes, the gentleman pays': the employers of Principal Officers

Introduction

In order to make sense of how the Principal Officers functioned in both the provinces and the capital, it is first necessary to understand the context in which they were employed, what they charged, how they claimed rewards, how their work differed in the provinces and London, and who employed them.

Cost of employing Principal Officers

The various ways in which Principal Officers were remunerated exercised both the numerous Committees convened to investigate the state of the police in the 1810s and 1820s and contemporary commentators such as John Wade and G. B. Mainwaring.[1] The basic stipend of a Principal Officer (when based in London) rose throughout the period 1792–1839. In 1793, the stipend was 11s 8d per week (rather surprisingly somewhat less than the 12s received by the Principal Officers based at the Police Offices created by the 1792 Middlesex Justices Act). This rose to 12s by October 1795, and by October 1802 the Principal Officers were receiving 16s. per week. From this period on, their salary seems to have been commensurate with the other Principal Officers at the various Police Offices, rising to 18s in 1807, one guinea in 1811 and reaching 25s in 1821.[2] It remained at this figure in the subsequent period up to their demise, despite Lord Melbourne's reorganisation of their expenses in 1831.[3]

However, at no time was this regarded as the sole source of income available to the Officers. With specific regard to provincial activities, the Principal Officers were also able to claim various amounts of money from their employer(s), be they private individual, public or private institution or the state. For the majority of the period under discussion the Officers received 14s per day for subsistence and lodging when engaged on what they termed 'country duties' or 'foreign service'.[4] On such investigations they also expected to be paid a guinea per day for what was euphemistically called their 'trouble', i.e. their services to their employers.[5] Finally, they could also claim travelling expenses, which by April 1820 had been officially set at 3d per mile.[6] Such expenses would obviously be beyond the capability of many individuals, thereby ensuring that the Principal Officers, when employed by private individuals, were only utilised by the relatively small sector of society that could afford to so do.

Other benefits available to Principal Officers

The Principal Officers were able to avail themselves of numerous benefits while working at Bow Street. On several occasions their medical expenses were paid after they had been injured in the line of duty – for example, in March 1833, George Leadbitter, a Principal Officer, was trodden on and injured while on duty at Ascot Races.[7] His medical bill of £13 7s was subsequently paid by Bow Street. Similarly, in March 1836, Richard Gardner, another Principal Officer, had his leg broken returning from Cambridge where he had been on official business, and was awarded medical expenses of £16 2s 6d.[8] The Officers could also call upon Bow Street to pay any legal costs resulting from their activities on behalf of Bow Street. For the quarter ending 10 October 1825, an allowance of £60 was made to defray the expenses of Harry Adkins, 'late one of the constables', who had been defending an 'Action at Law'.[9]

There seems to have been a system of superannuation in place with regard to Bow Street personnel from at least the first decade of the nineteenth century; Treasury accounts refer on numerous occasions to 'superannuated' or 'infirm' personnel – for example, Archibald Ruthven (George Ruthven's father) is referred to on 5 July 1811 as a 'superannuated or infirm Patrol member'.[10] In 1839, when the Principal Officers were disbanded, provision appears to have been made for them to receive pensions in order to compensate them for loss of earnings in a similar manner to the pension provisions for the Horse Patrol (see Chapter 7, note 2). The *Era* 31 March 1844 stated that 'Ruthven's allowance was £230 per annum, from the fact of his returned income as being £1,000 yearly'.[11] Surviving widows of deceased Principal Officers also received a portion of their husbands' pensions in the same way that widows of Bow Street magistrates appear to have; Mary Bond, the widow of magistrate Nicholas Bond received a pension from the State which she petitioned to have increased to £200 per annum in 1812.[12]

Claiming of rewards by Principal Officers

Despite the above expenses and benefits often adding up to a not inconsiderable amount, the major source of the Principal Officers' income was gained from claiming shares of any rewards offered as the result of the conviction of suspects. As private subjects of the monarch, the Principal Officers were allowed to share in any rewards offered by either the state or private individuals or institutions. The system of parliamentary rewards dated back to the seventeenth century – the Highwaymen Act of 1693 (4 & 5 William & Mary c.8) offered a £40 statutory reward for the capture of highwaymen – while the payment of private rewards had a similarly long history.[13] Only one major change to the payment of rewards was introduced in the intervening period, when in the Act of 25 Geo. II c.36 (1752), it became an offence with a fine of £50 to advertise a reward with 'no questions asked'.[14]

Although widely utilised by victims (the pages of *Hue & Cry* are full of private adverts offering often substantial rewards for the return of stolen property and the successful prosecution of the suspects), such a system of rewards could obviously be open to abuse, as demonstrated by the respective activities of Wild and McDaniel in the first decades of the eighteenth century. The 1816 Select Committee *Report* on the Police of the metropolis concerned itself to a great extent with the inherent problem, and contained evidence given by Sir Nathaniel Conant, Bow Street Chief Magistrate from 1813 to 1820, in which he strongly defended the system of private rewards. When asked: 'Have the Police officers any profits arising from being employed by individuals for the detection of robberies committed?' Conant replied in the affirmative, stating:

They are paid by the parties themselves, subject, sometimes, to a reference to the Magistrates; but in general the parties themselves induce the officers to assist them in their objects, and they pay them according to their private dispositions.[15]

When asked: 'Do you not think the effect of that is to lessen the exertions of the Police in those cases where the reward is not offered?' Conant replied:

I think not, according to my apprehension of the particular character of the men who are employed as officers at this time [...]; I think, though they would be stimulated by the views of greater reward, the exertion of their ordinary duty is not relaxed by the absence of it.[16]

Conant was questioned hard and at length on this issue, but defended the character of the Principal Officers. Pressed over the additional financial demands made by the officers on account of their endeavours to find an offender, Conant supported their requests, stating that the Officer

is entitled to say; I receive one guinea a week in my engagement as a Police Officer, and because a person wishes that I should go twenty miles off, at a minute's notice, and employ all my time, I do not think that guinea is the retainer for such excessive duty, possibly at the hazard of my life, and certainly at some expense.[17]

John Stafford, Chief Clerk, was similarly defensive when questioned over the expenses and rewards claimed by the Principal Officers:

We have no instance of any of the officers being induced from venal or corrupt motives to swerve from or betray the confidence reposed in them, and to their being more generally respected, and in many instances better paid, than at the other Offices; those circumstances altogether make them more anxious to do their duty correctly.[18]

The criticism of the methods of payments made to the Principal Officers came not only from those with a professional view on the matter; the *Monthly Review* of December 1816 makes it clear that it was not happy with the situation:

It appears to us that the fees which the officers receive from private individuals should not be suffered; the time of the officer belongs exclusively to the public, by whom he deserves to be paid liberally; there cannot be a divided interest; and the alternative is that the charges on individuals are an imposition on the employment of the officer's time in their service is a palpable neglect of public duty.[19]

Similarly, when Bow Street Officers gave evidence in court, the defence counsel often referred to the availability of rewards, implicitly suggesting that the Officer hoped to secure a conviction in order to benefit financially. An example of this line of questioning can be seen in a trial of 1821, when Principal Officer Stephen Lavender was asked the direct question, 'Does your remuneration depend on the prisoner's conviction?' he was careful to point out that he was not acting independently of his superiors, replying 'Certainly not; it makes no difference to me whether he is convicted or not. I went to his lodgings entirely by the direction of Sir Robert Baker.'[20]

Views of Principal Officers regarding their payment

The evidence of two of the Principal Officers is illuminating as to how they perceived the debate surrounding their payment. John Townsend was examined by the Committee on 7 June 1816. When asked about provincial activities, he candidly admitted that:

The great means of their living, in a measure, is that of their being employed, as I have always termed it, upon foreign service; that is out of their local jurisdiction, because the officer's salary is only a guinea a week.[21]

He stated (probably somewhat disingenuously) that he doubted if any of the officers made as much as £30 per year from Parliamentary rewards, but also admitted that the system was inherently flawed, commenting that:

I have always been of opinion, that an officer is a dangerous subject to the community, if he is not so kept and so paid as to afford him the means of being honest; for in some cases, God knows, it has been frequently the case.

Townsend may have been referring obliquely to the contemporaneous 'Blood-Money' scandal, which broke publicly a little later than his appearance before the Committee, but this affair certainly damaged the reputation of Bow Street in the eyes of the public. L. B. Allen, magistrate at Union Hall, when reviewing the situation in 1821, wrote perspicaciously that 'an odium had been thrown upon them [Principal Officers] as a body from the gross villainy of a few, which I admit to the fullest extent, but which I do not believe to be general.'[23]

As a means of preventing such possible abuses of the system, Townsend suggested a salary of two guineas a week and discretionary payments by magistrates and judges at assizes. He unsurprisingly wanted to keep the system of large rewards in cases such as smuggling or poaching as an incentive to encourage informers to ensure that the culprits were apprehended. He cited a recent 'notorious case' involving the murder of a Revenue officer, in which the government offered a £1,000 reward, 'to which I have no doubt they [Principal Officers and informers] will all be entitled'. To put these figures into context, in 1829 a Metropolitan Police Inspector was paid £100 per year, while Henry Goddard, upon his forced retirement from Bow Street in 1839, accepted the post of Chief Constable of Northamptonshire Constabulary at a salary of £250 per year. Stephen Lavender, another former Principal Officer, must be considered to have been fairly liberally paid as Deputy Constable of Manchester in 1821, receiving an annual salary of £400.[25]

John Vickery was also examined by the Committee. He had held office as a Principal Officer for five years, after having served at Bow Street and Worship Street Offices for a total of 17 years. With regard to the Parliamentary rewards system, echoing Townsend, he stated that:

> I do not think I have received, during the five years I have been at Bow Street, £20. Out of the six or seven principal officers at Bow Street I should not think there is one man who has received £40 in the year for it; I speak of the rewards under the Act of Parliament, I do not include those offered by advertisements by parties injured [i.e. victims of crime].[26]

It is significant that Vickery was careful to separate these rewards from those offered by private parties, as the latter would probably have made up most of his annual emolument. The statutory Parliamentary reward system was discontinued in 1818, although discretionary rewards could still be made in exceptional cases.[27]

The 1835 Municipal Corporations Act which allowed the creation of provincial police forces did not, as Jennifer Hart has pointed out, 'make it illegal for the police to receive fees or gratuities from private individuals or the public purse for services rendered or anticipated'.[28] Hay and Snyder remark that in 1836 Parliament was told 'There is a great abuse in this respect. There is the strongest reason for believing that constables prefer the most unfounded charges, and that upon oath.'[29] Rewards or voluntary donations could be received not just for a particular incident, but also for cumulative good service. The 1834 *Report* of the Police Association of Bourton on the Water, Gloucestershire contains a letter in which the writers (members of the local Police Committee) commend the Metropolitan Police Commissioners on the exertions of one of their former officers, George Cooper, who left the Metropolitan force to become head of Bourton's police. The writers state that due to his exceptionally good service, 'voluntary donations have been given him each year, above his regular salary'.[30]

Comparisons between provincial and metropolitan employment of Principal Officers

Although this book focuses primarily on the provincial activities of Principal Officers, the online availability of the Proceedings of the Old Bailey (OBP) from 1674 to 1913 in a searchable digitised format has allowed limited comparison to be made between provincial cases and cases in which they were involved within the metropolis. The Old Bailey (now known as the Central Criminal Court) dealt with the more serious and indictable crimes within the metropolis that were committed north of the River Thames. The OBP are a useful source of information about such trials and are especially valuable in comparing the activities of Principal Officers within and without the metropolis.

Detailed analysis of the OBP has established that during the period 1792–1839 there were 292 metropolitan cases that involved Principal Officers. This gives an average of just over six cases per year within the metropolis involving Principal Officers, compared to 601 recorded provincial cases, which in turn gives an average of just over twelve and a half cases per year. Although these figures are admittedly of limited statistical use and cannot be seen as a complete record of all provincial or metropolitan cases involving the Officers – both are partial, with caveats and limitations concerning both sources – they still tentatively suggest that the level of involvement in provincial cases was considerably higher than has been previously thought by many historians and that the Principal Officers were primarily utilised outside the capital.

The findings demonstrate at the very least that (a) much of the Principal Officers' work was undertaken outside the metropolis; (b) they appear to have been used relatively infrequently within the capital with regard to indictable crimes, perhaps due to the much greater availability of less senior ranks; and (c) they were increasingly used in the provinces as the period under discussion progressed.[31] The smaller percentage of metropolitan cases post-1829 (down from an average of 6.2 cases per year in the period 1792–1829 to an average of 5.2 cases per year in the period 1830–39), together with the concomitant increase in provincial usage in the last decade of the Officers' employment (from an average of 10.2 cases per year in the period 1792–1829 to an average of 20.3 cases per year in the period 1830–39), can be seen as both a direct result of the introduction of the Metropolitan Police with many metropolitan investigations being carried out by the new force and the increased availability of the Officers for provincial employment. However, it is pertinent to note that not all metropolitan activity by the Principal Officers ceased – there were 52 cases in the years 1830–39, mostly comprising larceny (33 cases) and fraud (13 cases), indicating that there were still occasions where their services were preferred to those offered by the Metropolitan Police.

While the number of provincial cases generally rises throughout the period, the opposite is true with regard to metropolitan cases. From 1808 there is not a single year in which the number of metropolitan cases exceeds the number of provincial cases. There also seems to be a sharp and generally sustained increase in provincial usage from 1810 onward. This may be a reflection of turbulent times in the provinces, especially with regard to Luddite and seditious involvement with France; such incidents account for almost one-third of the number of provincial cases in 1812. The decade from 1812 was particularly unsettled due to a combination of rising food prices and (from 1815) the rapid demobilisation and subsequent unemployment of hundreds of thousands of army and navy personnel. It is not stretching the bounds of possibility too far to suggest that such unsettled times in the provinces affected the propensity of provincial victims of crime to call in Principal Officers.

Comparison of the types of employer in the provinces and the metropolis

With regard to the composition of those who employed the Principal Officers, there are several comparisons to be made between their use in the metropolis and the provinces. The employers of Principal Officers can be divided into four main categories:

- private individuals;
- provincial magistrates;[32]
- institutions (private and public);[33]
- direct employment by the Home Department/Bow Street Magistrates.

The category of employer is recorded in over two-thirds of the 601 provincial cases and in all of the 292 metropolitan cases.

With regard to the 418 provincial cases in which the type of employer is known, the respective percentages of the four categories are shown in Table 3.1.

This breakdown is not as clear-cut as it may first appear, as the Bow Street magistrates were directly responsible to and financed by the Secretary of State for the Home Department, and therefore, at least in theory, that minister had the final say as to when and where the Principal Officers were employed. However, in practice the Bow Street Chief Magistrate enjoyed a considerable degree of autonomy in decisions as to the deployment of the personnel at the Police Office.

The practical level of autonomy seems to have fluctuated to an extent, depending on the respective personalities and approach of the Chief Magistrate and Secretary of State. For example, Lord Melbourne showed an extremely active interest in the running of Bow Street during his tenure as Secretary of State for the Home Department (1830–34), while Sir Frederick Roe (Chief Magistrate of Bow Street

Table 3.1 Types of provincial employers of Principal Officers, 1792–1839

	%	No. of cases
Private individuals	41.39	173
Institutions	25.12	105
Provincial magistrates	12.68	53
Home Department	20.81	87

1832–39) seems to have done all that he could to discourage what he considered as outside interference in his management of the Police Office.

With regard to the 292 metropolitan cases, the respective percentages of the four categories are shown in Table 3.2.

We now turn to an examination of each of the four categories in order to see what they can tell us about the usage of Principal Officers both in the provinces and in the metropolis.

Private individuals

Just over two-fifths of the provincial cases in which the type of employer is recorded were the result of individuals applying for the use of one or more Principal Officers. There were several ways in which these individuals or institutions could endeavour to procure the services of the Officers: they could write to the Home Department, requesting help from that source, they could contact Bow Street directly in person or by letter, or they could request help via an intermediary (usually their solicitor or an employee). In cases where the services of Bow Street had been previously utilised, Officers would obviously be known personally to the prospective employer(s), but even if they received a direct request from such an employer, they still had to obtain permission from the Chief Magistrate; they were not simply allowed to hire themselves out to the highest bidder without first gaining official permission.

Socio-economic status of private employers of Principal Officers

The percentage of private individuals who availed themselves of the services of the Principal Officers in metropolitan cases is considerably higher than in the provinces: over two-thirds of such cases were instigated by individuals. This seems initially to contrast sharply with the provincial figures, but when the socio-economic status of

Table 3.2 Types of metropolitan employers of Principal Officers, 1792–1839

	%	No. of cases
Private individuals	68.48	200
Institutions	23.163	69
Provincial magistrates	N/A	N/A
Home Department	7.88	23

such employers is taken into consideration a rational explanation can be seen to emerge. Table 3.3 shows the socio-economic status of individual employers of Principal Officers in metropolitan and provincial cases.

Secondly, the aristocracy and gentry, while often maintaining a residence in London, overwhelmingly based themselves in the more rural areas of Britain, whereas a considerable proportion of the mercantile class was located in what was at the time the pre-eminent commercial city in Europe. Therefore the socio-economic population of the capital was significantly different to much of the rest of the country and this is likely to be reflected in the figures.

Thirdly, the types of crime investigated in the metropolis by the Principal Officers were often very different to those for which they were employed in the provinces – this aspect is discussed below in greater detail in Chapter 4. If the magistrates considered that an applicant required the services of Bow Street, any suitable member of its personnel could be sent out, occasionally at Bow Street's expense, depending on circumstances. However, the vast majority of metropolitan crimes recorded in the Old Bailey Proceedings were of a fairly mundane and petty nature and were therefore dealt with by the less senior Bow Street officials, who were much more numerous than Principal Officers, totalling over 240 men, and would therefore have been the first choice of the Bow Street magistrates. The Proceedings contain almost 1,300 mentions of patrol members compared to 292 cases involving Principal Officers.[35]

By contrast, the ability to afford to employ such professional and experienced assistance as that offered by the Principal Officers seems to have been a crucial factor in their utilisation when employed by provincial individuals. In almost all provincial instances it was the ruling elite, i.e. those, invariably men, with the authority to create, maintain or influence law enforcement and judicial procedure at

Table 3.3 Socio-economic status of private individuals who employed Principal Officers in metropolitan and provincial cases

	Metropolitan cases %	Provincial cases %
Aristocracy	8.00	19.54
Gentry	33.50	59.20
Mercantile	58.50	21.26

local or national level, who decided whether or not a particular case warranted the employment and cost of a Principal Officer. The considerable expense incurred by private individuals when hiring the services of a Principal Officer in the provinces ensured that those who did employ their services were almost exclusively from the propertied and wealthier sectors of society. In such cases, the gravity of the crime often seems to have been less of an issue than the perceived need to employ (and perhaps as importantly, be seen to employ) a senior member of Bow Street.

While, as Peter King points out, it cannot be assumed 'that the propertied were a monolithic group who usually agreed about how the law should be used, about who should make decisions within it, or about the criteria on which those decisions were to be based', it is clear that despite any individual differences in legal and judicial matters, it was overwhelmingly the provincial propertied classes who made use of Principal Officers.[36] Apart from the obvious financial advantages possessed by members of this group, they were also more likely to have and make use of influential social contacts in positions of authority, such as justices of the peace or local political figures.

If such individuals therefore decided to employ Bow Street personnel privately, they were deemed liable for all costs incurred – as John Sayer succinctly remarked, 'if the gentleman writes, the gentleman pays'.[37] This axiom was certainly instigated in the vast majority of provincial cases – a note replying to the request of a Bow Street Officer in 1835 states 'when a police officer is sent into the country, it is usual for <u>the party applying to pay him</u>' (original underlining), while in the following year, a victim agreed to pay 'all expenses specified in the printed paper you sent me' in order to ensure that a London officer was sent to investigate a provincial crime, suggesting that by this time fees were set at a fixed rate and advertised as such to victims requiring such services.[38]

Similarly, a victim of arson at Weymouth in 1838 employed an Officer only after a memorandum of charges which had been omitted from previous correspondence was sent to him.[39] Such fees could often add up to a considerable amount and were undoubtedly sometimes a disincentive to provincial victims requesting assistance from Bow Street. In his research into the Dursley Association for the Prosecution of Felons (founded in 1773), Bryan Jerrard notes that:

One expense that was not allowed after 1820 was the employment of any officer from Bow Street or any other police office, probably because of the high charges that the Bow

Street 'Runner', Vickery, made to the Earl of Berkeley when his gamekeeper was shot in 1816.[40]

Similarly, following a case of suspected arson at Husbands Bosworth in Leicestershire, the victim wrote that he could not afford a London police officer at 'terms mentioned in memorandum' – and as an alternative he employed a Leicester officer incognito for several days.[41]

Absence of poorer victims in reported provincial cases

These costs undoubtedly deterred many victims from applying for the services of senior Bow Street personnel, and the absence of poorer or working-class victims in the provincial records is immediately apparent. Only in one of the recorded cases was either the victim or prosecutor specifically described as poor. Elizabeth Longfoot was murdered in Easton, near Burleigh Hall, Lincolnshire, in March 1838 and her cottage 'plundered of what little money she was supposed to possess'.[42] However, further research indicates that while not being wealthy, she was in fact 'possessed of a little freehold property' and her murderers also stole £100 in cash from her property; she was therefore not as poor as was originally reported.[43]

Through a combination of factors including their small number and their relative cost, it is clear that the Principal Officers were in no way a viable option to the vast majority of victims of provincial crime, i.e. those who could not afford to pay the not inconsiderable amounts for their services. Similarly, although the socio-economic positions of those employing Principal Officers in the capital were undoubtedly different to those of provincial employers, poorer victims of crime in either the provinces or the metropolis simply could not avail themselves of the services of the senior personnel.

There is, however, one category of provincial offence in which poorer victims do make a regular appearance: that of murder/attempted murder. Of the deaths investigated, while the majority seem to have been the result of robberies or burglaries of relatively prosperous individuals that escalated into serious and often fatal violence, the victims in almost one third (32.5 per cent) of such cases were working-class people.[44] This relatively large percentage of such victims is at first sight unusual – such people are otherwise almost entirely absent from the recorded cases.

Such a high proportion of working-class murder victims superficially may therefore appear to be somewhat at odds with the argument that poorer victims could not avail themselves of Bow

Street's services. However, the vast majority of such poorer victims were involved in law enforcement in one form or another, ranging from Revenue officers to gamekeepers and police constables, and as such, were employed by either wealthy private individuals or governmental bodies, both of whom had the means and desire to employ Bow Street to discover the perpetrators of the offence.

Although such victims were working-class, the instigators of the prosecution of suspects and therefore the employers of Bow Street's services were again from the classes that could afford to pay the going rate. Apart from the employers' ability to pay, the use of Principal Officers in such cases also sent out the explicit message that while the victims may be poor and from the lower social strata, the murder of an official or the employee of an aristocrat was also perceived as a direct threat to the status quo and this was not to be tolerated. Therefore every effort was made, and just as importantly, was seen to be made in order to catch and punish the perpetrators(s).

The apparent restriction of provincial and metropolitan use of Principal Officers to the propertied and moneyed classes clearly exercised the concern of contemporary critics of Bow Street. The 1816 Committee often homed in on this factor, but in his evidence the Chief Magistrate at Bow Street, Sir Nathaniel Conant, was adamant that ability to pay was not a prerequisite of acquiring the services of Bow Street.[45] When asked: 'Supposing the party lodging a complaint be poor; or that no prosecutor is to be found, can you state any other way in which the expenses of the prosecution can be defrayed?', he replied:

> If the party injured is extremely poor, and incapable of carrying on his own prosecution, the Magistrate will, and frequently does at his own private expense, direct a constable to carry on the prosecution, and in some instances even to maintain the party injured, till the time of the trial.[46]

This statement seems to have referred primarily to the situation within the metropolis, where any member of the public could enter the Police Office for assistance, as such professed egalitarianism is certainly not reflected in the reported provincial cases. Even in metropolitan cases, where the percentage of mercantile/middle-class employers is much higher than in the provinces, there are no recorded cases in which the victim appears to be poor. Apart from the obvious reason that the poor had little enough to lose that would justify the expense involved in employing the services of Bow Street and the subsequent cost of prosecution, the fact that rewards were offered by victims or prosecutors as inducements to both the general public and the Principal Officers could also have further diminished the ability of poorer people to engage the Officers' services, by perpetuating the widely held belief that the Officers would not take a case on without the possibility of financial reward, although it was in fact always the magistrates and not the Officers who decided whether or not to accept cases.

The Bow Street magistrates were also financially accountable to the Home Department for the running of the Office, and with regard to provincial cases involving poor victims therefore were likely to have been reluctant to send out an Officer knowing that they would not be able to recoup any or most of the costs involved in his employment. It also has to be considered that in a largely illiterate and geographically static age, when responsibility for prosecution of a crime fell on either the victim or his/her family or friends, poorer victims may not have even been aware of this avenue of detection. Bow Street and metropolitan London must have seemed a world removed from the daily lives of the provincial poorer classes.

Use of less senior personnel in cases involving poorer victims
Limited evidence suggests that if a provincial victim was poor, there was a chance (though still remote) that upon the unlikely circumstance of receiving a request for help, the Bow Street magistrates would send out a salaried Patrol member rather than a Principal Officer. This occasional provincial use of Patrol members is borne out by Sir Richard Birnie's evidence to the 1828 Select Committee. When questioned as to the provincial use of Patrol members, he stated that he occasionally sent Patrol officers 'as far as Yorkshire sometimes', and later repeated that 'we avail ourselves of the patrol occasionally' but that if he sent a patrol, unlike a Principal Officer (who charged a guinea a day for his services and 14 shillings a day for his expenses), 'he does not charge any such sum'.[47]

Such use of the less senior Bow Street personnel remained very much the exception to the rule throughout the period – of the total provincial cases researched for this book only 5.6 per cent employed Bow Street personnel other than the Principal Officers. Unlike the more senior Bow Street personnel, Patrol members seem to have been available at much less cost, usually being paid directly by Bow Street, though from the available evidence, they were still not employed widely outside the metropolis, most probably because of the fear of escalating the cost of sending such officials outside London, the costs having to be met directly by the government rather than by the victim(s). Such victims therefore seem to have been generally prevented from utilising the more highly skilled and experienced Principal Officers due to the high cost of their employment. As has been shown above, this contrasts sharply with the metropolitan situation, where less senior personnel were used on a much more regular basis.

Provincial magistrates

The role of the propertied and landed gentry in administering and dispensing provincial justice is demonstrated in Carl H. E. Zangerl's examination of the returns of Justices of the Peace from 1831 to 1887 (reproduced as Table 3.4).[48] He found that the magistracy in 1842 was overwhelmingly comprised of the gentry with the next largest group being the clergy, while the emergent mercantile/middle classes were not yet represented.

Despite an apparent close correlation between the type of private provincial employers of Bow Street and the composition of the provincial magistracy, i.e. while both groups were mainly comprised of the gentry with a smattering of aristocrats, provincial magistrates are only rarely recorded (in 31 cases) as having applied directly for the use of senior Bow Street personnel. This appears at first sight to be somewhat anomalous to generally perceived opinion: Alan Pike refers to the Bow Street Police Office as the body which 'magistrates all over the country would ask for their assistance if they were stuck with a serious crime', while Roger Wells quotes from the 1798 Select Committee *Report* that the Bow Street office was 'the office with which the County Magistrates correspond, and from which arises much Business for the magistrates, clerks and officers.'[49]

Table 3.4 Social composition of magistrates,*
England and Wales, 1842

	%
Aristocracy	8
Gentry	77
Clergy	13
Middle Classes	0
Others	1

*No. magistrates in 1842 = 3,090.

Similarly, in his evidence to the 1822 Select Committee, John Stafford, Chief Clerk at Bow Street, specifically refers to applications from provincial magistrates regarding arson cases, stating that 'it is very seldom that the farmers write themselves, they apply to the magistrates, and the application comes from the magistrates', and it is certainly the case that over two-fifths of the 52 recorded cases in which provincial magistrates applied directly to Bow Street were concerned with arson or other similar and serious damage to property (the vast majority (13) of the other cases being murder/attempted murder).[50]

However, this apparent discrepancy can be explained by the fact that such magistrates more often seem to have communicated with the Home Department rather than with Bow Street directly, and therefore their role in instigating the involvement of Bow Street remains somewhat masked in the statistics. That there was only limited direct correspondence with Bow Street or the other London Police Offices is suggested by Patrick Colquhoun's letter sent to George Rose MP on 3 May 1798 regarding the formation of the Central Board of Police Revenue in which he favoured the establishment of 'a correspondence with a select number of the most active and intelligent Magistrates in every part of Great Britain, for the purpose of communicating and receiving intelligence relative to criminal offences', suggesting that such correspondence was therefore not commonplace at the time.[51] Similarly, in his evidence to the 1816 Select Committee, Sir Nathaniel Conant indicated that regular communication with provincial magistrates was not kept.[52]

The reasons for this apparent lack of direct communication remain uncertain; perhaps the provincial magistracy, who for much of the period were not stipended individuals and who have been described as both 'a local oligarchy, appointed for life and responsible to no-one' and 'a self-constituting political elite', considered themselves as above direct contact with mere stipendiary magistrates, preferring to deal with their perceived social equals in the upper echelons of the Home Department.[53] Certainly, local magistrates were not required by law to instigate the executive pursuit of criminals, and although there were exceptions such as Samuel Lister (magistrate for the West Riding of Yorkshire 1751–69), research suggests they 'were rarely involved in detecting and apprehending offenders'.[54]

Another possible reason for the seeming reluctance of magistrates to deal directly with Bow Street could be that they were concerned with having to pay an often not inconsiderable sum for the expertise of the Principal Officers. By applying indirectly to the Home

Department, they may have hoped that the expense would have been paid by centralised government rather than from borough, parish or county coffers – and there is certainly evidence that when the Home Department considered the crime to be detrimental to the political or economic stability of the area, the Department would fund the cost of employing Principal Officers. An example can be seen in the following case in which, following the murder of a parish constable in the Forest of Dean in 1817, the magistrates of Ruarden sent a letter to the Home Department stating that 'we beg to suggest that an active Bow Street officer would be of essential service in the pursuit of [three murder suspects]', adding that:

> The state of the Forest of Dean and its neighbourhood is become so truly alarming, that […] the magistrates of the district have in contemplation to hold a meeting to consider the propriety and necessity of strengthening the police.[55]

The situation was clearly thought to be of a serious nature by Henry Addington (Viscount Sidmouth), Secretary of State for the Home Department, who subsequently drafted a reply that a Bow Street Officer was to be sent down without claiming expenses from the local authorities. This was by no means de rigueur, however; there are several recorded occasions in which similar requests for assistance from Bow Street via an application to the Home Department were acceded to only on the parochial authorities agreeing to fund the Officer'(s) expenses. Such an example can be found in a letter written in 1834 from the Secretary of State for the Home Department to Bow Street, following a number of arson attacks near Hereford. The Secretary desired the most intelligent officer to investigate, but specifically stated that 'the officer's expenses will be paid by the local authorities'.[55] Many magistrates must therefore have been relieved if the victim(s) decided to apply to Bow Street on their own behalf, therefore becoming responsible for the financial implications of such an action and not reducing county or borough coffers.

Institutions

Tables 3.5 and 3.6 show the types of institutional employer in recorded provincial and metropolitan cases.

These figures do not include any applications by such institutions that may have been made to the Home Department and then indirectly to Bow Street.

Table 3.5 Composition of provincial institutional employers

	%
Governmental institutions	47.2
Private institutions	52.8
Composition of these private institutions:	
Banks	49.1
Insurance companies	14.5
Other private institutions	36.4

Table 3.6 Composition of metropolitan institutional employers

	%
Governmental institutions	62.3
Private institutions	37.7
Composition of these private institutions:	
Banks	88.5
Insurance companies	3.8
Other private institutions	7.7

The overall institutional figures of provincial and metropolitan cases have been shown in Tables 3.1 and 3.2 above to be broadly consistent with each other. However, there is a considerable discrepancy in the percentage of government or private institutions when the provincial and metropolitan figures are compared. The government appears to have been much more willing to utilise Principal Officers in the metropolis than in the provinces; there are several possible explanations for this including the most obvious of expense – the Officers were much cheaper to employ in the environs of the metropolis. Another factor could be that many governmental institutions were based in the capital, and that there was a concomitant rise in the number of cases involving such institutions compared to in the provinces.

That banks are proportionately the most common type of private institutions to avail themselves of the services of Bow Street is perhaps not surprising considering both the often large amounts of money involved in robbery or forgery cases and the rapid proliferation in the growth of provincial banking during the period.[57] The number of country banks in England and Wales increased by over 224 per cent in the period 1793–1830, and this, together with the introduction of paper currency from 1797 following a shortage of coinage, led to a huge increase in forgery cases.[58]

Banks (both provincial and metropolitan) utilised numerous methods in endeavouring to trace the culprits of both bank robberies and forgeries, including the employment on occasion of Principal Officers. The Officers were employed primarily in the investigation of forgery cases or in detecting the perpetrators of bank robberies. Such crimes resulted from the loss (either actual in terms of stolen money or potential as in forgery cases) of considerable amounts, and unsurprisingly banks often invested a great deal of time and expense in the resultant investigations.

Although the expenses and charges incurred as a result of employing Principal Officers could on occasion be considerable, such costs were by no means unique to Bow Street – other forms of detection were also used by both the Bank of England and country banks on a regular basis, and subsequent investigations could often result in similarly high costs.[59] Randall McGowen estimates that in 1820 alone the Bank of England spent over £50,000 on the prosecution and investigation of forgery.[60]

Two examples show the often considerable costs involved in such investigations. Firstly, in 1779 a forgery investigation carried out by two Bank of Scotland employees is recorded as reaching a total cost of £56 16s 7d. Successful prosecution of the case cost a total of £128 17s 11d, justice obviously coming at a high price in this instance.[61] Secondly, an investigation of a forgery case at Cockermouth in 1812 carried out on behalf of Freshfields, the Bank of England's solicitors, cost the Bank over £93 for the services of their investigator Mr Christian and his deputy.[62] That investigating agencies other than Bow Street were utilised by provincial banks is further indicated in a letter to the Bank of England's solicitors from Plymouth Bank. The letter details 'an alarming degree of forged £1 and £2 notes', and requests 'a person for the purpose of tracing this evil to its source'.[63] Freshfields employed several investigators on at least a semi-permanent basis, one of the best known being Thomas Glover, who is referred to in correspondence from West Country sources concerning widespread rumours of forgeries.[64]

The above cases indicate that while banks were the most prevalent employers of Principal Officers among private institutions, there may have been a number of reasons for the relatively infrequent appearance of banks in the total of recorded cases. Firstly, it is clear that banks employed a variety of individuals and bodies to investigate crime, choosing not to rely solely on Bow Street or the other London Police

Offices, despite the fact that Sir Richard Birnie, in his evidence to the 1822 Select Committee, specifically mentions such usage when asked: 'What is the sort of business on which you think it desirable to dispatch those officers into the country?' He gives two examples, with 'forgery, as under Bank cases' being one of them.[65] Secondly, banks and indeed insurance companies may not appear as frequent employers due to their wish not to damage their public standing by publicly admitting breaches in their security measures.

In the case of banks, there is considerable evidence showing that private rather than public negotiations to retrieve stolen money often took place between the bank and the criminals, with a third party often acting as an intermediary. As has been shown above, such negotiations could involve Bow Street personnel on occasion, and the desire on behalf of banks and similar institutions to keep such matters out of the Press could explain the apparent infrequency of such cases.[66]

Similarly, other institutions seem to have regarded Bow Street as one constituent in the pantheon of options for detecting the perpetration of crimes against the respective bodies. Insurance companies appear surprisingly infrequently as employers in the recorded cases in both provincial and metropolitan records, with only a couple of fraudulent insurance claims and a few arson investigations involving Principal Officers being recorded.[67] An explanation for this relatively small number of cases could be that insurance companies have a long history of employing 'in-house' surveyors, investigators and assessors, the first post of Fire Surveyor being created in 1696 by the Hand in Hand Fire Insurance Office.[68] The majority of cases involving the employment of Bow Street officials by insurance companies related to attempts to discover the perpetrators of arson, but there is the occasional case in which large insurers such as Lloyd's of London employed Bow Street in both a detective and preventive capacity – see Chapter 6 for the case involving the plundering of the *Adamant*.

Such cases seem to have arisen when the insurance company was of the opinion that their own agents were not up to the task of investigating such complex cases. Lloyd's employed their own agents to carry out preliminary investigations in cases of plundering, but these agents, being locally employed and therefore conscious of their vulnerability within their immediate community, often proved ineffectual when confronted with a situation in which the perpetrators were protected by many fellow inhabitants. A letter from a local magistrate and owner of Heysham Hall, near Lancaster, regarding the prevention of plundering on the Lancashire coast, sums up the situation:

I feel that it is my duty as Magistrate to request that something may be done to check the practice of wrecking which prevails upon this coast. The agent for Lloyd's in this district has approached me and says "I must be supported by those who are placed in situations to render me assistance". The Parish Constable receives 2 shillings and 6d. per annum. I cannot expect him to be on the lookout for offenders in rough and stormy weather.[69]

Other institutions, both private and governmental, also employed Bow Street, but this was very much on an ad hoc basis, with specific circumstances leading to their involvement – for example, the forging of military service or pay certificates at Greenwich Pay Office, or the robbery of mail coaches. The one governmental institution which did utilise the services of Bow Street on a regular basis in the provinces was the Home Department, and it is to this body that the discussion now turns.

The Home Department

Surprisingly little research has been carried out into the early development of the Home Department (the term Home Office not entering into general use until the 1840s), but even these limited studies show that from its inception in 1782 the Home Department was surprisingly small and remained so for much of the period under discussion. Clive Emsley states that 'at the close of the eighteenth century the Home Office was a tiny organisation, consisting of less than two dozen individuals', while R. R. Nelson notes that 'only four rooms made up the Home Office quarters in Whitehall'.[70]

As Emsley comments, 'with no permanent police force in the country and no official centralised intelligence service, perhaps the greatest problem facing the Home Office during the 1790s, was knowing exactly what was going on in the kingdom'.[71]

Nelson suggests that this problem was at least partially met by the employment of King's Messengers, who fulfilled a number of duties: 'The corps [...] carried important dispatches and messages both in the British Isles and abroad, but it also acted as a kind of national police.'[72] The corps, never large in number, did increase from 16 men in 1772 to 30 in 1795.[73] It was undoubtedly a similarly dangerous profession to that of the Bow Street Officers, with perhaps an even wider remit, both in terms of jobs undertaken and geographical area covered. The King's Messengers routinely operated abroad, normally, though not exclusively, in Europe.[74] Bow Street certainly collaborated with The King's Messengers on several occasions, most notably on treason or sedition cases, as both organisations had gained considerable experience in investigating such matters.[75]

Roger Wells, in his study of the British secret service at the end of the eighteenth century, suggests that Bow Street was used by the fledgling Home Department as its information-gathering centre: 'the London police, and the metropolitan stipendiary magistracy, with their nerve centre at Bow Street were involved in the creation of the Home Office's intelligence system', while Emsley similarly remarks that 'after the creation of the London Police Offices in 1792 the Home Office increasingly called on the stipendiary magistrates of these offices to conduct investigations'.[76] Emsley also suggests that Sir Richard Ford, Bow Street Chief Magistrate from 1800 to 1806, could in some ways be regarded as a 'quasi' permanent Under-Secretary, coordinating Bow Street's assistance to the Home Department in its investigative work.[77] In 1800 Ford was also appointed as a Superintendent of Aliens, responsible for the monitoring of foreigners within Britain.[78]

An example of this is illustrated towards the end of September 1800, when Ford, described by Wells as 'one of a small number of officials responsible for the furtive creation of the British secret service', ordered two Bow Street officials to spend six weeks undercover in the Nottingham area following unrest and food-rioting.[79] The two men apparently successfully infiltrated the 'seditious' society, and they became 'immediately [...] acquainted with the disaffected persons in Nottingham, and were received into their company [...]. The conversation was always of the most seditious nature [...] they were under no fear of the Magistracy.'[80]

Use in sedition cases

Such use of Bow Street personnel, including Principal Officers, appears to have been fairly commonplace and was an important part of Bow Street's existence – the Principal Officers were used in over 30 recorded provincial cases in the period. A typical example of this type of investigation was reported in the *Staffordshire Advertiser* of 10 March 1798, which carried the following correspondence from Margate, dated 28 February 1798:

Five persons have been apprehended here this morning by two of Bow Street Public Officers, upon suspicion of carrying on a Treasonable Correspondence with the French Government. [...]

Rivett and Fugion, two of Bow Street's Public Officers, were the persons appointed by the Government to apprehend them. It is pretended that these officers were down in Kent, at Gravesend, on other business; but we believe they were sent from London specially on this business, and that Government had good intelligence of the proceedings of the parties now in custody. [...] The officers had previously consulted some Custom House officials, whom they engaged in their cause, together with a party of the military.

This particular use of Bow Street personnel was clearly widely known and continued throughout the period under discussion; in July 1815, the Mayor of Leicester applied unsuccessfully for the use of Principal Officers as spies to defeat seditious and threatening meetings in his town, and in July 1835 Sir Frederick Roe, Bow Street Chief Magistrate, was sent to investigate rioting in Wolverhampton.[81] In early December 1838, Henry Goddard was directed by Roe to proceed to Leigh Bury, Todmorden, Ashton-under-Lyne and other places to

take notes, observe and obtain what information I could as to the names of the authors and ringleaders attending these seditious and Torchlight meetings. [...] All I have to do, Sir Frederick said, requires silence, discretion and activity, to have assistance at hand, but not to cause alarm by shewing it.[82]

Numerous Bow Street personnel were also involved in the Luddite disturbances in Nottinghamshire and Derbyshire during 1811 and 1812; the reports often do not make it clear whether or not the personnel involved were Principal Officers or Patrol personnel, but several sources indicate that there was a considerable contingent from Bow Street. A letter sent in early January 1812 from Nathaniel Conant to the magistrates at Nottingham states that 'you may be assured that no assistance on our part or of the force we have with us shall be wanting', and he proposed to 'get our men sworn in as Special Constables both for this County and Derbyshire, that they may be ready to act at any moment [that] opportunity may arise.'[83]

The presence of Bow Street personnel in the streets of Nottingham excited considerable interest in the local press, including the following somewhat unusual report of a case of mistaken identity (thus illustrating a problem of lack of local knowledge that must have often been faced by the Officers), which poked fun at the efforts of the Bow Street Officer involved:

On Tuesday, several prisoners were brought in from the county, by military escorts, among them was John Waplington, a well-known wandering maniac [...]. He [...] was apprehended as a suspicious character [...]. But what excited the attention of the public more than usual, was, to see this unfortunate offspring of our father Adam, confined in a cart by the side of a lusty Bow Street Public Officer, who drove along the streets with dashing fury, attended by about half a score Hussars.[84]

The report is also interesting in that it confirms that Principal Officers often collaborated closely with military personnel when they were sent to investigate rioting or similar such 'seditious' behaviour. It is perhaps not surprising that the Bow Street personnel sought out the aid of a body of armed men, as many such disturbances involved considerable numbers of angry and unpredictable 'rioters'.

Other uses by the Home Department

It was not just for cases of sedition, rioting or treason that the Home Department utilised Principal Officers; they were often used in conjunction with other governmental bodies in various preventive and detective roles. In several of the reported smuggling cases, Principal Officers were engaged by the state to work in conjunction with other law-enforcement bodies such as the Revenue or the Coastal Blockade.[85] Reports of the arrest of one particularly notorious group of smugglers known as the Aldington Gang show that Principal Officers were used in conjunction with members of the Coastal Blockade and that the Officers appeared to be subordinate to the leader of the Blockade. This determined and well organised group could reputedly call upon over 200 men in smuggling runs and gained long-standing notoriety after the murder of a Coastal Blockade Officer, Richard Morgan, in 1826.

On 16 October 1826 an attack on the Aldington Gang was led by Lieutenant Sam Hellard of the Coastal Blockade, assisted by two Principal Officers, Daniel Bishop and John J. Smith, who acted under his instructions. This attack was partially successful, and most of the gang were arrested. On 14 November 1826, Lieutenant Hellard led another raid to capture the remnants of the gang, but the weather was atrocious and the conditions proved too much even for an experienced and hardy Principal Officer: 'Some roads were nearly three feet deep in mud and the police officer [John James Smith] said he must give up [as] he could not proceed any further.'[86] The raids by Hellard and the Principal Officers netted a total of 19 men, most of whom (including the gang leader, George Ransley) were transported to Australia after what appears to have been frantic 'plea-bargaining' in order to calm the local situation.

The Principal Officers were also utilised by the Home Department for other less dangerous and onerous tasks; they were often called upon to guard the King and his retinue from pickpocketing gangs when the monarch visited the provinces. The Sheriff Deputy of Leith wrote to the Home Department in July 1822 stating that it was 'necessary that two or three Bow Street Officers who know by sight the principal London pickpockets should be in Edinburgh for the purpose of pointing them out to the officers of the Edinburgh police', while in the previous year, Vickery and Bishop had been sent to Ireland after the King's watch was pickpocketed by an enterprising thief.[87] On one occasion in 1837 a Bow Street Officer was somewhat unusually directed to Brixworth in order to investigate the payment of Poor Relief:

Soon after the Workhouse had opened the Secretary of State had to send a Bow Street Runner to Brixworth to investigate the strict policy being adopted by the Guardians regarding the payment of 'out relief' to the poor and needy.[88]

Attitude of the Home Department to provincial authorities' use of Principal Officers

The Home Department had the final say with regard to the Bow Street magistrates' decision to send Principal Officers at public (i.e. state) expense to the provinces, and it is clear from correspondence that the Home Department frequently refused applications from local authorities when the Department considered that they were failing in their duty. There are several instances where applications made by local magistrates or other provincial bodies were not accepted by the Home Department.

Quite apart from what was perceived as an unsustainable drain on the resources of Bow Street, the Home Department seems to have been reluctant to employ the services of the Principal Officers in provincial cases except when absolutely necessary because of the precedents this would create. It clearly wished the onus of arresting and prosecuting offenders to remain within the remit of the local authorities and therefore discouraged a reliance on central government. The sending of Principal Officers would also lend weight to the oft-repeated assertions that local authorities were inefficient and unable to maintain law and order without central government backing.

During the Luddite disturbances of 1811–12 in Nottinghamshire, the Home Department originally 'refused requests for Bow Street Public Officers or a Special Commission, and had been unwilling to accept financial and other responsibility for prosecuting offenders and preparing witnesses', although Bow Street personnel were sent after the situation continued to deteriorate.[89] In a similar manner, requests from the magistrates of Huddersfield for the creation of a Night Watch under the auspices of Bow Street were also refused.[90]

Apart from having the ultimate sanction with regard to Bow Street personnel's employment, the Home Department also had overall control of most other aspects of the functioning of the Police Office: it approved or disallowed appointments from Patrol Constables to Chief Magistrates, and also controlled the purse-strings. Bow Street personnel were recommended for appointment or promotion by a wide variety of individuals – for example, Richard Gardner was recommended to serve as a Bow Street Patrol Constable by the Duke of Bedford in February 1824 – but there is at least one example of a recommended applicant being refused office by the Home Department.[91] In December 1831, the magistrates at Bow Street recommended Thomas Ford, Bow Street gaoler to replace Bishop, who had reached the age of superannuation, 'there being no one better informed of the haunts of known thieves and pickpockets'. Samuel March Phillips (Under-Secretary of State) wrote on the back of the recommendation request that 'he cannot be appointed – he has been guilty of corruption'.[92]

Similarly, the Home Department seems to have been reluctant to use Principal Officers in metropolitan cases of sedition or treason; only two such cases are recorded in the OBP. An explanation could be that the Home Department was unwilling to involve Principal Officers who were undoubtedly well-known figures throughout much of London for fear of being seen to admit that such matters were taking place in the metropolis. No such reservations seem to have applied in regard to private requests for the provincial use of Principal Officers – the Home Department seems to have been much less concerned if private money was at stake.

Conclusion

From the above discussion, it is apparent that Principal Officers were employed by a wide variety of provincial employers, ranging from wealthy individuals to governmental bodies and private companies. With regard to the provincial employers (apart from the Home Department), it is equally clear that the connecting thread between all of them was the ability to pay handsomely for the services of Bow Street; this does not seem to have been the case to anywhere near as large an extent in the metropolis. The discussion has shown that poorer provincial victims rarely if ever enjoyed the use of experienced Principal Officers, the prohibitive nature of the costs involved preventing them from availing themselves of such service, whereas the mercantile class made much more use of them in London. That such provincial costs could be considerable has been demonstrated, but the chapter has also indicated that investigations carried out by other bodies could be equally as expensive.

The decision to employ Principal Officers rather than rely on other available methods of investigation seems to have been largely dictated by a combination of the individual circumstances of each crime together with the economic, social or political standing of the victim(s) – this is especially relevant with regard to their employment by bodies or institutions such as insurance companies or banks which possessed 'in-house' investigators. That Bow Street personnel were sometimes chosen in preference to these other forms of detection suggests that the Principal Officers were often held in high regard and considered to provide the best opportunity of recovering the companies' losses and arresting the culprits. Similarly, wealthy private individuals seem to have turned to Bow Street in the expectation that it would offer the best return from an often considerable investment in terms of detection of perpetrators and recovery of goods or money.

The next chapter turns from a discussion of who employed the Principal Officers to the contemporary perception of crime and the types of crime investigated by them in both the provinces and the capital.

Notes

1 John Wade, *The Black book or Corruption Unmasked* (London: John Fairburn, 1820); John Wade, *A Treatise on the Police and Crimes of the Metropolis*, intro. J. J. Tobias (Montclair, NJ: Patterson Smith, 1972; original published

1829); and G. B. Mainwaring, *Observations on the Present State of the Police of the Metropolis* (London: John Murray, 1821).

2 Figures abstracted from T 38/673 Treasury: Departmental Accounts, Public Office, Bow Street 1793–1816 (1793–1802 figures); 47 Geo. III c.CXLII (1807 figure); HO 65/2 Police Entry Books Series I 1795–1921, letter dated 18 October 1811 (1811 figure); HO 60/1 Police Court Entry Books 1821–30 (1821 figure).

3 In a letter from Melbourne to Bow Street, 5 January 1831 (HO 60/2 Police Court Entry Book, p. 86) Melbourne's secretary detailed the ordered changes: 'Viscount Melbourne [...] observes that these allowances are much higher than are necessary and though they have been hitherto admitted his lordship does not feel himself justified in sanctioning their continuance. He therefore directs that in future the following scale of allowances may be adopted in lieu thereof: All reasonable expenses of conveyance to be allowed. Twelve shillings per day for expenses of subsistence and lodging. Ten shillings per day in addition to their regular pay, for their extra services.'

4 The figure of 14s per day applied from at least 1816 to 1831.

5 The earliest mention of a guinea per day while on provincial duties is in 1812 (T 38/673), and this continued until Melbourne's reforms in 1831.

6 HO 65/2, letter dated 17 March 1819.

7 HO 60/2, letter dated 27 March 1833. It is not clear whether the injury was caused by a spectator or a horse.

8 HO 60/2, letter dated 24 March 1836.

9 HO 60/1, Expenses for Quarter ending October 1825, p. 190. This must have been a protracted legal case, as Adkins left Bow Street in late 1820.

10 TNA T 38/673, Treasury Accounts 1793–1816.

11 The pensions seem to have varied according to length of service; William Ballard received a superannuation of £100 per year following 16 years of service, as did Henry Goddard (Les Waters, 'The Bow Street Runners: A Hand Book of Police in London Working for Bow Street and the other Middlesex Justices Act Offices 1750–1839' (Huntingdon: unpublished work for the Police History Society, undated *c*.1992), pp. 5 and 8).

12 HO 42/130 f. 182, letter dated 22 December 1812. Widows' pensions appear relating to the spouses of William Barnett (who was murdered while on duty) in TNA T 38/673, Treasury Accounts 1793–1816.

13 Such rewards could reach considerable sums: Beattie remarks that 'rewards paid in London for the conviction of street robbers, which for the twenty-five years between 1720 and 1745 were supplemented by royal proclamation [...] amounted to £140 for each defendant – a staggering sum that approached three or four years' income for even a skilled workman' (J. M. Beattie, 'Early Detection: the Bow Street Runners in Late Eighteenth-Century London', unpublished essay).

14 A. H. Manchester, *Sources of English Legal History: Law, History and Society in England and Wales, 1750–1950* (London: Butterworth, 1984), p. 237.

15 PP 1816, p. 4.

16 Ibid., p. 4.

17 Ibid., pp. 8–9.

18 Ibid., p. 42. The same Committee did in fact later hear evidence of the dismissal of two Principal Officers from the Hatton Garden Office, who were sacked for corruption and were not replaced, thus causing the Hatton Garden Office complement of Principal Officers to be temporarily reduced to eight.

19 *Monthly Review or Literary Journal*, vol. LXXXI, September–December 1816 (London: J. Porter, 1816), p. 196.

20 OBP, January 1821, trial of Thomas Williams, t18210110-46.

21 Ibid., p. 196.

22 Ibid., pp. 139–40.

23 Lucas Benjamin Allen, *Brief Considerations on the Present State of the police of the metropolis: with a few suggestions towards its improvement* (London: Joseph Butterworth, 1821), p. 32.

24 PP 1816, p. 138. This was probably the murder of four Revenue Officers by a smuggling gang at Deal in Kent in 1815, in the investigation of which Principal Officer John Vickery played a leading role.

25 Metropolitan Inspector's salary taken from C. T. Clarkson and J. Hall Richardson, *Police!* (London: Field & Tuer, 1889), pp. 67–8; Goddard's salary taken from Henry Goddard, *Memoirs of a Bow Street Runner*, ed. Patrick Pringle (London: Museum Press, 1956), p. xxiii; and Lavender's salary taken from the *Manchester Guardian*, 9 June 1832.

26 PP 1816, p. 174.

27 Bennet's Act of 1818. Henry Grey Bennet was the Chairman of the 1816 Select Committee. Bow Street was not the only law-enforcement agency to benefit from the system of statutory or discretionary rewards – the system was in use throughout Britain. See J. L. Hammond, and Barbara Hammond, *The Town Labourer 1760–1832: The New Civilisation*, 2nd edn, 2 vols (London: Guild Books, 1949), vol. 1, p. 85 for an account of the scandals surrounding 'blood-money' in provincial towns.

28 Jennifer Hart, 'Reform of the Borough Police 1835–1856', *EHR*, vol. 70 (1955), pp. 411–22, at p. 419. Discretionary rewards continued well into the twentieth century – Crewe Borough Petty Sessions Register for 1918 contains numerous cases in which police officers (of various ranks ranging from Constable to Inspector) are noted as receiving rewards ranging from ten shillings to one pound for the capture of deserters from the Armed Forces (Chester Archives QPCr 3863/21). Similarly, Detective Inspector Richard Tanner (who achieved a degree of fame in 1864 for capturing Franz Muller, the first person to be found guilty of carrying out a murder on a railway train) recorded in his notebook (which lists cases from 1856 to 1867) that he received numerous rewards ranging from 10s to £50. See

Martin Fido and Keith Skinner, *The Official Encyclopedia of Scotland Yard* (London: Virgin, 1999), p. 259 for further details of Inspector Tanner's career. Such rewards (although from public funds) are still occasionally allowed; section 31 of the 1996 Police Act states that: 'A police authority may, on the recommendation of the chief officer of police, grant out of the police fund to members of the police force maintained by that authority rewards for exceptional diligence or other especially meritorious conduct.'

29 Select Committee Report into County Rates PP 1836 xxvi, quoted in D. Hay and F. Snyder (eds), *Policing and Prosecution in Britain, 1750–1850* (Oxford: OUP, 1989), p. 46.

30 HO 73/4 Report to the Royal Commission on a Rural Constabulary, 1834.

31 It is unlikely that the Principal Officers would routinely have been used within the metropolis in the investigation of minor misdemeanours, for the same reasons that they were rarely used on such cases in the provinces.

32 This category is obviously redundant with regard to metropolitan cases.

33 Private institutions include insurance companies, banks, mail coach companies, etc. Public institutions are classed as governmental bodies other than the Home Department, such as the Marine Pay Offices, the Admiralty, the Bank of England, etc.

34 That this required permission seeming to have been fairly common knowledge is implied by the fact that it appears in Richmond's fictional account entitled *Scenes in the life of a Bow Street Runner*, where one of the Officers states, when requested to attend to a case, that 'I have no power, Sir, to do any thing of myself to serve you without the orders of the presiding magistrate' (Anon, *Richmond – Scenes from the life of a Bow Street Runner*, vol. 2, p. 119).

35 An exact comparison between the rate of employment of Principal Officers and less senior Bow Street officers must not be drawn from these figures, however, as the figure of almost 1,300 refers to the total number of mentions of the various Bow Street Patrols in the OBP, and of course more than one Patrol member could be involved in the same case. With regard to the Principal Officers, the figure of 292 is by contrast the total number of cases involving one or more Principal Officers rather than mentions of individual Officers.

36 Peter King, *Crime, Justice, and Discretion in England 1740–1820* (Oxford: OUP, 2000), p. 354.

37 PP 1816, p. 215.

38 HO 64/5 f. 68, letter dated 8 May 1835 and HO 64/4 f. 199 note on letter dated 24 November 1834. It is not clear in this instance as to whether the correspondence referred specifically to a Bow Street Officer, but all the London Offices operated a similar system of charging.

39 HO 643/8 ff. 43–46 8 July 1838.

40 Bryan Jerrard, 'Early Policing in Gloucestershire', *Transactions of the Bristol and Gloucestershire Archaeological Society for 1992*, vol. C (1993), pp. 221–40, at pp. 229–30.

41 HO 64/6 ff. 234–5 8 January 1836. Such charges also applied to the sending of Metropolitan Police officers outside London – several of the letters do not make it clear whether or not they are referring to Bow Street Officers or Metropolitan personnel. The use of Metropolitan personnel to investigate cases originating in the provinces, while relatively rare, was by no means unknown, but such usage normally related to government-instigated and funded investigations.

42 See Goddard, ed. Pringle, *Memoirs*, pp. 144–7 for a detailed account of the case.

43 *The Times*, 12 March 1838. It is not clear who paid for the services of the Bow Street Officer.

44 The murder/attempted murder figures relating to working-class victims are one King's Messenger, one steward, one Poor Law official, three Bow Street personnel, one Watchman, ten Gamekeepers, two Parish Constables, twelve Revenue/Coastal Blockage Officers and one Turnpike Keeper.

45 That the Officers could behave humanely and compassionately towards the poor is demonstrated in a story carried by *Bell's Weekly Messenger* of 28 November 1830, in which Townsend is reported to have found a young woman in straitened circumstances and with an illegitimate baby wandering in Green Park. Townsend established that she was destitute, having been deserted by her lover. He supplied her with new clothes and 3s at his own expense, and persuaded some of his friends to raise £5 for her support. She was then conveyed back to her native parish in Kingswood, Gloucestershire. Townsend seems to have been quite a caring man; the *Morning Chronicle* of 30 November 1807 carried a story of his procuration of a 'presentation' – a financial gift – to Christ's Hospital for one of three orphan boys, the sons of his wife's sister – when he grew richer he looked after the boy himself.

46 Ibid., p. 10. Conant does not make it clear whether or not he is referring solely to the situation within the metropolis.

47 PP 1828, pp. 37, 43 and 42.

48 Carl H. E. Zangerl, 'The Social Composition of the County Magistracy in England and Wales, 1831–1887', *Journal of British Studies*, vol. XI (November 1971), p. 93. For a detailed discussion of the social composition of a particular county magistracy in the early nineteenth century, see Helen Johnston, 'Policing, Punishment and Social Institutions in the Nineteenth Century: The Role of the Shropshire Magistracy', in David J. Cox and Barry Godfrey (eds), *Cinderellas and Packhorses: A History of the Shropshire Magistracy* (Logaston: Logaston Press, 2005), pp. 43–64.

49 Alan R. Pike, 'A Brief History of the C.I.D. of the London Metropolitan Police', *Police Studies*, vol. 1, no. 2 (June 1978), pp. 22–30, at p. 22, and Roger Wells, *Insurrection: The British Experience 1795–1803* (Gloucester: Alan Sutton, 1983), p. 37.

50 PP 1822, p. 26.

51 Letter reproduced in PP 1798, p. 355.

52 PP 1816, p. 12.

53 David Philips, 'The Black Country Magistracy, 1835–1860: A Changing Elite and the Exercise of Its Power', *Midland History*, vol. III, no. 3 (Spring 1976), p. 163, and David Eastwood, *Government and Community in the English Provinces 1700–1870* (Basingstoke: Macmillan 1997), p. 96.

54 John Styles, 'An Eighteenth-Century Magistrate as Detective: Samuel Lister of Little Horton', *Bradford Antiquary*, New Series, Part XLVII (October 1982), pp. 98–117, and King, *Crime, Justice, and Discretion in England 1740–1820*, p. 62. This research is borne out with regard to the few surviving Justices' Books; there is little mention of an investigative role played by the magistrates. For a detailed analysis of such a notebook, see Ruth Paley (ed.), *Justice in Eighteenth-Century Hackney: The Justicing Notebook of Henry Norris and the Hackney Petty Sessions Book* (London: London Record Society, 1991).

55 HO 42/165 f. 320, letter dated 15 May 1817, and reply from Addington, HO 41/3, letter dated 26 May 1817 (latter quoted in Leon Radzinowicz, *A History of English Criminal Law and Its Administration from 1750*, vol. 2 (London: Stevens & Sons, 1956), p. 80).

56 MEPO 1/49, letter dated 28 June 1834.

57 The Bank of England was founded in 1694 as the first public bank in Britain, with the Bank of Scotland being founded in the following year. Their respective success led to the creation of provincial or 'country' banks throughout Britain. For a history of the Bank of England see Richard Roberts and David Kynaston (eds), *The Bank of England: Money, Power and Influence 1694–1994* (Oxford: Clarendon Press, 1995), and for a history of the Bank of Scotland, see Alan Cameron, *Bank of Scotland 1695–1995: A Very Singular Institution* (Edinburgh: Mainstream Publishing, 1995).

58 Percentage increase abstracted from Jeremy Gregory and John Stevenson, *The Longman Companion to Britain in the Eighteenth Century* (London: Longman, 2000), Table 9.2: Country Banks in England and Wales, 1784–1830, p. 273.

59 *Crime and Punishment Police vol. VIII* (IUP Reprints Series): *First Report on the Constabulary Force in England and Wales*, PP 1839 (169) vol. XIX, p. 5.

60 Randall McGowen, *The Bank of England and the Policing of Forgery, 1797–1821*, paper delivered at the European Centre for Policing Studies, Open University, Milton Keynes, 28 November 2003. For further details on how the Bank of England prosecuted forgery and coining, see also Randall McGowen, 'Managing the Gallows: The Bank of England and the Death Penalty, 1797–1821', *Law and History Review*, vol. 25, no. 2 (Summer 2007), pp. 241–82

61 Alan Cameron, *Bank of Scotland 1695–1995*, pp. 102–3.

62 *Bank of England Freshfields' Papers F22/8 AB64/2: Correspondence concerning forgery in Cockermouth 15 April–8 July 1812*. This case shows that the Bank

of England employed its own investigators as well as occasionally calling upon the expertise of Bow Street or the other Police Offices.

63 Bank of England Freshfields' Papers F2/165 AB 179/5, letter dated 10 January 1807. The person was presumably one of the Bank of England's own investigators.

64 Bank of England Freshfields' Papers F2/155 AB 91/12, various letters dated 6 April–21 April 1801. Thomas Glover sent back a detailed series of reports, together with his own comments on how and why the rumours had started. He visited Brixham, Totnes, Torquay, Dartmouth and Exeter in his exertions to find the culprits.

65 PP 1822, p. 14. He may of course have been referring purely to Bank of England cases.

66 Such a system of negotiation with bank robbers or fraudsters continues to occur in the present day. On 21 April 2002 a BBC Radio 4 programme, *Staunching the Flow*, dealt with the same subject with regard to present-day robberies and frauds. Several experts were interviewed regarding bank fraud and robbery, with a former MI5 officer remarking that 'banks are so sensitive about protecting their public image that they are willing to allow those who steal their money to keep it'. Similarly, in the same programme a financial investigator stated that 'banks prefer to investigate fraud themselves rather than making them public'. He also claimed that deals are regularly struck with regard to insurance companies: 'They are basically a hostage to a crime that has already occurred. Therefore, their vested interest is, as with any Board of Directors of any Bank, to make as much [of] a recovery as possible.' These deals clearly often involve a third party acting as intermediary and negotiator in much the same way as Principal Officers (with the implicit support of both their magistrates and the parties involved) did in the early nineteenth century.

67 For details of Principal Officers' involvement in arson cases, see Chapter 4.

68 David T. Hawkings, *Fire Insurance Records for Family and Local Historians 1696 to 1920* (London: Francis Boutle, 2003), p. 19. For a comprehensive account of the development of insurance companies, see David Jenkins and Takau Yoneyama (eds), *The History of Insurance*, 8 vols (London: Pickering & Chatto, 2000).

69 HO 44/32 ff. 110–111.

70 Clive Emsley, 'The Home Office and Its Sources of Information and Investigation 1791–1801', *English Historical Review*, vol. XCIV (July 1979), pp. 532–61, at p. 532, and R. R. Nelson, *The Home Office 1782–1801* (Durham, NC: Duke University Press, 1969), p. 71.

71 Emsley, 'The Home Office and Its Sources of Information and Investigation 1791–1801', p. 536.

72 Nelson, *The Home Office 1782–1801*, p. 149.

73 Ibid., p. 149.

74 A King's Messenger was murdered at Romford in 1795 and was

investigated by Bow Street – see Herbert Hope Lockwood, 'The Bow Street Mounted Patrol on Essex Highways', in Kenneth Neale (ed.), *Essex 'Full of Profitable Thinges': Essays Presented to Sir John Ruggles Brise* (Oxford: Leopard's Head Press, 1996), pp. 311–30, at pp. 315–16. Much more research is needed to clarify the position and role of such personnel, as little of significance appears to have been written about them, despite them having frequently played an important role (often in espionage) in the diplomatic history of England. The only serious history of them remains V. Wheeler-Holohan, *The History of the King's Messengers* (London: E. P. Dutton, 1935).

75 For an example of collaboration between King's Messengers and Bow Street, see Francis Place, *The Autobiography of Francis Place*, ed. Mary Thale (London: CUP, 1972), p. 176.

76 Wells, *Insurrection: The British Experience 1795–1803*, p. 37, and Emsley, 'The Home Office and Its Sources of Information and Investigation 1791–1801', p. 532.

77 Emsley, 'The Home Office and Its Sources of Information and Investigation 1791–1801', p. 532.

78 This post was thought necessary due to the continued hostilities with France and the perceived increase in continental (especially French) immigration to England.

79 Roger A. E. Wells, *Riot and Political Disaffection in Nottinghamshire in the Age of Revolutions, 1776–1803* (Nottingham: University of Nottingham, 1983), p. 1. The two named Bow Street officials (Amsden and Mayhew) are referred to by Wells as 'Runners' but they were not Principal Officers. Thomas Amsden appears in both OBP, July 1797, trial of Patrick Keogh, t17970712-1 and OBP, May 1820, trial of Benjamin Meredith, t18200517-66 and describes himself on both occasions as a Patrol Officer, while Thomas Mayhew is similarly described in OBP, February 1802, trial of James Mackenough, t18020217-15. This use of non-Principal Officers on such protracted provincial cases is unusual; they may have had specialist knowledge of the individuals concerned in the sedition.

80 HO 42/55, letter from R. Ford to Home Secretary, Duke of Portland, enclosing the deposition of Amsden, 9 December 1800 (HO 42/55, f. 40), quoted in Wells, *Riot and Political Disaffection in Nottinghamshire in the Age of Revolutions, 1776–1803*, p. 1.

81 Frank Ogley Darvall, *Popular Disturbances and Public Order in Regency England* (London: OUP, 1969), pp. 150–1, and the *Manchester Guardian*, various editions during July 1835. Investigation into whether or not Sir Frederick Roe involved any of the senior Bow Street personnel in his investigations or came to the Midlands alone has proved inconclusive.

82 Henry Goddard, *Memoirs* (4-volume manuscript dated 1875–79), vol. 4, p. 216.

83 HO 42, letter dated 22 January 1812. The swearing-in as Special Constables was obviously carried out to negate the need for Bow Street officials to

be accompanied by parish constables, who may well have been known to the suspects.

84 *Nottingham Review and General Advertiser for the Midland Counties*, 31 January 1812.

85 The Coastal Blockade was created in 1817 and was the forerunner of the modern Coastguard. It ran from Sheerness to Chichester, a distance of some 200 miles, and employed over 3,000 men. For an account of its history, see Roy Philp, *The Coast Blockade: The Royal Navy's War on Smuggling*, 2nd edn (Horsham: Compton Press, 2002).

86 Ibid., p. 109. This is a rare documented case where a Bow Street Officer is reported as admitting failure.

87 John McGowan, 'The Emergence of Modern Civil Police in Scotland: A Case Study of the Police and Systems of Policing in Edinburghshire 1800–1833' (unpublished PhD thesis, Open University, 1996), p. 265, and *Manchester Guardian*, 8 September 1821.

88 Extract from *Brixworth – A Village Appraisal* (Brixworth: Brixworth Village Appraisal Committee, 1994), reproduced at http://www.brixworthhistory.org/.

89 Darvall, *Popular Disturbances and Public Order in Regency England*, p. 82.

90 Ibid., pp. 109.

91 MEPO 4/508 Foot Patrol Register 1821–29.

92 HO 44/13, letter dated 31 December 1831.

Chapter 4

'Contending with desperate characters': the types of crimes investigated by Principal Officers

Introduction

This chapter begins with a brief discussion on perceptions of crime and then analyses the types of crimes investigated by the Principal Officers in the provinces, debating the reasons for their use in each of the different categories of crime shown in Table 4.1 below. It suggests reasons for the use of Principal Officers in such cases and why the other available law-enforcement agencies were considered to be unsuitable by those employing the services of Bow Street. It also compares and contrasts the types of provincial crime with those investigated in the metropolis.

Perceptions of crime

The nineteenth century was a period of unparalleled conflict and change in many aspects of British society, and perceptions of crime and criminality were modified as a result of this socio-economic and political upheaval. Throughout the century, as a result of various changes including the reform of criminal codes and the growth in availability of, and refinement to, statistical information these perceptions were altered and occasionally deliberately manipulated by both an increasingly sophisticated socio-political system and an emergent media.[1] The fear of losing political control contributed to the promulgation in the minds of many middle- and upper-class individuals of the creation of a class of itinerant, idle and often drunken working-class men – what Sir Archibald Alison, the Tory Sheriff of Lanarkshire, referred to in 1844 as 'the dangerous classes'.[2]

The legal definitions of crime were very much a construct of the ruling social and cultural milieu – witness the reform of the criminal codes and penalties from a concentration on crimes against the person to a concentration on crimes against property. Frank McLynn suggests that the attitude of employers towards perks of the job had constantly hardened throughout the preceding century – he states that 'in the woollen trade alone, eleven new embezzlement statutes were passed from 1725 to 1800'.[3] Private wealth and property had become an important sign of affluence and respectability – those who had amassed it (by whatever means) were increasingly unwilling to forfeit even a small part of it – and were willing to expend considerable time and effort to regain it if lost. These changing views toward crime are discussed below in relation to the types of crime investigated by the Principal Officers.

Provincial cases

Rationale and limitations of provincial case types

Table 4.1 below shows the types of provincial cases involving Principal Officers investigated in this book. It does not include any cases which originated within London and subsequently involved provincial activity by the Principal Officers, for example the capture of a fleeing suspect from a crime committed in the metropolis, all such crimes instead being shown in Table 4.3 below.

In order to render the analysis more manageable, a degree of rationalisation has been made in the nomenclature of the categories of crime shown in both Tables 4.1 and 4.3. There has therefore been a concatenation of similar types of crime into a more encompassing category. Counterfeiting, forgery and fraudulent behaviour have been grouped under the category of forgery/fraud, while rioting, sedition and treason have similarly been grouped under a single category.

It must also be recognised that some of the recorded cases involved more than one type of crime; for example, several of the cases recorded under the category of murder/attempted murder resulted from poaching affrays that escalated to the shooting of gamekeeper(s), while other murders/attempted murders resulted from the attacking of Revenue officers by smuggling gangs. In such instances the case

A Certain Share of Low Cunning

is recorded under the more serious category of murder/attempted murder.

With regard to Table 4.1, all the crimes have been categorised according to the nature of the offence reported rather than any subsequent charges that may have been formally laid before the suspect at respective trials – the crime reported was not always the exact offence for which the suspect was tried. It must also be stressed that for some of the cases recorded details are extremely sparse, giving little more than the briefest description of the case and its location. With regard to Table 4.3, all crimes are the offence for which the suspect was tried.[4]

Serious nature of majority of provincial cases

It is clear from a perusal of Table 4.1 that while Principal Officers were involved in a wide variety of investigations involving numerous different types of criminal activity, the vast majority of cases involved crimes of a serious indictable and often capital nature.

Even when the reforms of 1832 (which greatly reduced the number of capital offences) are taken into consideration, almost two-thirds of recorded cases theoretically still carried the statutory penalty of death (although research by Gatrell suggests that such ultimate sanction was not effected in many such instances, especially towards the end of the period under discussion).[5]

This finding suggests that in the majority of instances, Principal Officers were employed in the provinces by a variety of individuals or institutions in order to investigate serious and often capital crimes that were deemed worthy of detailed, prolonged and often expensive professional investigation. It would therefore appear that such crimes were thought by those who suffered from them to be beyond the capabilities of local law-enforcement agencies, necessitating the employment of more skilled and experienced personnel in order to achieve a satisfactory outcome to subsequent investigations.

Analysis of categories of provincial crime

Six categories of crime dominate the findings shown in Table 4.1, accounting for almost four-fifths (79 per cent) of the total number of cases.[6] The remaining categories of crime occur in the records on a much less regular basis. This book does not aspire to discuss the causes or underlying reasons behind the many different types of criminality recorded – rather it relates the categories of crime to the employment of Principal Officers, discussing why they were called

104

Table 4.1 Types of recorded provincial cases, 1792–1839

	No. cases	%
Abduction/elopement/bigamy/adultery	9	1.50
Arson/damage to property/threatening behaviour	93	15.47
Burglary	66	10.98
Duelling/prizefighting	11	1.83
Fraud/forgery/embezzlement/counterfeiting	71	11.81
Larceny	86	14.31
Murder/attempted murder	99	16.47
Others/Not recorded	15	2.50
Pickpocketing	14	2.33
Poaching	9	1.50
Recapture of escapee(s)	14	2.33
Robbery	61	10.15
Smuggling	11	1.83
Spying/sedition/treason/rioting	42	6.99
Total	601	

out to investigate such cases. The seven main types of cases are dealt with below in descending order of occurrence.

Murder/attempted murder

Murder was the most common crime investigated, with a total of 99 cases of murder/attempted murder being recorded, such cases being present in over three-quarters of years within the 48-year period; only eleven years do not include a murder investigation.

Many of the murder/attempted murder victims (over a quarter of the total) were employed by the government or private individuals in various law-enforcement capacities. This seems to have underwritten the willingness on behalf of the Home Department to employ Bow Street Officers at governmental cost in an attempt to trace and prosecute the perpetrator(s) of such offences. It is clear that in many such cases, the local and national authorities either could not or did not wish to rely on local or parish constables to bring the murderers to justice. If the parish constable was the victim, there was an obvious concomitant difficulty with regard as to who was left to conduct an investigation.

Such an example can be found in a botched robbery attempt in March 1814, in which parish constable Henry Trigg of Berden was murdered by Thomas Turner and William Pratt, two thieves who had broken into Trigg's shoe shop with the intention of stealing a large quantity of shoe leather.[7] The local authorities, being both at a loss as to how to proceed and shocked by the cold-blooded murder which had been witnessed by both of Trigg's elderly parents, requested Bow Street's assistance. John Vickery, Principal Officer, and Daniel Bishop (at the time a Patrol member) subsequently carried out an extensive investigation at the expense of the Home Department, finally arresting the suspects in Bishop Stortford in February 1815.[8]

This particular case illustrates several of the factors that influenced the relatives or friends of victims to request the use of Principal Officers. The first of these was the length of time that the Officers could be involved in investigations. Whereas parish constables could be reasonably expected to expend their energy on one particular and simple investigation for a short period of time in a localised area, Principal Officers were frequently engaged for considerable periods of time, with investigations also covering a large geographical area.

Many of the provincial cases involving Bow Street personnel could be long drawn-out affairs, necessitating an investigation that lasted several weeks or even months.[9] In his evidence to the 1816 Select Committee, Townsend stated that

> there are certain cases in which we may be employed longer; there have been officers for eight to ten days on [a] poaching case. Vicary [sic] was down for a fortnight in Gloucestershire, with Colonel Berkeley; frequently it takes a great deal of time to detect a Banditti like that.[10]

Further examples can be found in a case that was investigated in July 1812. Following the murder of a mill-owner in Huddersfield, an anonymous Principal Officer spent over three weeks in the area, infiltrating Luddite societies and eventually assisting in the arrest of some fifty men for various charges of murder, rioting and sedition.[11] The following year, Harry Adkins spent over a week disguised as a country labourer in an Aldwych doss-house in order to arrest a murder suspect, after being on his trail for several weeks (see Chapter 6 for further details of this case).

The second factor, not exclusive to murder but often prevalent in the investigation of such a crime, was the threat of danger to life and limb. Many local law-enforcement officials who served as elected officers on a part-time basis for a fixed period (usually a year, although they could be re-elected) were understandably often reluctant to tackle potentially dangerous murder suspects. The problems of elected officials holding office for a relatively short period (and occasionally against their will) were recognised by many of those who were involved in provincial law enforcement; petty sessions magistrates in 1839 summed up the perceived problems with regard to parish constables:

> As far as our experience extends, we are convinced of the incompetency and inefficiency of the old parish constable. He holds his office generally for a year; he enters upon its duties unwillingly; he knows little what is required of him; is scantily paid for some things, has no remuneration in many cases; he has local connections, is actuated by personal apprehension, and dreads making himself obnoxious.[12]

By contrast, a Principal Officer was an experienced and professional investigator, with little to fear from local unpopularity with regard to long-term recrimination. That said, the job of Principal Officer was often a dangerous one, calling for reserves of both physical and mental strength; many of the characters apprehended by the Officers were desperate and violent.

Although no serving Principal Officer appears to have been murdered in the period under discussion, several were seriously injured during the course of their duty. While investigating a metropolitan case in London in early 1814 John Vickery was attacked by three men and narrowly escaped death, having his head cut open five times with a poker and his fingers broken; he took several months off from his employment in order to recuperate from his injuries and seems never to have fully recovered – his health being further damaged following another violent assault in 1822 – while in 1836 Francis Keys was similarly badly injured in the course of his duty.[13]

Prior to 1792, it appears that at least two Principal Officers were murdered, Thomas Hind in April 1755 and William Barnet in August 1779. Several members of the Patrol were certainly killed during the period, including Duncan Grant, a Conductor of the Patrol, in December 1798, and Richard Smithers in 1820, who was run through with a sword during the arrest of the Cato Street Conspiracy.[14]

The Officers were frequently well-armed for self-protection; as there was a common-law right to bear firearms, pistols as well as cutlasses were regularly carried by the Principal Officers. Weapons seem to have been provided and maintained at Bow Street's cost; quarterly expenses detailed for July 1801 include the cost of repairing 'firearms belonging to the officers' (£1 16s) and expenses for the quarter ending July 1802 include the cost of repairing 'cutlasses etc. for the officers' (£6 1s).[15] On 25 March 1834 Henry Goddard was ordered to go to investigate the murder of the steward of Earl Arden at Epsom and he records that 'as I [...] will have to contend with desperate characters, I was not to forget to go armed with a brace of loaded pistols which Mr Stafford, the Chief Clerk would provide me'.[16] Percy Fitzgerald, the Officers' earliest biographer, remarks that while 'their ensign of office [...] was a tiny baton with a gilt crown on the top malefactors knew perfectly well that their pockets held pistols as well as handcuffs'.[17] By contrast, parish officers were normally unarmed and understandably often somewhat reluctant to tackle dangerous and reputedly armed suspects.

Another factor influencing the employers of Principal Officers over local alternatives in murder cases was the relative infrequency of the crime. A parish constable or other local law-enforcement official would have been highly unlikely or unfortunate to encounter such a crime during his relatively short term of office, and would therefore have had little or no experience of how to conduct subsequent investigations, there being no formal training available for his position. By contrast, Principal Officers often had years of experience gained through employment in the less senior posts of Patrol Constables or Patrol Conductors, as several of them seem to have undergone a period of probationary training, accompanying more experienced colleagues on complex and dangerous cases. Benefiting from this training, such Officers could be expected to act

> like the experienced detectives of the Metropolitan Police Murder Squad, who in the twentieth century could be called upon to help the detectives of an area [who] were not fully experienced in the investigation of the most complex offences.[18]

By contrast with the yearly service of most parish constables, the average length of service for Principal Officers was just under twelve years, and it is stressed that this figure does not include any service in the other ranks at Bow Street. Such service was often of several years; for example, Richard Gardner was appointed as a Patrol Constable in 1824 but did not become a Principal Officer until 1831; similarly, George Ruthven began his career at Bow Street in 1811 (following in the footsteps of his father, Archibald, who had been a Conductor of the Patrol for many years) but did not reach the rank of Principal Officer until 1818. Officers therefore had plenty of opportunity to learn and refine their detective and investigative skills over a considerable period of time.

This state of affairs was extremely rare among law-enforcement officials of the pre-Metropolitan Police period. Apart from a handful of Scottish police forces and some extra-ordinary parish constables, Principal Officers were the only force that could hone their policing (and perhaps more importantly) their detective skills over a long period.[19] They also had the advantage of being able to draw upon a wealth of experience from their fellow Officers, who had similarly learnt their trade in a system that itself remained relatively unchanged for almost a century.

Arson/damage to property

This category accounts for almost one in eight of the total number of cases, and includes arson, animal maiming and breaking down trees. It is one of the few categories that can be seen to follow a distinct chronological trend. Over 89 per cent of such cases are recorded in the last two decades of the Bow Street Officers' existence, i.e. 1820–39. Prior to 1820, the crime was investigated by Bow Street relatively rarely – there are only two cases of arson before 1810. This discrepancy may be somewhat tempered by the choice of sources, with one of the main sources (accounting for 35 arson cases) being HO 64 Home Office: Criminal (Rewards and Pardons) Correspondence and Secret Service Reports 1820–1840. However, even if this source is removed from the equation, over three-quarters of remaining cases still occur in the period 1820–39.

This increased reported activity of Bow Street reflects the growing number of reported arson and property damage cases throughout England during this period. John Archer remarks in his work on incendiarism and animal maiming in East Anglia between 1815 and 1870 that 'as a weapon of social protest incendiarism can be located fairly exactly in the first half of the nineteenth century, more especially the second quarter', and he goes on to state that: 'Moreover, contemporaries were convinced that the identities of the incendiary was widely known but that communities shielded them from prosecution, despite the enormous rewards offered.'[20] The statistics certainly reflect the increase in arson nationwide – between 1834 and 1849, reported arson cases rose by 250 per cent, and this in turn seems to have led to something of a 'moral panic', with farmers and landowners frequently writing to the Home Department stating their fears and requesting help to tackle the problem.[21]

Arson was undoubtedly often both seen and conducted as a protest crime – that is one by which the protagonist was making a point about prevailing social or economic conditions in the immediate area, for example the price of staple foods or the enclosure of previously common land. An example of such anger is quoted by Roger Wells (further details of this case can be found in Chapter 6):

> Attempts to restrict commoners' rights in Ashdown Forest in 1810–11 galvanised so many threatening letters, and the burning of buildings and stables, that [a] vicar was alleged to have used it as a cover for firing his own house in order to claim the insurance.[22]

By the 1830s such illegal activity was often linked to the introduction of the New Poor Law system, 'signalling the start of an escalation in violence, riot, meetings, and arson', further concerning parish officials as well as farmers and landowners who were already attempting to deal with the situation.[23]

One of the main problems involving the investigation of such crimes and the detection of offenders was the inability or unwillingness of large sections of the respective local community (usually the labouring class) to cooperate with the parish or other authorities.[24] In a similar manner, parish constables were often understandably loath to investigate such crimes too thoroughly for fear of reprisal and the disapprobation of much of the community in which they worked and lived. By contrast, the Principal Officers as visitors to the district would not have had to contend with that threat after they had arrested any suspects – though, as has been demonstrated above, the immediate circumstances of an arrest may have proved very dangerous. This is probably the main reason why such Officers were employed on crimes of this nature, including plundering and smuggling – there was little to fear from long-term reprisal, despite the immediate threat of considerable physical danger. Consequently, it would have been much more difficult for the Officers to be intimidated by threats to their family or friends.

Larceny

Despite the prevalence of arson in the types of case investigated by Bow Street, George Rudé states in his study of crime in the nineteenth century, *Criminal and Victim*, that:

> In nineteenth-century England, even in the days of angry protest, crimes of violence were the exception rather than the rule [...]. By far the most common form of crime was larceny, or theft.[25]

This view is reflected in the fact that larceny was the third most common type of provincial crime investigated by the Principal Officers. The majority of provincial larceny, petty in both nature and amount, undoubtedly did not merit the involvement of senior Bow Street personnel, or even much serious consideration from local law-enforcement officials. The *First Report on the Constabulary Force in England and Wales 1839* states that:

> Magistrates in Newcastle under Lyme reported that in thefts of a trifling character (as to the amount taken), a great disinclination to take the trouble of prosecuting exists. In the rural districts the constables are mostly farmers, who are often deterred from interfering with old offenders, or with beer-houses, or other resorts of the dissolute, by an apprehension of injury to themselves or property.[26]

Some of the provincial larcenies investigated by Principal Officers would probably be regarded as of a 'trifling character' today: 13 cases involving stolen horses, with another involving the theft of rare plants from Kew Gardens, and in one very unusual case, the theft of seven pineapples. However, in many such cases the involvement of Bow Street seems to have owed more to the social or economic standing of the victim than the intrinsic value of the stolen property. The investigation of the theft of plants was instigated by the Royal Botanical Society, while the investigation of the theft of the pineapples (which were extremely rare and relatively expensive at the time, each being valued at nearly £1) was instigated by the victim, a clergyman (and resulted in their successful return, being discovered for conspicuous sale in Covent Garden Market).[27]

The majority of larceny cases utilising Principal Officers involved a considerable amount of money or goods; this was particularly the situation with regard to thefts from mail coaches which could often run into thousands of pounds (for example a case in Higham Ferrers, Northamptonshire in 1812, where £15,000 was stolen, or a theft from the Norwich mail coach the following year, which exceeded £13,000). Similarly, as Table 4.2 shows, in fraud, burglary, robbery or larceny cases where the value of the goods stolen or misappropriated is recorded, it is overwhelmingly large amounts of money or goods that are involved, ranging from £2 to over £100,000. Rarely was the sum a negligible amount.

Table 4.2 Value of goods/money in provincial cases, 1792–1839

Value	No. cases
Under £10	9
£10–£99	84
£100–£999	52
£1,000–£9,999	22
£10,000–£99,000	11
£100,000+	1

Over half (51.9 per cent) of the cases involved amounts between £2 and £99, while almost a third (29.1 per cent) related to sums between £100 and £999. One in eight (12.3 per cent) involved amounts of over £1,000, while 6.2 per cent were in excess of £10,000, and one plundering case was reported to have involved £100,000 of insured goods (see Chapter 6 below for further details of this case).[28]

These often considerable sums are perhaps not unexpected as the victims of the relevant crimes were, as previously discussed in Chapter 3, predominantly wealthy individuals or property owners, men or organisations of financial substance. However, it also suggests that the victims considered the Principal Officers capable of justifying the often not inconsiderable expense incurred in the investigation of such cases and the hopeful recovery of at least some of the goods or money involved.

Forgery/fraud

Principal Officers were involved in 71 recorded cases of forgery/fraud during the period, the fourth most prevalent type of crime that they investigated, perhaps not unsurprisingly when, as, Randall McGowen remarks, 'by some estimates forgery accounted for a third of the capital legislation of the period'.[29]

The number of forgery/fraud cases is perhaps at first sight surprisingly large, given that the period covered is somewhat earlier than that usually associated with what is now often considered to be a peculiarly 'white-collar' crime. However, many of the individual crimes within this category were relatively crude attempts to defraud the state or other institutions by forging military service records in order to gain additional pensions or making forgeries of individual promissory notes rather than more elaborate and ambitious frauds perpetrated by the emergent middle-class employees of banks or similar financial institutions. Examples of such relatively minor fraud include a case at Maidstone in 1799, in which a £1 note was altered to a face value of £5, or a case from 1825, where Principal Officers managed to catch a fraudulent game of chance in progress during race-day at Ascot. The London Police Offices were not themselves exempt from forgery: in 1812, the Chief Clerk of Queen Square Police Office, George Skene, was sentenced to hang as a result of his forgery of receipts totalling £65 7s, while Richmond, the aforementioned disgraced clerk at Bow Street, seems to have been suspected of fraudulent behaviour.

That is not to say that forgery, fraud or counterfeiting was negligible in the period; thousands of forged banknotes were presented for payment – as Malcolm Gaskill has remarked, 'counterfeiting [...] had a history as long as the monetised economy'.[30]

Forgery in the form of counterfeiting increased dramatically in the years following the decision to suspend payment in gold by the Bank of England in 1797; the subsequent paper notes issued in lieu by the Bank often proved irresistible to forgers, causing one caustic anonymous correspondent to write to the Bank of England in 1809 suggesting that every time a forgery was discovered, a Bank of England director should be publicly hanged. This measure, contended the writer, would rapidly improve note design and quality of printing.[31] The government had attempted to rectify the situation with regard to coinage in 1804, when on 8 March of that year the Privy Council requested blank dollars of Spanish silver to be stamped by Matthew Boulton of Birmingham and circulated at 5s. By 11 May 1804 dollars were being stamped at the Soho Mint in Handsworth. The *Manchester Guardian* of 12 May 1804 reported that:

> The new coinage of crown pieces from Dollars is now going on with all possible dispatch, at Mr Boulton's manufactory, the Soho, near Birmingham. Within these few days three waggons loaded with dollars were sent from the Bank, under a proper escort, to that place, each waggon contains about seven tons weight.

The 'proper escort' seems to have been a contingent of Bow Street Officers, presumably accompanied by armed guards; Fitzgerald reports that Vickery and Lavender were often used for such purposes.[32] Similarly, in 1812 the *Morning Chronicle* of 18 August reported that Adkins had conveyed the huge sum of £33,000 in dollars (over £3 million in today's terms) to Portsmouth in order to supply the Army Pay Officer with cash to pay the army.

Many counterfeiting cases investigated by Principal Officers involved the forging of provincial banknotes, which were often easier to pass off than Bank of England notes; for example, forged notes of the Salisbury Bank were discovered in 1818 and a large quantity of Salop Bank notes were counterfeited during 1820.

Most of the recorded instances of fraud, forgery or counterfeiting were indeed carried out against institutions rather than individuals – over 80 per cent of such crimes where the instigator of the investigation is recorded. Provincial private individuals who were the victims of minor cases of counterfeiting – for example, unknowingly being the recipient of a single forged note or coin – may well have been unlikely to go to the time, trouble and expense to involve the services of Bow Street in order to recover what was a relatively minor financial loss.

During the period under discussion Principal Officers investigated several large frauds, forgeries and embezzlements that were carried out in the provinces or originated abroad. Forgery could be an international affair, the senior Bow Street Officers being employed by both British and European governments in attempts to prevent and detect large-scale counterfeiting. The *Manchester Guardian* of 11 August 1821 reported details of a large forgery in London on the Prussian government. Foy and Clements, two of the senior Marlborough Street officers, were reported as being involved in solving the case, but Bow Street may well also have been involved, as Fitzgerald reports that George Ruthven, a long-serving Principal Officer, retired in 1839 with a pension from the Prussian government for his services in discovering forgeries connected with that country, and it seems likely that this was the case to which the pension referred.[33] Similarly, in 1837, a Bow Street Officer was sent to Birmingham at Home Department expense to investigate counterfeit French currency after the case had been reported to the British government by a French Minister at Court.[34]

Cases such as those above, or the embezzlement of some £40,000 from the Leipzig Bank in 1821, often involved a huge sum of money, while counterfeiting cases such as that from 1828 in which an engraver was asked to create false Bank of England engraving plates could also potentially have netted the criminal tens of thousands of pounds had he been successful.[35] It is therefore likely that victims would often go to considerable lengths to discover and prosecute the perpetrators of such crimes.

However, the majority of recorded forgery/fraud cases were less ambitious in their financial scope, and the use of Bow Street frequently seems to have been as much a statement of preventive intent by the victims to do everything in their power both to ensure that the culprits were caught and to publicly demonstrate that such matters were taken extremely seriously by the relevant institutions, despite the often relatively small amounts of money involved. This two-pronged intention seems to have been particularly practised by insurance companies in cases involving fraudulent claims such as the deliberate arson of hayricks by a farmer in Offerton, Cheshire, in 1834 in order to claim an inflated amount of insurance, and by the Army or Navy Pay Offices which, with the aid of Bow Street, instigated investigations into several fraudulent pay claims or prize-money certificates.

Forgery cases could often be difficult to prove; a letter written in 1812 from the Bank of England's solicitors, Kaye, Freshfield & Kaye, to a magistrate in Cockermouth laments the fact that 'in short, some of our judges seem to expect positive evidence of knowledge' of the possession of forged banknotes – the letter specifically refers to a case in Warwick where a man was found with a few good notes together with several forged ones and was acquitted.[36] The availability of Principal Officers to carry out detailed and time-consuming investigations must have therefore been a major factor in the decision to utilise their services.

Burglary

Burglary was the fifth most common type of recorded crime, with the victims being primarily private individuals. This is reflected in the fact that of the known types of employer in such cases, three-quarters (75 per cent) were private individuals. Such burglaries were frequently described as involving large quantities of stolen goods, providing one reason why the victims were prepared to invest time and money in the employment of Bow Street Officers. Burglaries, through their very nature, i.e. occurring at night, often without witnesses being present to describe any suspects, required a considerable amount of detective analysis and experience to solve, but such detection was often beyond the capabilities of the local, annually elected (and therefore often inexperienced) parish constabulary. Apart from rounding up the 'usual suspects' there was often little that such constables could do, especially if the suspects had fled to another parish or county. By contrast, Principal Officers could call on considerable knowledge and experience with regard to forensic detective skills – these are discussed in greater detail in Chapter 6.

With regard to burglary as with larceny, in such cases where property in the form of goods or cash was illegally appropriated, the amount involved was almost invariably considerable. The amounts mentioned range from two guineas (equivalent to c.£200 in today's terms) to burglaries which netted the criminals involved over £2,000. It is clear that if at least some of the goods or cash involved in such cases was recovered as quickly as possible, the financial losses suffered by the victims could be minimised. There was also a strong desire on the part of insurance companies and other financial institutions that the swift capture and punishment of those involved in burglary or larceny should act as a deterrent to would-be law-breakers.

Robbery

This category covers a wide range of offences, from a robbery of a tollgate keeper in 1818, in which £40–50 was taken, through to large-scale bank robberies involving many thousands of pounds (for example, the 1815 robbery of the Newbury Bank involved some £20,000+ plus, and it was reported that the entire contents of the bank had been taken). The category also includes highway robbery, which was much more prevalent in the earlier part of the period under discussion, no cases of this type being investigated by Principal Officers after 1814.[37] However, Edwin Chadwick's claim in 1829 that 'the race of highwaymen is extinct' was a slight hyperbole, with a handful of such crimes being tried at the Old Bailey between 1830 and 1839. However, none of these involved the Principal Officers.[38]

Robbery is one of the most immediate offences in two ways: it takes place in the presence of the victim, often being accompanied by the threat of violence, and the loss of property is directly apparent, in contrast to other offences such as fraud or forgery in which it may be some time before the gravity of the crime is discovered. It was also one of the major fears of the wealthier sectors of society throughout the early-modern period; the crime of highway robbery in particular was one of the first to attract a statutory reward of £40 in an attempt to stem the perceived inexorable rise of the offence in the late-seventeenth century.[39]

Indeed, the activity of gangs of highwaymen was one of the primary reasons given by Henry Fielding for the need to create the Bow Street force. Both he and his half-brother John stressed the immediate availability of their men to investigate such crimes, stating that 'many thieves and robbers daily escape justice for want of immediate pursuit'.[40]

This is perhaps the primary reason why the Principal Officers were employed to a considerable extent in the investigation of robberies of one type or another; such crimes required prompt and detailed investigation in order to increase the chances of the perpetrator(s) being apprehended. It is recognised that investigation of such cases could be delayed by the practicalities of the Principal Officer travelling to the locality of the crime, but as the Officers were full-time, once in the locale, they could dedicate their whole time to the investigation, unlike the parish constable who was often in other full-time employment. Many highway robberies were also investigated by the Bow Street Horse Patrol, which concentrated its efforts on known 'hotspots' for highway robbery, and were consequently stationed on the major turnpiked roads leading into London. Such detailed and swift action may well have often been beyond the capability of the annually elected parish constable, who would have had little opportunity to gain the necessary experience of such investigatory work and who could often ill-spare the time required to investigate thoroughly any crime that had occurred.

Any delay or prevarication through inexperience or ineptitude was recognised to be detrimental to the investigation of such crimes; in his evidence to the 1839 *Report* of the Constabulary Force Commissioners, the High Constable of Stockport, Mr Sadler, was asked. 'Do you find that by investigating the case of a robbery immediately after it has occurred, you are enabled to secure evidence, that if no investigation took place you would lose?' He replied in the affirmative, stating that he had

> known instances where some time has elapsed before the information has been given of the robbery having been committed, to the police, and in which, when an investigation has taken place, the witnesses who have before made statements to other parties not connected with the police, which would have led to the conviction, have been tampered with in the intermediate time, or from the idea, that it would be attended with inconvenience, or from mistaken motives of humanity to screen the thief, have withheld that evidence and the guilty parties have by that means escaped.[41]

It was similarly recognised that experience and detective skill played a large part in the successful outcome of robbery investigations. Sir Peter Laurie, administrator for the City of London, referred in his evidence to the 1837/38 Select Committee to the need for such experience in the form of the Principal Officers of the various London Police Offices:

> The men of whom I am speaking have no other pursuit; they have been what are commonly called thief-catchers all their lives [...] if you do away with such useful men as those I have alluded to, and leave the offices without their assistance, you will never, in my opinion, detect a robbery at all.[42]

In the vast majority of the recorded robberies in which the instigator of the investigation is known, they were either private individuals or institutions, i.e. the victims. The Home Department seems to have had little interest in employing Principal Officers on such cases – in the two recorded cases (from 1795 and 1798 respectively) where they did employ their services, both occasions were in order to track down and apprehend gangs of highway robbers that had been plaguing their respective haunts for weeks or even months, and had consequently been causing much criticism of the failure of government to deal with such problems.

Consequently, potentially lucrative employment on such investigations was popular among the Principal Officers – private individuals or institutions often paid a great deal more handsomely for the services of Bow Street than did the Home Department. Fitzgerald dryly comments that 'where some great robbery [...] had been committed, handsome gratuities were looked for and received. It was noted that the men were always anxious to leave their town duties for these "country services".'[43] In return for their often considerable financial outlay, wealthy victims clearly considered that they were employing the best available personnel to maximise their chances of recovery of the stolen goods or money.

The Principal Officers had two main advantages over their provincial law-enforcement colleagues in investigating robberies. Firstly, as discussed above, they had an unrivalled amount of experience in the investigation of such offences, often gained during their service in a more junior capacity. Peter King, in his research into the activities of a group of Bow Street personnel in Becontree Hundred in Essex in the late 1780s, states that:

> Between 1784 and 1787 [...] these men [West Ham-based thieftakers] and five Bow Street runners were involved in at least 60 per cent of the burglary and highway robbery convictions in the Becontree hundred and about a third of those in the other south-western hundreds.[44]

The Horse Patrol and Dismounted Horse Patrol in particular had widespread experience of dealing with highway robbery, while members of the Foot Patrol would have gained considerable knowledge of how to investigate robberies during their day-to-day employment in the streets of the metropolis. This experience would have been further honed should they have subsequently been promoted to the rank of Principal Officer.[45]

Secondly, the Principal Officers were able to travel throughout the length and breadth of the country, unlike their parochial counterparts who were confined to their immediate parish. Many of the recorded robbery cases show that the perpetrators of such offences did not remain in the vicinity of the crime for long, and that subsequent detection of such offenders necessitated considerable time and travel. An example can be seen in a case from 1836, where Goddard's investigation into a robbery from the mail coach *Defiant* between Dover and London necessitated his travelling the entire route, calling at every mail-station on the way.

The Principal Officers could also liaise with their counterparts throughout the country in a way in which parochial officers would have found difficult; a large jewellery robbery in Manchester in 1828 involved officers from Bow Street, Liverpool Police Office and Manchester Police Office (run at the time by former Principal Officer Stephen Lavender) in a successful joint venture which led to the guilty parties being transported for life. By contrast, parochial officers would have found it difficult to cooperate with fellow officers within their own county, let alone nationwide.[46]

Other types of provincial crime investigated by Principal Officers

The remaining categories of crime account for just over one-seventh of the provincially instigated crimes investigated by Principal Officers. Although such crimes do not feature heavily in the records, they are still useful in discussing the wide variety of ways in which the Principal Officers were employed in the provinces. As in the case of poaching offences detailed in Chapter 3, the level of under-reporting was undoubtedly high with regard to other types of offence, especially in relation to less serious or more personal cases. Examples of such crimes include a number of abductions or elopements, together with cases of bigamy and adultery. The presence of these types of case, although infrequent, suggests that either (or both) the ability to pay handsomely for the services of Bow Street personnel and the status of the victim could prove more important factors than the nature of the crime in the decision to employ Bow Street Officers.

Although such abduction/elopement cases account for only a small percentage of the total recorded, they usefully illustrate the point that Principal Officers were occasionally employed on relatively trivial matters by those who could afford to so do. The majority of the cases involved the elopement of rich, naive young heiresses and older, poorer men, with the girls' fathers willing to employ Bow Street personnel to find them and (hopefully) prevent the otherwise inevitable and socially damaging consequences.

Elopements in particular could involve considerable distances – for example Edward Gibbon Wakefield's 1826 abduction/elopement of the Turner heiress involved a pursuit from Lancashire via London to France.[47] In such cases, it would have been impossible for parish constables or other parochial authorities to have traced or pursued suspects. Bow Street personnel, on the other hand, were experienced and adept at pursuing suspects over long distances and were willing to devote as much time and effort as their employers wished, as long as they were suitably recompensed for their diligence.

Another possible reason for the use of Bow Street personnel in such cases is that they could conduct their enquiries discreetly with little publicity, thus avoiding any ensuing embarrassment or disapprobation of the victims' families. The low number of recorded cases may be a tribute to their efforts – such cases occasionally did come to the attention of the press, but many more may have escaped the glare of contemporary publicity. This may well have been the case with duelling, which the Principal Officers were occasionally called upon to prevent. However, several of these duelling matches featured high-profile protagonists – most notably the aborted match in 1815 between Sir Robert Peel and Daniel O'Connell. In such cases, it is clear that the Officers were at hand in order to witness that the honour of the protagonists was satisfied as much as to prevent genuine injury from taking place in what was technically an illegal activity.[48]

The Principal Officers were similarly called upon to carry out preventive policing in the provinces or in Ireland with regard to pickpocketing gangs likely to be present at any important gathering, especially those involving royalty. The *Manchester Guardian* of 8 September 1821 reported that during a visit to Ireland by George IV, his retinue was accosted by pickpockets, and that:

One of them had the address, whilst his Majesty was shaking hands with one of his 'Pall-Mall' acquaintances, to slip his hand under his upper tog [coat] and extract his thimble [watch]; on which Lord S. sent off an express to the head government of the metropolis at Bow Street, to send two of his first ministers (Vickery and Bishop) of that establishment, to Dublin; but on arrival there the gentlemen of the fancy had taken their departure for London, where they arrived safe and cashed their flimsies [stolen goods].

Similarly, in advance of a visit by King George IV to Scotland in August 1822, Sheriff Deputy William Duff wrote to the Home Department in July 1822, requesting that it was 'necessary that two or three Bow Street Officers who know by sight the principal London pickpockets should be in Edinburgh for the purpose of pointing them out to the officers of the Edinburgh police'. Four Principal Officers were subsequently despatched by steamship to Leith.[49] In both cases it is clear that the Principal Officers were employed as much for their deterrent and preventive effect as their ability to recognise known pickpockets, and they were also clearly expected to work in close collaboration with the local police.

The Officers were also occasionally sent out of the metropolis to identify escaped suspects or felons who had committed crimes in the provinces, and on at least two occasions became involved in the capture of resurrectionists. Evidence connected with the first case of bodysnatching, that took place at Plymouth in 1828, intriguingly suggests that Ellis (who served as a Principal Officer from 1824 to 1836) was seconded as head of the Plymouth Police for a period in the late 1820s. Fitzgerald states that Ellis was at the time of the bodysnatching case 'placed at the head of the Plymouth Police'.[50] Ellis was certainly present in Plymouth in August 1829 when he arrested a gang of housebreakers, but he was still receiving his quarterly pay from Bow Street in 1829.[51] Plymouth Borough Police was not created until 1836, but a system of Watch and Ward had been created in 1812 – it may be that Ellis had been temporarily seconded to help train this body of men.[52] The second case in which Principal Officers were involved was instigated following the discovery of a suspicious box in October 1830 at a public house by the Constable of Stafford, Robert Jones. He contacted Bow Street and an Officer was despatched to Stafford after the box had been opened and found to contain a human cadaver.

In stark contrast to the Home Department's apparent disinterest in provincial robbery cases, provincial seditious crimes, including rioting and spying, occupied them greatly. The Home Department, as has been shown above, used the services of Bow Street for a variety of reasons, but by far the most common usage was the investigation of seditious crimes – in every such recorded case, it was the Home Department that instigated the employment of Principal Officers.

Francis Sheppard states that 'the elimination of riot and disorder as an endemic feature of British life' was a prime consequence of the 1829 Metropolitan Police Act.[53] This undoubtedly overstates the case with regard to the activities of the Metropolitan Police and also ignores the contribution made by Bow Street and the other Police Offices, both within and without the metropolis. The Principal Officers were called upon to investigate a wide range of potentially seditious occurrences, from treasonable correspondence between France and revolutionary sympathisers, through the marches of colliers demanding a fair wage, to the Luddite Riots of 1812–13 in Nottingham and the 1830–31 'Captain Swing' Riots.[54]

In the case of the 'Colliers' March' of 1816, the Bow Street Officers, together with Sir Richard Birnie, managed to successfully diffuse a potentially dangerous situation through a combination of tact and pragmatism. Poorly paid and underfed colliers from Bilston in Staffordshire had hand-hauled a full coal-waggon weighing over two tons to Maidenhead on their way to London in an effort to publicise their plight and shame the government into taking action over their protest against the coal-mine owners. Sir Richard Birnie and his men met the angry miners outside the town and through skilful and patient negotiation they persuaded the colliers to depart peacefully.[55]

In sedition or rioting cases the Principal Officers had two advantages over other agencies: they were experienced at going undercover for long periods of time, and they were unlikely to be recognised by their suspects as local law-enforcement officers would often undoubtedly have been. An example of the length of time spent on an investigation into claimed sedition is illustrated in Goddard's *Memoirs*. In early December 1838, Goddard was sent by Sir Frederick Roe to Leigh Bury, Todmorden, Ashton under Lyne and other places throughout the north of England, spending several weeks in the area searching for suspected Chartist agitators.

Similarly, several Principal Officers, along with other Bow Street personnel, were in the Nottingham/Derby area in 1811–12 for several months, searching for the ringleaders of the Luddite riots.[56] Such long-winded and geographically extensive campaigns could not easily have been undertaken by other law-enforcement agencies.

Use of single Principal Officers in provincial cases

For the vast majority of cases, Principal Officers worked as individuals, rarely working in pairs or other combinations. This may have been due to the severe limitations imposed by their small force – never more than eleven in number at any given time – but the type of provincial crime being investigated may also have influenced the Bow Street magistrates in their decision to send out one or more Officers. On average, Principal Officers worked alone on 76 per cent of recorded provincial cases.[57] This figure appears to be somewhat at odds with Beattie's findings from his research into the earlier history of Bow Street. He states with regard to 1766–67 that:

> Each of the Runners worked from time to time on their own, but most often when they went out on patrol or in search of a suspect they worked together in various combinations – a third of the time [...] with one partner, occasionally in larger groups. In those two years groups of three or four were in action on eighteen occasions'.[58]

However, this was prior to the permanent creation of the various Bow Street patrols that operated throughout London in the later period, and consequently the Principal Officers would have been on duty within the metropolis to a far greater extent than in the post-patrol period. Such work may have been less specialised, requiring more physical strength and numbers than mental or detective work.

The percentage variation from the average is remarkably consistent over a wide range of cases, from a high of 90 per cent with regard to murder cases and a low of 63 per cent with regard to duelling/prizefighting cases, suggesting that the use of individual Officers was considered sufficient in most circumstances in most types of crime. For all types of cases that involved the use of multiple Officers, it is significant that the employer tended to be either the state or an institution; such bodies could more readily afford to employ numerous Officers on cases that it was felt imperative to solve as quickly and efficiently as possible.

The Officers, although largely left to their own devices while on provincial investigations, were, however, expected to make regular progress reports when involved in lengthy and complex detective work and a few of these reports have survived. One written by Samuel Taunton on 4 November 1830 from the Bull Inn, Sittingbourne, details the situation regarding a spate of arson attacks in the area:

Sir,

I beg leave to inform you [J. J.] Smith arrived here on Saturday last. He is at Newington endeavouring to ascertain what he can. Nothing has transpired of any consequence at present since my last letter on Thursday evening about 10 o'clock a fire broke out two stacks of hay burnt at L[illegible] Hill about ten miles from this place yesterday evening a Fire at Mr Catt a farmer at Chartham near Canterbury a barn destroyed on Tuesday morning last I see [James] Ellis and Duke pass through this place on their way to Canterbury since the troops have been here the meetings seem [illegible]. We have a great number of special constables sworn in about this part and the farmers are on the watch nightly tomorrow the 5th November they are in the habit of [illegible] the night with fireworks and putting masks on their faces.[59]

It is clear from this letter that on this occasion the Principal Officers were part of a large and varied force of people who were employed to prevent the outbreak of more arson attacks connected to the 'Captain Swing' riots and to discover the perpetrators of those attacks already committed. James Ellis was another Principal Officer, while Duke may well have been a member of the Horse Patrol, or even a Metropolitan Police constable. On such large-scale investigations, it was not unusual for the Principal Officers to be accompanied by one or two less senior personnel – this not only increased the manpower of Bow Street, but also provided valuable experience for the more junior ranks.

Another letter from the period survives, dated 11 November 1830, in which Daniel Bishop describes his solitary attempts to infiltrate the society of those thought to be responsible for a spate of arson attacks:

I have gone to the different Pot Houses in the Villages, disguised among the Labourers, of an evening and all their talk is about the wages, some give 1s. 8d. per day, some 2s., some 2s. 3d. [...] all they say they want is 2s. 6d. per day and then they say they shall be comfortable. I have every reason to believe the Farmers will give the 2s. 6d. per day after a bit [...] they are going to have a meeting and I think it will stop all the outrages.[60]

This letter is interesting not only for illustrating that investigation into arson could be carried out by either single Officers or groups, but also for the way in which the Officer went undercover in order to gain information; this seems to have been common practice for the Officers when working in areas where they could safely assume that they would not be recognised.

The Officers would generally go about their provincial business incognito, as they wore no uniform and would not have been recognised in many areas outside London, but they often resorted to specific disguises in order to infiltrate 'seditious' groups or to get closer to those they wished to arrest. These disguises often took the form of dressing as itinerant labourers or out-of-work servants; Goddard mentions in his *Memoirs* that on one occasion he disguised himself as a 'countryman' and visited Weedon Fair in order to observe suspected robbers more closely.[61]

Such use of non-uniformed police was deeply unpopular in early nineteenth-century Britain; for many it smacked too much of 'continental' methods of surveillance and spying, being regarded as 'entirely foreign to the habits and feelings of the nation'. In 1812 the Earl of Dudley, referring to calls for the creation of a new police force following a series of grisly murders in the Ratcliff Highway, London, remarked:

> They have an admirable police at Paris, but they pay for it dear enough. I had rather half a dozen peoples' throats be cut in Ratcliff Highway every three or four years than be subject to domiciliary visits, spies, and all the rest of Fouché's contrivances.[62]

Although a few Scottish police forces had employed plain-clothes officers in the first quarter of the nineteenth century, it was not until the end of the century that the majority of English provincial police forces created plain-clothes detective branches, and it has been suggested that many of these were set up as a result of the fear of mainland terrorism by Irish nationalists.[63]

Metropolitan cases

Table 4.3 shows the types of crime investigated by Principal Officers within the metropolis between 1792 and 1839 and recorded in the OBP. There are only three statistically significant crimes: larceny, forgery/fraud and burglary, and of these larceny is by far the most prevalent. This category of crime accounts for over half (54.8 per cent) of the total number of crimes, with forgery/fraud supplying just over one-fifth (21.6 per cent) of the total, and burglary almost a tenth (8.6 per cent). These figures suggest that not only was the provincial usage of Principal Officers considerably greater than their use in the metropolis, but also the types of cases were much more numerous than their metropolitan equivalent, with provincial employers prepared to enlist their help on a broader range of crimes.

As has been demonstrated above in Chapter 3, due to a combination of factors including the lack of travel costs and the relatively highly developed mercantile economy of the capital, the employers of Principal Officers in the metropolis were far more likely to be from the mercantile/middle class than their employers in the provinces. This is the most obvious explanation for the preponderance of metropolitan larceny cases. Just over half (51 per cent) of the victims were merchants or shopkeepers who applied to Bow Street in an attempt to recoup their losses quickly by tracing where their stolen goods had gone, while 27 per cent of victims were members of the gentry, who often owned or rented property in the metropolis as well as having a country house – many of the metropolitan cases involved larceny by the servant or employee of the victim.

The personnel at Bow Street had an unrivalled knowledge of the fences and receivers of stolen property within the metropolis and were probably the first choice for those who could afford to pay for their services, being both more experienced and more professional than the alternative of the various watches or parish constabulary. This situation is repeated with regard to the victims of burglary: 48 per cent of the victims were again members of the mercantile class, with 40 per cent being from the gentry.

Table 4.3 Types of recorded metropolitan cases, 1792–1839

	No. cases	%
Arson/damage to property	3	(1.03)
Burglary	25	(8.56)
Forgery/fraud	63	(21.58)
Larceny	160	(54.79)
Murder/attempted murder	6	(2.05)
Pickpocketing	7	(2.40)
Recapture of escapees	12	(4.11)
Robbery	14	(4.79)
Sedition	2	(0.68)
Total	292	

Only in the cases of forgery/fraud does the situation change, with over 75 per cent of the victims unsurprisingly being institutions rather than individuals. In the fraud cases, in 21 instances the employer was a bank (including the Bank of England), in eight cases the Post Office and in six cases the Stamp Office.[64] In a large urban and commercial centre such as London, the opportunities to carry out fraud were infinitely more available than in the provinces, and the authorities would have been keen to prevent such crimes wherever possible.

In a similar vein, the average value of goods involved in metropolitan cases investigated by the Principal Officers was much lower than in provincial cases. Table 4.4 shows that over two-fifths of cases (46.4 per cent) involved sums less than £10, with crimes of goods valued between £10 and £99 accounting for a further third (32.3 per cent). Less than one in five cases (17.0 per cent) involved values of between £100 and £999, and only 6.2 per cent had values of more than £1,000.

The preponderance of cases involving values less than £10 in the metropolis suggests that victims were more willing to employ Principal Officers in the capital than in the provinces for crimes involving lower values as the expense of employing such an Officer was considerably less due to the absence of travel expenses. The large number of larcenies includes a significant proportion of thefts from shops or warehouses. This is not surprising considering the vast number of retail and wholesale outlets for goods concentrated in what was then the mercantile capital of the world.

This suggests a strong correlation with the preponderance of the mercantile/middle class as employers of Principal Officers; they were much more likely to be the most common group of victims of such relatively low-value crimes and would have been keen to recoup their losses if possible. Such victims readily utilised the services of

Table 4.4 Value of goods/money in metropolitan cases, 1792–1839

Value	Number of cases
Under £10	122
£10–£99	85
£100–£999	44
£1,000–£9,999	12
£10,000–£99,000	0
£100,000+	0

Bow Street and the other Police Offices; as detailed in Chapter 3 there are over 1,500 cases involving Bow Street recorded in the OBP in the years 1792–1839, with over 83 per cent of such cases using less senior Bow Street personnel. It must, however, be remembered that the metropolis was, quite apart from the presence of Bow Street personnel, relatively densely policed in relation to the rest of the country, and as such, metropolitan residents had a much greater choice with regard to whom to turn in order to investigate relatively minor crime.

Elaine Reynolds' work on the pre-Metropolitan Police situation in the capital has demonstrated that the various watches were not always as inefficient as previously supposed, while Drew Gray's research into the policing of the City of London in the late-eighteenth and early-nineteenth centuries has revealed a surprisingly high ratio of officers to residents; his findings suggest an average of 82 dwellings per constable's patch in the City – this is by any standards fairly intensive policing.[65]

Other metropolitan duties of Principal Officers

Not all of the Officers' involvement in policing activities was of the more interesting or exciting variety; they were occasionally used for much more mundane tasks. Several of the Officers were regularly employed within the metropolis by the Bank of England; John Sayer and John Townsend attended the Bank for ten days each quarter, when dividends were paid out, despite the Bank having its own security force known as the Picquet.[66] The practice of employing Principal Officers seems to have begun in November 1794, when the *Court Minute Book* records the decision to pay for 'two officers to attend every Dividend time for the first ten days, and to be allowed 21s. *per diem*'.[67] However, it seems that by the early 1820s the Bank of England was more usually employing the services of John Foy, Principal Officer at Marlborough Street – the *Manchester Guardian* refers to him in its edition of 19 May 1821 as 'the police officer who is in the constant employment of the Bank of England', and Home Office records state that he was seconded to the Bank of England for considerable periods.[68] Superannuated Officers and Constables from Bow Street also attended the Opera House in Covent Garden, where they would warn the crowds of known pickpockets and thieves.[69]

Despite the fact that the Principal Officers were not regularly deployed within the metropolis, they seem to have been favoured by both King George III and the Prince Regent to undertake duties of royal security. Bow Street personnel were often used within the capital on state occasions such as royal investitures and funerals. On 4 June 1811 and 7 January 1812, eight personnel were paid 10s 6d each for their attendance at Saint James' on His Majesty's birthdays.[70] On 1 June 1812, three Officers were paid £3 3s for attending the installation of the Knights of Bath at Westminster Abbey, while a full complement of Officers and Constables formed part of the security force guarding the streets for Queen Caroline's funeral in 1821. The funeral procession of Queen Caroline turned into a farce; at least one man was killed in rioting and several were badly injured, with the result that Sir Robert Baker, Chief Magistrate of Bow Street, who had been placed in charge of the procession's organisation, was forced to resign, despite evidence that events were beyond his control and that he was used as a scapegoat.[71] From 1792 at least two Principal Officers were also permanently stationed at Windsor after the King had received several death threats. These Officers were considered to be part of the royal retinue and as such were regarded as otherwise unconnected to the Bow Street Office. Consequently, these Officers were not included in the complement of Principal Officers employed at Bow Street in any of the official returns concerning the numbers based at Bow Street.[72] There seems to have been a degree of two-way movement between Bow Street and Windsor, with Bow Street Officers such as Dowsett and Edwards beginning their careers at Bow Street and then being transferred to Windsor, while William Anthony, who became an active Principal Officer by 1800, had originally launched his career by attending the King at St James and was transferred to Windsor in 1796. However, for the majority of Officers so employed such posts appear to have been little more than sinecures to which they could aspire once their most active days were over.[73]

Conclusion

From the above analysis it is clear that the provincial activities of the Principal Officers were extremely diverse in nature. The role of the Home Department has been shown as important in several of the provincial duties of the Officers, and several facets have revealed themselves. The socio-economic status of the employers of the Officers was clearly important in determining what types of crime were investigated and the absence of poorer victims is explained.

The metropolitan use of the Principal Officers, while in many ways mirroring their activities in the provinces, seems to have been on a much more limited basis, with larceny providing the main reason for their use. Their use in the provinces was obviously far more varied, perhaps reflecting the fact that they were generally employed on provincial duties by the more affluent members of society who could afford to employ them on cases that were not deemed financially viable by members of the mercantile/middle class that were their main employers within the metropolis.

The next chapter examines the alternatives available to victims of provincial crime and then concentrates on the geographic spread of the recorded cases involving Principal Officers to see if any conclusions can be drawn from their use in particular areas.

Notes

1 For discussions about the validity of criminal statistics throughout the nineteenth century, see Howard Taylor, 'Rationing Crime: The Political Economy of Criminal Statistics since the 1850s', *Economic History Review*, vol. 51, no. 3 (1998), pp. 569–90; Chris Williams, 'Counting Crimes or Counting People: Some Implications of Mid-Nineteenth Century British Police Returns', *Crime, Histoire & Sociétés*, vol. 4, no. 2 (2000), pp. 77–93; and Robert M. Morris, '"Lies, Damned Lies and Criminal Statistics": Reinterpreting the Criminal Statistics in England and Wales', *Crime, Histoire & Sociétés*, vol. 5, no. 1 (2001), pp. 111–27.

2 Quoted in David Philips, *Crime and Authority in Victorian England: The Black Country, 1835–60* (London: Croom Helm, 1977), p. 13.

3. Frank McLynn, *Crime and Punishment in Eighteenth-Century England* (London: Routledge, 1989), p. 302.

4 The exception that proves the rule is the crime of embezzlement, which the OBP categorise as theft while this book treats all such cases as fraud in order to match the categories used in the analysis of provincial cases.

5 For a detailed study of the use of the death penalty in the late-eighteenth to mid-nineteenth century, including a brief list of those crimes which carried the death penalty and the dates at which such sentence was abolished, see V. A. C. Gatrell, *The Hanging Tree: Execution and the English People 1770–1868* (Oxford: OUP Paperbacks, 1996), and for a critique of Gatrell's impassioned subjective style and findings, see Randall McGowen, 'Revisiting The Hanging Tree: Gatrell on Emotion and History', *British Journal of Criminology*, vol. 40, no. 1 (January 2000), pp. 1–13.

6 The high percentage of arson/damage to property may be particularly influenced by the source data consulted – see pp. 109–10 for a discussion on this topic. With regard to the creation of different categories of theft,

robbery and burglary, the generally accepted definitions are utilised of the respective crimes: burglary being the crime of house-breaking, robbery being theft from the person with the use, or implied use, of force, and theft being the dishonest appropriation of property. Bank robberies have been included in the category of robbery, because (a) they were invariably referred to as robberies in the sources, and (b) it is often not clear in the sources whether the crime committed was actually robbery or theft.

7 Like the overwhelming majority of parish or petty constables at the time, Trigg was a part-time constable and relied on another occupation for his living.

8 For a fuller account of this investigation, see Fred Feather, 'The Slaying of Parish Constable Trigg', *Essex Police History Note Book No. 2* (undated).

9 Such investigations may not of course have involved the respective Principal Officer(s) on a full-time basis – the Officers often worked on several cases concurrently.

10 PP 1816, p. 138.

11 *Staffordshire Advertiser*, 11 July 1812.

12 *First Report on the Constabulary Force in England and Wales, PP 1839* (169) vol. XIX 9-240, p. 146. This unambiguously critical view of the parish constabulary has been subject to increasing revision in recent years; in 1983 Jim Sharpe presented a more sympathetic and balanced view (J. A. Sharpe, 'Policing the Parish in Early Modern England', *Past and Present Colloquium: Police and Policing* (1983), unpaginated), while Jerrard, and Morgan and Rushton, have similarly shown that the provincial policing situation was not uniformly appalling – see Brian Jerrard, 'Early Policing Methods in Gloucestershire', *Transactions of the Bristol and Gloucestershire Archaeological Society for 1992*, vol. C (1993), pp. 221–40; Gwenda Morgan and Peter Rushton, 'The Magistrate, the Community and the Maintenance of an Orderly Society in Eighteenth-Century England', *Historical Research*, vol. 76, no. 191 (February 2003), pp. 54–77.

13 For Vickery's injuries, see *The Times*, 1 January 1814, T 38/673 and PP 1816, p. 177. For Keys' injuries, see HO 60/3, 29 December 1836. The latter source unfortunately does not state what type of crime Keys was investigating at the time he sustained his injuries.

14 For a comprehensive list and brief details of murdered law-enforcement officers prior to the introduction of the Metropolitan Police in 1829, see the National Police Memorial website at: http://www.policememorial. org.uk/Forces/Metropolitan/appendix2.htm.

15 T 38/672 Public Office Accounts, Expenses for Quarters ending July 1801 and July 1802. The need for repair suggests that these weapons were used or at least carried by the Officers on a fairly regular basis.

16 Henry Goddard, *Memoirs* (4-volume manuscript, 1875–96), vol. 3, p. 170. Colin Greenwood remarks that 'the Seizure of Arms [1820] was the only means prior to the twentieth century, which, in any real way, imposed

on the right to keep arms, which by this time clearly included firearms' (Greenwood, *Firearms Control: A Study of Armed Crime and Firearms Control in England and Wales* (London: Routledge & Kegan Paul, 1972), p. 17), although section 4 of the Vagrancy Act 1824 provided limited means by which to penalise anyone armed with intent to commit a felony. Despite further legislation such as the Gun Licence Act of 1870, it was not until the Pistols Act of 1903 that the carrying of sidearms was effectively limited and controlled.

17 P. Fitzgerald, *Chronicle of Bow Street Police Office: with an account of the Magistrates, 'Runners' and Police*, 2 vols (London: Chapman & Hall, 1888), vol. 1, p. 93. This fact was capitalised on by Gill & Co. of St Bartholomew Square, Birmingham and 6 Princes Street, Soho, who in January 1812 advertised firearms for self-protection 'as made by them for, and most approved of, the Bow Street and other Police officers' (*Staffordshire Advertiser*, 4 January 1812). The advertisement seems to have been an entrepreneurial if somewhat cynical exploitation of the widespread fear and revulsion following the Ratcliff Highway murders of the previous year. The pistols that Bow Street officers used seem to have been made by a variety of gunsmiths both in the capital and the provinces; a flintlock travelling pistol dated *c*.1801–10, engraved 'Bow Street' and made by Tatham & Egg (whose premises were located in Charing Cross) has recently been sold at auction for £500 (http://www.thomasdelmar.com/catalogues/as071206/page3.htm).

18 J. J. Tobias, *Crime and Police in England 1700–1900* (Dublin: Gill & Macmillan, 1979), p. 47. Such 'extra-parochial' use of experienced detectives still occurs in the present day.

19 A few parish constables were popular and repeatedly re-elected, often serving for several years; for example, Thomas Poole of Arlington, near Bibury, served continuously from 1796 to 1811, while Thomas Franklin similarly served from 1813 to 1818 (Jerrard, 'Early Policing Methods in Gloucestershire', p. 221). Robert Jones, the constable of Stafford, served from at least 1830 to 1834 (*Staffordshire Advertiser*, 8 January 1831 and 8 February 1834) – see Chapter 5 for more details of Jones' work.

20 John E. Archer, *By a Flash and a Scare: Incendiarism, Animal Maiming and Poaching in East Anglia 1815–70* (Oxford: Clarendon Press, 1990), p. 7. With regard to the proliferation of arson, he also raises an interesting point concerning the widespread introduction of the safety match (tellingly nicknamed the 'Lucifer') by 1830 – this simple invention made the setting of such fires much easier and quicker than the tedious (and dangerous) process of flint and tinderbox. This period also saw a considerable growth in insurance with regard to farms and land – John Archer has informed me that the majority of farmers and landowners were not insured prior to 1830 (John Archer, personal communication, July 2005). It is recognised that then, as now, arson could also be committed by individuals purely for the 'thrill' of seeing the results of their handiwork rather than having any particular societal axe to grind.

21 Ibid., p. 22.
22 R. Wells, 'Social Protest, Class, Conflict and Consciousness in the English Countryside, 1700–1880', in Mick Reed and Roger Wells (eds), *Class, Conflict and Protest in the English Countryside* (London: Frank Cass, 1990), pp. 121–214, note 106.
23 Archer, *By a Flash and a Scare*, p. 49.
24 Archer's research suggests that some 83 per cent of incendiarism was perpetrated by members of the pauper or labouring classes (Archer, *By a Flash and a Scare*, pp. 177–8).
25 George Rudé, *Criminal and Victim: Crime and Society in Early Nineteenth-Century England* (Oxford: Clarendon Press, 1985), p. 10.
26 *Crime and Punishment Police vol. VIII* (IUP Reprints Series): *First Report on the Constabulary Force in England and Wales*, PP 1839 (169) vol. XIX, p. 5.
27 The victim of the sapling theft, for example, was the Duke of York. It is also recognised that horse-stealing was often regarded in the early nineteenth century as a particularly abhorrent form of larceny, and that horses during the period could often fetch considerable prices – indeed the first recorded Association for the Prosecution of Felons was created in Stoke-on-Trent in 1693 following a spate of horse thefts (see Douglas Hay, 'Manufacturers and the Criminal Law in the Later Eighteenth Century: Crime and "Police" in South Staffordshire', *Past and Present Colloquium: Police and Policing* (1983), unpaginated) – but in general the horses stolen (judging by the rewards offered for their return) were not extremely expensive thoroughbreds, as these would undoubtedly have proved difficult for thieves to dispose of without questions being asked.
28 See Table 4.4 for a comparison of the values of stolen goods involved in metropolitan cases.
29 Randall McGowen, 'Making the "Bloody Code"? – Forgery Legislation in Eighteenth-Century England', in Norma Landau (ed.), *Law, Crime and English Society 1660–1830* (Cambridge: CUP, 2002), pp. 117–38, at p. 119.
30 Malcom Gaskill, *Crime and Mentalities in Early Modern England* (Cambridge: CUP, 2000), p. 25.
31 Bank of England Freshfields' Papers, F2/166 AB 179/6. It has been estimated that between 1805 and 1823 there were some 263,990 forged notes in circulation (*First Report on the Constabulary Force in England and Wales*, PP 1839, p. 5).
32 Fitzgerald, *Chronicle of Bow Street Police Office*, vol. 1, p. 111.
33 Ibid., p. 116.
34 HO 60/3 1836–39, correspondence dated 23 October 1837.
35 The majority of well-known cases involving large amounts of money originated in London and are therefore not discussed in detail in this book. Such cases could involve spectacular sums of money; for example, the case of Rowland Stephenson, reported in the *Manchester Guardian*, 10 January 1829, involved fraud apparently in excess of a contemporary

amount of £200,000. This would equate to around £15–20 million in the present day. Similarly, Bank of England Freshfields' Papers F2 Forged and Other Imitation Bank Notes 1812–1905 and the OBP (o18040215-1) contain details of a somewhat ambitious attempted fraud carried out by Robert Aslett, who was tried 'with having feloniously secreted and embezzled property belonging to the said Governor and Company of the Bank of England, to the amount of 2,000,500 l. against the statute, and against the King's peace' from the Bank of England in April 1803 in exchequer bills and other securities – equivalent to over £200 million in today's terms.

36 Bank of England Freshfields' Papers F22/8 AB64/2 Correspondence Concerning Forgery in Cockermouth April 15th–July 8th 1812, letter dated 25 May 1812 to J. Christian, magistrate, Cockermouth from Kaye, Freshfield and Kaye. This particular case did not involve the services of Bow Street.

37 For a detailed study of the history of highway robbery and its eventual demise see Gillian Spragg, *Outlaws and Highwaymen: The Cult of the Robber in England from the Middle Ages to the Nineteenth Century* (London: Pimlico, 2001). Spragg elsewhere states that the crime had almost died out by 1815 and that the last mounted highwayman was tried in 1831 (http://www.outlawsandhighwaymen.com/history.htm).

38 E. Chadwick, 'Preventive Police', *London Review*, vol. 1 (1829), pp. 252–308, at p. 261. The last provincial highway robbery investigated by Principal Officers was in 1814 when a man was robbed at gunpoint of £20 near Bedfont in Middlesex. The last metropolitan case of highway robbery involving Principal Officers was when a hatter was robbed of £20 in 1813.

39 Highwaymen Act of 1693 (4 & 5 William & Mary c.8).

40 *Public Advertiser*, 17 October 1754.

41 *Crime and Punishment Police vol. VIII* (IUP Reprints Series): PP 1839 (169) vol. XIX, p. 109.

42 PP 1837/8, p. 128.

43 Fitzgerald, *Chronicle of Bow Street Police Office*, vol. 1, p. 123.

44 Peter King, *Crime, Justice, and Discretion in England 1740–1820* (Oxford: OUP, 2000), p. 142. The 'Runners' referred to were not in fact Principal Officers as this area was patrolled by either the Horse Patrol or the Dismounted Horse Patrol, but as the vast majority of Principal Officers worked their way 'through the ranks', such activities would have provided invaluable experience.

45 Although, as mentioned above, many of the Principal Officers were promoted from the ranks, such promotion was rare due to the very limited number of Principal Officers and there must have been fierce competition to obtain such a promotion. This competition is likely to have stimulated the more ambitious Patrol Officers to prove their worth in the eyes of their superiors.

46 John Styles' study of the investigations of a provincial magistrate, 'An Eighteenth-Century Magistrate as Detective: Samuel Lister of Little Horton', *Bradford Antiquary*, New Series, Part XLVII (October 1982), pp. 98–117, illustrates the extremely limited (at best) or (at worst) often non-existent level of cooperation or correspondence between provincial law-enforcement agencies. This lack of cooperation was still present in the 1830s; Les Waters, in his Foreword to the Police History Society reprint of the *Police and Constabulary List* of 1844 (which gave details of the various police forces throughout England), states: 'There can be no doubt that the "List" fulfilled a real need. We know from the first report of the Constabulary Commissioner in 1839 that there was virtually no co-operation between the police forces in existence at that time. Without such a publication how would police forces have known who to communicate with should they have wished to seek the help of colleagues elsewhere?' (Captain Adderley W. Sleigh (ed.), *The Police and Constabulary List 1844*, reprinted as Police History Society Monograph No. 3, 1991).

47 For further details of this case, see Chapter 6.

48 O'Connell had previously killed an opponent in a duel at Kildare, Ireland on 1 February 1815. He shot dead Captain John D'Esterre over a dispute concerning a toll bridge at Rosmanagher, County Clare, and apparently swore afterwards that he would never fight anyone again. This implies that the aborted duel later the same year between O'Connell and Peel would have been a face-saving exercise rather than a serious contest to the death, although there was a profound and long-standing enmity between the two potential participants.

49 John McGowan, 'The Emergence of Modern Civil Police in Scotland: A Case Study of the Police and Systems of Policing in Edinburghshire 1800–1833' (unpublished PhD thesis, Open University, 1996), p. 265.

50 Fitzgerald, *Chronicle of Bow Street Police Office*, vol. 2, p. 219.

51 T 38/674 Treasury: Departmental Accounts, Public Office, Bow Street 1816–35.

52 Research carried out at Plymouth has as yet neither substantiated nor denied this possibility (Brian Moseley, personal communication, September 2005, and see http://www.plymouthdata.info). Ellis' time in Plymouth may have been a similar abortive appointment to that of Rivett to the Dublin Police, mentioned in Chapter 2, note 70.

53 Francis Sheppard, *London 1808–1870: The Infernal Wen* (London: Secker & Warburg, 1971), p. 35.

54 For a detailed account of the 'Captain Swing' riots, see Eric Hobsbawm and George Rudé, *Captain Swing*, 2nd edn (London: Phoenix Press, 2001).

55 For further details concerning the Colliers' March of 1816, see David J. Cox, 'Civil Unrest in the Black Country, 1766–1816', in *The Family*

and *Local History Hand Book*, 9th edn (Nether Poppleton: R. Blatchford Publications, 2005), pp. 30–3.

56 Goddard, *Memoirs*, vol. 4, p. 216.

57 This figure excludes the crimes of pickpocketing (in which cases Bow Street Officers were normally sent out in groups in order to circulate among the crowds) and sedition (again Bow Street Officers were normally utilised in larger numbers in order to infiltrate crowds at meetings).

58 John Beattie, *English Detectives in the Late Eighteenth Century*, paper delivered at the European Social Science History Conference, The Hague, March 2002.

59 HO 44/22 ff. 45–6. The reference to James Ellis and Duke reinforces the under-reporting of cases; Ellis's investigation does not appear elsewhere in any of the utilised sources.

60 Letter quoted in J. L. Hammond and Barbara Hammond, *The Village Labourer 1760–1832: A Study in the Government of England before the Reform Bill*, 4th edn, 2 vols (London: Guild Books, 1948), vol. 2, p. 49. This probably refers to outbreaks of arson and machine-breaking in Kent.

61 Goddard, *Memoirs*, vol. 4, p. 210. This refers to a case in which a poaching gang in Northamptonshire was also responsible for a series of thefts.

62 Letter written by John William Ward, 1st Earl of Dudley, to his sister and quoted in Clive Emsley, *The English Police: A Political and Social History*, 2nd edn (London: Longman 1996), p. 22. Fouché had been appointed by Napoleon as Minister of Police in Paris. For a detailed account of the Ratcliff Highway Murders see P. D. James and T. Critchley, *The Maul and the Pear Tree: The Ratcliff Highway Murders 1811* (London: Faber & Faber, 2000).

63 Glasgow had employed plain-clothes detectives from 1821; see Alistair Dinsmor, 'Glasgow Police Pioneers', *Journal of the Police History Society*, 15 (2000), pp. 9–11, at p. 11.

64 For a detailed examination of a Metropolitan forgery case of the late eighteenth century, see Donna T. Andrew and Randall McGowen, *The Perreaus and Mrs. Rudd: Forgery and Betrayal in Eighteenth-Century London* (Berkeley, CA: University of California Press, 2001). For the official history of the Stamp Office, see H. Dagall, *Creating a Good Impression: 300 Years of the Stamp Office & Stamp Duties* (London: Stamp Office, 1994).

65 Elaine A. Reynolds, *Before the Bobbies: The Night Watch and Police Reform in Metropolitan London: 1720–1830* (Basingstoke: Macmillan, 1998); and Drew Gray, 'A Well-Constructed and Efficient System of Police'? *Constables, Substitutes and the Watching Systems in the City of London c.1750–1839*, paper presented at the European Centre for Policing Studies, Open University, July 2002.

66 In 1780 the Court Minute Book of the Bank of England records that the force consisted of one officer, two sergeants, two corporals, one drummer and 29 privates.

67 Bank of England Archives, Court Minute Books Index 1780–1899.

68 HO 59/2. Randall McGowen has researched the Bank of England's approaches to tackling forgery and an interim report was given by him in a paper entitled *The Bank of England and the Policing of Forgery, 1797–1821*, delivered at the European Centre for Policing Studies, Open University, Milton Keynes, November 2003. An expanded version of this paper can be found in Randall McGowen, 'The Bank of England and the Policing of Forgery 1797–1821', *Past and Present*, no. 186 (2005), pp. 81–116, and the subject is further explored in Randall McGowen, 'Managing the Gallows: The Bank of England and the Death Penalty, 1797–1821', *Law and History Review*, vol. 25, no. 2 (Summer 2007), pp. 241–82.

69 John Wade, *The Black Book or Corruption Unmasked*, p. 97.

70 Since 1748 the ceremony of Trooping the Colour, held in June, has been used to celebrate the official birthday of the reigning monarch. The monarch also usually celebrates his or her real birthday on the relevant date.

71 T 38/673, and see J. L. Lyman, 'The Metropolitan Police Act of 1829: An Analysis of Certain Events Influencing the Passage and Character of the Metropolitan Police Act in England', *Journal of Criminal Law, Criminology and Police Science*, vol. 55 (1964), pp. 141–54.

72 John Townsend's evidence to the 1816 Select Committee, p. 137. The situation continued throughout the period under discussion: the *Staffordshire Advertiser* of 16 January 1807 refers to Dowsett as 'one of the resident police officers at Windsor', while Pigot's 1823 *Directory of Windsor* contains a listing of the address of the resident Bow Street Officer, and a letter from the Home Department dated 15 November 1837 (HO 63/3) details the superannuation of two of the Windsor officers.

73 HO 65/3, letter dated 31 March 1796.

Chapter 5

'Police officers for the country at large': the nationwide role of the Principal Officers

Introduction

This chapter begins with a brief discussion of the pre-1829 provincial policing situation, considering the alternative avenues of investigation available to provincial victims of crime. It also details the geographical spread of the reported use of Principal Officers, suggesting reasons for their widespread use in certain areas and their limited presence in other parts of Great Britain. There is also a debate concerning the level of success enjoyed by the Principal Officers with regard to their investigations.

The pre-1829 provincial policing situation

Principal Officers were clearly not the only avenue to which a provincial victim of crime could turn. There was a limited range of alternatives available, not all of which were necessarily as inefficient as they have been portrayed by historians throughout much of the nineteenth and twentieth centuries. An increasing amount of research in recent years has gone some way to modifying the consensus of opinion about the pre-1829 policing situation in the provinces. Whiggish assertions that the 'New Police' – those created by the 1835 Municipal Corporations Act, 1839 Rural Constabulary Act and the 1856 County and Borough Police Act – 'quickly ended a long period of uncontrollable crime and disorder which had lasted, in some parts of the country, for more than a century' can no longer be accepted at face value.[1] Research by historians such as Robert Reiner and Cyril D. Robinson has, as Stanley Cohen and Andrew Scull remark, 'destroyed for ever the idea of a simple, linear progression from "bad" old parish constables and watchmen to "good" new, uniformed police forces'.[2] This book does not aspire to provide a comprehensive analysis of the earlier policing situation; rather it synthesises the findings of recent research into the subject and relates it to the provincial activities of the Principal Officers.

Perceived inefficiency of parish constabulary system

There was undoubtedly considerable and widespread contemporary criticism of the parish constabulary system in the early decades of the nineteenth century. This system probably predated Edward Ist's reign (1272–1307); the 1839 Royal Commission remarked in its *Report* that 'we incline to the opinion that the office of constable is an office at common law, that it was regulated, not created by the Statute of Winchester (13 Edw. I. C.6 sec. 1 2 3 and 4)'.[3]

In 1829 Edwin Chadwick memorably berated parish watchmen in London as being nothing more than '"ambulating lighthouse[s]" to direct their [thieves'] perilous course'.[4] Similarly, several of those provincials giving evidence to the 1839 Royal Commission (especially magistrates) were particularly harsh in their blanket criticism of provincial parish constables. In answer to the query, 'what is the number of constables in your division and how are they appointed?' magistrates of the petty sessions at Alfreston in Derbyshire stated 'about fourteen, appointed generally by the inhabitants of the parish and townspeople, and, in almost every instance, persons quite unfit and afraid to perform the duties of the office.' Similarly, in Newnham, Gloucestershire, parish constables were 'generally chosen [...] without any regard to their fitness for the office', while 'in the rural districts the constables are mostly farmers, who are often deterred from interfering with old offenders, or with beer-houses, or other resorts of the dissolute, by an apprehension of injury to themselves or property'.[5]

However, despite the considerable amount of opprobrium heaped upon the parish constabulary and judiciary system, and while there remains, as Alastair Dinsmor remarks, 'a tendency to dismiss any policing organisation before 1829 as not being "real" policemen, just a collection of old nightwatchmen or bumbling parish constables', an increasing body of evidence is emerging to suggest that the system was not necessarily always inefficient.[6]

Work by both James Sharpe and John Styles has shown that in some locations, both the parish constabulary and the local magistracy could occasionally prove effective in preventing and detecting crime.[7] Similarly, R. W. England's work on the investigation of murders in Northern England deals with four northern counties (Cumberland, Yorkshire, Westmoreland and Northumberland) in the period 1800–24, and suggests that magistrates within the Northern Circuit often relied heavily on the investigative skill and prowess of their local constables. R. W. England provides summaries of four cases showing constables' detective skills and tenacity, and also indicates that this skill was not exclusive to the North of England, giving several examples from further afield. At murders in Bitton parish, Gloucestershire (1824), and in Tilhurst parish, Berkshire (1817), successful prosecutions resulted from the forensic examination of footprints. The former case also involved the investigation of trouser marks made by sitting ambushers, while the latter involved measuring footprints and stride lengths and comparing heel marks, boots and shoes at the time all being handmade and therefore individual.[8]

The records published in *A Village Constable's Accounts (1791–1839)* go some way to illuminating details of the wide-ranging day-to-day duties of provincial parish constables, which were often far removed from criminal investigation, including public highways maintenance, collecting dead foxes, paying poor relief to soldiers, widows, etc.[9] Some parish constables undoubtedly did their duty honourably and to the best of their ability, often serving for several years. In Stafford, newspaper reports indicate that their parish constabulary was considered effective by many in positions of power. In March 1827 Baron Vaughan, one of the Lent Assize judges, addressed the Grand Jury at Stafford Court with the following words: 'I believe there is no County – as far as my knowledge of it enables to judge – in which the Police is [sic] more vigilant and the magistrates more active.'[10]

Throughout the early 1830s the *Staffordshire Advertiser* reports numerous cases involving the constable of Stafford, clearly holding him in high esteem (which did not, however, preclude him from having to resort to the following unusual method of raising money for himself):

Mr R. Jones, our active and intelligent constable, whose constant labours are not confined to this borough alone, but are extended to the protection of the property of farmers and others, in the surrounding county, will, by favour of the Mayor of Stafford, take a benefit on Tuesday evening next. The inadequate manner in which his effective services have hitherto been remunerated, inclines him to avail himself of this means of seeking some additional recompense for his exertions on behalf of the public.[11]

Whether or not the parish constable should be seen as a 'most ancient, most constitutional, and most useful officer' or as a completely inefficient and outdated institution, one of the main problems with the parish constabulary system seems to have been the lack of manpower. Roger Swift's research into the policing of Wolverhampton reveals that in the first decade of the nineteenth century the town had a population of c.13,000 and possessed only two parish constables; in 1814 a night watch of ten men was finally created to supplement this meagre force.[12] Similarly, in 1812, Stourbridge in Worcestershire had a population of c.4,500 and one parish constable.[13] However, contemporary commentators occasionally throw a different light on policing issues; Marc de Bombelles, a minor French aristocrat, recorded in his private diary kept during an extended visit to England in late 1784 that:

Among the 60,000 people which make up the population of Birmingham [...] there is no need for any establishment of a police force. But as everyone is continually at work, public holidays offer no more than an indispensable period of rest, which the artisan uses without too much abusing.[14]

This may be seen as nothing more than the uncritical musings of an ingenuous member of the French upper class, but throughout the rest of his diary, Bombelles (who circumstantial evidence suggests was probably engaged on an industrial espionage mission) often shows himself to be capable of considerable analysis and perspicacity.

Provincial alternatives to the parish constable

The parish constable was one of the few means by which victims of crime could hope for redress; there remained, however, no system of public prosecution during the period. Consequently, one of the most popular alternatives for those who could afford it was to belong to a private prosecution society funded by subscription. These were known as Associations for the Prosecution of Felons and were usually comprised of members from either a single county or borough. As has been noted, the earliest known such association dates back to 1693, but by the end of the eighteenth century they had multiplied throughout the country.

Craig B. Little and Christopher P. Sheffield provide an interesting comparison between English and American ideas of how to deal with the problems of law enforcement; in both countries they argue that it was the failure of the executive to implement the legislature that led to the respective creation of vigilante societies and Associations for the Prosecution of Felons: 'Neither the concept of the law nor its content were in question – only problems surrounding the effectiveness of the law's enforcement.'[15]

David Eastwood suggests that these problems were dealt with at least to some extent by the creation of such associations, which he regards as 'the most significant components in a programme to deter crime in later Hanoverian England without abandoning traditional forms of communal policing'. However, in reality they often had little effect on serious crimes such as those investigated by Principal Officers. Very few murders appear to have been prosecuted by such associations, and because of the relatively high subscription costs, they were not seen as attractive or viable alternatives by many poorer members of the local community, who often suffered disproportionately from crime but were largely unable to pursue suspects due to the prohibitive cost of private prosecution.[16]

The *Wolverhampton Chronicle* of 6 January 1813 contains advertisements for over half a dozen such associations in the immediate area around the town, many containing preambles such as that of the Tettenhall Association: 'Whereas several burglaries, felonies, grand and petit larcenies have frequently of late been committed [...] and the Offenders have escaped Justice with impunity, for want of proper Pursuit'.[17]

Prosecution associations and associations of manufacturers or organisations did occasionally employ their own force of constables or detectives. Freshfield's, solicitors to the Bank of England, employed their own agents for detecting and pursuing suspects, while the Dursley Association created a short-lived police force in 1814, consisting of 36 men on night patrols.[18] It would seem, however, that most Associations or private businesses were unwilling or unable to meet the expense necessary for the creation of such forces. Philips remarks: 'A number of associations [did] establish their own private police forces or patrols, but the majority did not go to this extent, preferring to work through their relationship with the parish constables, or later, with the new police forces.'[19] In 1839 the railway companies that had created their own police force were criticised in the Royal Commission *Report*: 'It has already been a subject of complaint that the railway police protect the companies against the passengers, without protecting the latter, and that they suppress and conceal information of accidents.'[20]

Attitude of local authorities to the use of Principal Officers in provincial cases

During the period under discussion Bow Street personnel were utilised on a regular basis throughout the United Kingdom, and therefore some analysis of the attitudes of local authorities to their employment needs to be attempted.

Any fears of centralised or metropolitan control over law enforcement seem largely to have been overruled in cases where Principal Officers were called in to investigate; as has been shown in Chapter 3, the overwhelming majority of investigations by Bow Street were instigated at the request of members of the local elite. Traditional communal methods of policing were clearly thought to be unsuitable in these cases – perhaps because many of the crimes such as poaching or smuggling involved a large proportion of the local community, leading to concomitant problems of local law officers being unable to proceed effectively with their enquiries due to fears of reprisal or future communal sanction.

The local authorities turned to Bow Street for numerous reasons: there may have been a localised epidemic of a particular type of crime, such as arson, and the parish constabulary were not experienced or capable of dealing with such matters over what could be a relatively large area. Similarly, crimes such as the murder of gamekeepers often occurred on large private estates and the landowner wanted to investigate the matter with the help of an outside agency which would not be intimidated by local feelings of sympathy for the perpetrator.

The advantages of a plain-clothes detective in the investigation of a localised crime, where the parish constable would have been instantly recognised and suspicions therefore aroused are obvious – although the Principal Officers were well-known by reputation in many areas, their individual identities would only have been known by a relatively small number of people in and around the metropolis.[21]

No other such force existed in England during the period, and it is therefore not surprising that they were frequently used in such a capacity by both local elites and the state.

There seems to have been little antipathy among the local authorities to the use of Principal Officers; no evidence suggests that magistrates appear to have thought that their authority or capability was being questioned by the use of such individuals. In practice, the local magistrates were still fundamentally in charge of the proceedings as the Principal Officer was usually employed directly by the magistrate, or by the victim(s), and was therefore responsible to local figures rather than a central body. Any warrant issued in the provinces also had to be signed by a local magistrate and served by a parochial law-enforcement official.

In several cases, magistrates and other local law-enforcement bodies seem to have been glad to avail themselves of Bow Street's services; in 1798 the *Staffordshire Advertiser* reported that the magistrates of Manchester wrote to Bow Street stating that 'treasonable proceedings were taking place in that town, and its neighbourhood, against the parties concerned in which they did not exactly know how to proceed, and therefore requesting that some of the London magistrates and Officers of Police might be sent to their assistance'.[22] Similarly, local magistrates occasionally wrote to Bow Street after the successful conclusion of an investigation, praising the quality of the respective Principal Officer; in 1836 the magistrates of Tunbridge Wells praised Henry Goddard for his investigation of an arson attack:

> Considering the very slight clue we had as to the offenders, the conduct, activity and intelligence of Mr Goddard cannot be too much commended. I can only express my own approbation and thanks of the principal inhabitants of this place of his exertions in this matter.[23]

In such cases, it can be seen that the local magistrates were happy to utilise the services offered by Bow Street, despite the fact that such use could be seen to reflect poorly on the existing provincial law-enforcement system.

Nationwide role of the Principal Officers

Although it has been demonstrated above that the Officers were used in the metropolis, it has been shown that much of their work related to the provinces, and it is to this aspect that the discussion now turns.

In marked contrast to the lesser members of Bow Street, the Principal Officers did not usually sully themselves with the more mundane activities of preventive policing.[24] Richard Birnie, when asked about the role of the Principal Officers in 1822, remarked that 'in general they do not patrol the streets or any thing of that sort; they are, more properly speaking, police officers for the country at large, than for any actual service to us'.[25] This situation has often been overlooked or ignored by many historians, who have persisted in conflating the work of the Principal Officers with that of their less senior colleagues, who fulfilled a largely preventive role. The use of Principal Officers in 1822 was therefore fundamentally unchanged from the time of the Fieldings, and remained so until their disbandment in 1839.

As has been demonstrated in Chapter 2, the Principal Officers were always regarded by the Fieldings and subsequent Chief Magistrates as more than simply a metropolitan force. This was a new and unique approach to crime prevention and detection. Principal Officers can therefore be regarded as the first law-enforcement body to operate throughout Britain, albeit on a very numerically limited basis.

That the Fieldings were happy for their new force to be employed throughout Britain is clear enough. Establishing the extent to which the Fieldings envisaged a national adoption of their plans by the creation of similar offices throughout the country is more vexatious. Henry Fielding's *An enquiry into the causes of the late increase of robbers* together with Sir John's *A Plan for Preventing Robberies within Twenty Miles of London* which set out the latter's views on how to provide an effective law-enforcement body, both concentrated almost exclusively on the problems resulting from perceived vastly increased criminal activity in the metropolitan area. However, Sir John made it clear in his series of notices in the *Public Advertiser* that the Bow Street personnel were available to travel throughout Britain.

However, there appears to be little evidence that either of the Fieldings, despite their prodigious output on the subject, or their successors, ever seriously considered the creation of a nationwide system of policing based on Bow Street lines. Stanley Palmer remarks that 'even the great police reformers, Henry and John Fielding and Patrick Colquhoun, steered clear of recommending the creation of a large, salaried, professional police force'; such an idea would have been anathema to many people.[26] In the event little came of any such subsequent nascent ideas that either of the Fieldings may have held in regard to the country as a whole.

Opposition to a national police force

The reluctance of the Fieldings and later Bow Street Chief Magistrates to actively cultivate such measures may have been largely due to an inherent awareness that the idea of a national police force has always met with stiff resistance.[27] The only practical attempt to create such a force took place in August 1655 when Oliver Cromwell introduced a scheme to divide England into districts under the command of Major-Generals.[28] This abortive plan, which contained an especially unpopular militaristic element, lasted less than two years, causing bitter and lasting resentment, and there was no more serious political momentum for the creation of a national police force until the early decades of the nineteenth century, by which time the reported excesses of Napoleon's militaristic gendarmerie had immeasurably soured public opinion against the creation of such a body of men.

Similarly, in 1829 the indefatigable commentator on policing matters, John Wade, indignantly stated that:

> The system established by Fouché and Savary, and continued under the administration of M. de Villèle, is quite sufficient to disgust us with refined and complicated organisations of preventive justice, and cannot have the most distant resemblance to any establishment required in this country.[29]

The above views were typical of many of those in authority; there was widespread antipathy to any proposed system that would reduce the power and authority of local unpaid magistrates. Such opponents argued that a centralisation of law enforcement was to be avoided at all costs because of the fear of centralised control over what were considered primarily local issues of crime and punishment. They argued that such a system would lead to state coercion, with attendant spying and surveillance. These views were based on a fundamentally rural and pre-industrial outlook on crime, with little consideration being given to the burgeoning populations in rapidly industrialising towns and cities. Even a rapidly industrialising area such as the Black Country, a domain largely controlled and owned by the Earl of Dudley, was fundamentally at this time still predominantly rural in nature – the population, although working in industries such as coal-mining, lived largely in small village-based communities (admittedly not always immediately distinguishable from one another to strangers) in which everyone knew nearly everyone else, and in which outsiders were immediately noticed.[30]

Conversely, some of those directly involved in law enforcement, including Principal Officers, did perceive that benefits would accrue from the creation of a national system. John Vickery, a highly experienced and erudite Principal Officer who served from 1811 to 1822, in his evidence to the 1816 Select Committee on the Police of the metropolis, tentatively suggested that a force of national officers could be created: 'Whether it would be considered at all a trespass upon the liberties of the subject, to make a certain number of officers constables for England, is a consideration I would submit.'[31] How pleased Vickery would have been to know that his ideas were echoed by a convicted recidivist some 23 years later is open to conjecture; in the 1839 Royal Commission *Report*, the statement of a 21-year-old habitual thief – the 'son of honest parents at Manchester' – included his view that:

> It would be one of the best things as ever was established if there were forty or fifty clever constables to travel through England, and go to all fairs, races, etc. [...] and they would soon know the faces of thieves and drive them off; they should change their rounds. [32]

Research by David Philips and Robert Storch has suggested that toward the end of the period under discussion there was more detailed consideration of the possible adoption of a national policing system. Their investigation has thrown new light on the Grey Ministry's ultimately abortive National Police scheme of 1832, in which a national system of stipendiary magistracies was proposed, with the magistracies being closely modelled on the London Police Offices.[33] It is interesting to speculate what would have happened as this scheme, had it been implemented, could have changed the face of the development of what is now regarded as our 'modern' policing system and would have created a national force based largely on Bow Street's lines.[34]

Despite the reservations concerning the creation of a national force, the Principal Officers can be seen to have operated, on an admittedly small scale, as a de facto national force (in the respect that they were utilised throughout Great Britain), and as Sidney and Beatrice Webb point out, 'The Bow Street Police Office gradually became the centre of the police administration, not only of the metropolis, but, to some extent, also of the whole country.'[35]

Location of reported provincial cases involving Principal Officers

Table 5.1 shows the number of cases reported involving Principal Officers in each county of England, Wales and Scotland.[36] It can be seen that the Officers are recorded as being active throughout Great Britain. Their widespread geographical use is not perhaps too surprising in a period when there was no system of public prosecution; victims had to undertake the often onerous and expensive task of organising the detection and apprehension of suspects themselves. It has already been shown that wealthy individuals or institutions did not baulk at the cost of employing Principal Officers when they were deemed necessary to ensure a successful investigation and prosecution; in many cases they were the only viable alternative in a situation when 'as late as the mid-nineteenth century no public official was responsible for ensuring that even the most serious offences were prosecuted', despite there having been frequent calls for the creation of a public prosecutor.[37]

A third (157) of the provincial cases reported were in the four counties in which Bow Street magistrates and Officers had official legal jurisdiction above and beyond that of the normal subject

Table 5.1 Number of cases in each county of England, Scotland and Wales that Principal Officers were called out to investigate, 1792–1839

Aberdeenshire	2	Gloucestershire	24	Nottinghamshire	5
Argyllshire	1	Hampshire	33	Oxfordshire	11
Ayrshire	2	Herefordshire	7	Renfrewshire	1
Bedfordshire	5	Hertfordshire	30	Rutland	1
Berkshire	24	Huntingdonshire	3	Shetland	1
Breconshire	2	Kent	86	Shropshire	5
Buckinghamshire	22	Lanarkshire	2	Somerset	14
Cambridgeshire	10	Lancashire	11	Staffordshire	9
Cheshire	3	Leicestershire	7	Suffolk	9
Cornwall	6	Lincolnshire	9	Surrey	32
County Durham	3	Middlesex	38	Sussex	27
Cumberland	3	Midlothian	4	Warwickshire	11
Derbyshire	3	Monmouthshire	1	Westmoreland	2
Devon	10	Montgomeryshire	1	Wiltshire	27
Dorset	5	Norfolk	9	Worcestershire	2
Dumbartonshire	1	Northamptonshire	10	Yorkshire	15
Essex	30	Northumberland	4	*Total*	582

during much of the period under discussion (namely Middlesex, Surrey, Essex and Kent).[38] These increased legal powers would have significantly simplified the job of the Principal Officer, negating the need for him to seek out local magistrates and constables for the issue of arresting warrants. This bias is therefore perhaps unsurprising, given the additional fact that travelling distances in such counties were obviously relatively short and therefore involved less expense to the prosecutor(s). The time delay between offence and subsequent investigation would also be significantly diminished the lesser the distance from London.

Travel was extremely expensive and slow at the time; private chaise hire in particular (which the Principal Officers seemed to have favoured because of its relative speed) between London and the provinces was especially dear, with costs reaching several pounds over even fairly short distances.[39] Many of the Principal Officers' investigations sent them throughout Britain, involving lengthy, expensive and slow journeys by coach or chaise. Alternative methods of transport were available but remained restrictive in terms of both speed and geographical area served.

By 1830, the first steam-driven passenger railway ran from Manchester to Liverpool, while almost seventy destinations throughout England and Wales were served by Pickford's 'fly-boats' – relatively fast horse-drawn passenger barges that had precedence over all other canal traffic. Steam-packets were one of the fastest forms of transport with an average speed of over 10 m.p.h., but were similarly limited in their routes, being confined to coastal or estuarine settlements. Travel by private chaise or mail coach averaged around 10 m.p.h., and was widely deemed to be more comfortable, safer and prestigious than most other forms of travel.[40]

Travel and other expenses could therefore easily amount to a considerable sum. Following George Ruthven's investigation into a particular case in February 1831, he submitted an expenses claim of £50.[41] Berkshire magistrate, J. Sawyer, replied to an unknown writer concerning a query about this large amount:

> I have the honour to acknowledge the receipt of your letter of the 21st instant. I can inform you that Ruthven was employed in investigating the case against Greenaway the time that he states, and that he was not otherwise employed. He has sent in a bill to the amount of £50 and upwards for his attendance and expenses [to] which Dr Vansittart has been applied to pay.[42]

Similarly, on 25 September 1830 a letter from Sir Richard Birnie details the situation regarding a suspected murder at Chard in Somerset.[43] Samuel Taunton, Principal Officer, had submitted an expenses claim of £51 12s 5½d, and Birnie's letter details the costs: 'Taunton's bill is very heavy and a considerable portion of it is money laid out in coach and chaise hire in going to various places by order of the local justices'.[44] A note on the rear of the letter written by Sir Richard categorically states that 'I never send a Bow Street Officer to investigate a spurious case of this kind – without assurance as to the payment of the expenses that may be incurred.'[45]

Kent seems to have been the county which most employed Principal Officers on provincial investigations: almost 15 per cent of the total number of cases. Apart from the proximity to London, its relative affluence, high proportion of wealthy property owners and long coastline which provided ample opportunities for often large-scale smuggling helped to ensure that it was a fairly constant source of employment for the Principal Officers.

The number of cases does not, however, seem necessarily to diminish proportionately to the distance from the metropolis – the map does not show a simple gradual decline in the number of cases in counties radiating from London, although there is an admittedly strong southern bias. Somerset or Lancashire, for example, cannot have been the easiest of places to reach from London in the early nineteenth century, despite the advent of turnpikes, metalled roads and rapidly expanding canal and rail networks, but both have a significant amount of cases, despite the inevitable time-lag between detection of the offence and subsequent investigation. With regard to communication systems over long distances, this obviously presented a major problem for Principal Officers when working in the provinces. Letters, even when travelling by the fastest mail coaches, would still have taken days to travel relatively short distances.

The period under discussion pre-dates the invention of the electric telegraph, though a mechanical system of shutter telegraph was installed between London and Portsmouth in 1795–96, and a network of semaphore towers was constructed at the end of the Napoleonic Wars. These, however, seem to have been exclusively used by the Admiralty, and there is no evidence of them being used to communicate details of crimes, although they were undoubtedly the fastest means of communication then available. According to the *Annual Register* of 28 January 1796, a message from Dover to London was transmitted by 'this ingenious and useful contrivance' in seven minutes. However, the innovation seems to have been regarded as little more than an interesting curiosity. Further research is needed into this little-known form of rapid communication; such a method, if it had been widely adopted, could have benefited crime investigations.[46]

In many of the more remote provincial counties, however, there were concentrations of landed gentry and self-made industrialists who possessed significant land and property and who would not have had to worry too much about the often considerable cost of financing private prosecutions. However, in all cases where property or valuables were stolen or misappropriated, those concerned with prosecuting suspect(s) must have had to consider a balance between the loss of property and the expense of prosecution.

Perhaps more significantly, Lancashire and Somerset in particular also possessed respectively the second and fourth largest centres of population in Britain: Manchester and Bristol. In 1801, Manchester had a population of c.80,000, while Bristol, although by this time declining in economic importance, was still home to over 50,000 people. Also by this period Liverpool in Lancashire had become the third most populous settlement in Britain.[47] All of the Lancashire cases reported emanated from either Manchester or Liverpool, while almost three-quarters of the Somerset cases originated in either Bristol or the nearby popular (and relatively populous) spa town of Bath, suggesting that at least in these areas of provincial Britain, the larger towns provided one of the main sources of employment for the Principal Officers.[48]

Lancashire's criminal fraternity is claimed to have been particularly active by some historians. A. G. L. Shaw states that 'Lancashire, with about a twelfth of England's population, supplied about one-eighth of her crime; in these two centres [London and Lancashire], with less than a fifth of the English population, more than a third of the crime was committed.'[49] The provincial policing of Bow Street was not, however, uniquely urban in nature; many cases were instigated by rural landowners, especially in the more southern arable counties of England, in which the victims and instigators of many of the investigations were farmers. Wiltshire, a predominantly agrarian county, had 27 cases, almost half of which involved arson or damage to farm property.

Distribution of cases

Looking at Table 5.1 there is an obvious southern bias to the distribution of identified cases – taking the north of the nation to be that area north of a line from the Dee estuary to the Wash, 71 cases are recorded (just under 12 per cent of the total), while the Midlands, taken as that area to the north of a line drawn from Hereford to Ipswich, has 92 cases (15.3 per cent of the total). By contrast, the remaining 16 counties of England account for 419 reported cases (almost 70 per cent of the total). The relative nearness of these counties to the metropolis, and the concomitant comparative ease by which they could be reached from London was undoubtedly a major factor for this preponderance of identified cases and must not be underestimated.

However, this large concentration of cases may also be partially explained by the economic and demographic dominance of many of these counties in what was still an overwhelmingly agrarian society. The south of England generally enjoyed more productive agriculture than the rest of Britain, and consequently there was a disproportionate number of landed gentry or aristocrats based in this area. These wealthy landowners (who were often also magistrates or similar such office-holders) could generally easily afford to employ the services of Bow Street and the sources suggest that they frequently so did. As discussed above with regard to Wiltshire, many of the identified cases involving damage or threatened damage to property or possessions, e.g. arson, threatening behaviour, poaching etc., were located in the south of England and this would appear to at least go some way in providing a possible reason for the overwhelming amount of identified cases in this area of Britain.

Scottish cases

There is also a marked discrepancy between the number of cases in each of the three mainland countries. In 1821, Scotland had a population of *c*.2.1 million (14.8 per cent of the total mainland population of *c*.14.2 million), but only 2.3 per cent of cases reported are from Scotland.[50] This may be largely related to the time-consuming distance involved in travelling from the capital to Scotland, and, once there, the difficulties of travel due to the terrain and lack of maintained roads.[51] Scotland also had a different legal and police system, with several large towns in Scotland possessing well-established and often effective police forces during the period under discussion, and this factor may have lessened the need for outside assistance in detecting and arresting the perpetrators of crime.

There is also the possibility that there was simply less crime to investigate in Scotland; David G. Barrie has recently remarked that 'statistically, serious crime in Scotland appeared to be less common than in England', but he also provides a caveat that 'differences between the Scottish and English criminal justice systems preclude meaningful comparison between the two countries'.[52] The likelihood is that the reasons for the lack of Scottish cases involving Principal Officers were many and varied, but the existence of well-established police offices (sometimes with a detective contingent) was probably *primus inter pares*.

The Glasgow police force in particular seems to have been innovative in its outlook: Apart from having created its own detective branch by 1821, a Central Police Office had been opened by 1825, which was extremely progressive for its time and 'unlike the "Police Offices" of the English Magistracy, functioned just as the police administrative and custodial centres we know today.'[53] Table 5.2 shows Scottish towns with police forces and the dates they were established.[54]

Welsh cases

Turning to the remaining mainland country, Wales, only four cases are reported – less than 1 per cent of the total. This almost complete absence of identified cases remains problematical, despite there being a multiplicity of possible explanations for this apparent anomaly. Relatively little academic investigation into either the policing history of Wales or the history of Welsh crime has taken place, an honourable exception being research carried out in recent years by David J. V. Jones, who has contributed greatly to our still limited knowledge of the subject. [55]

The most obvious explanation (but probably the least likely) for the lack of identified cases is simply that less crime was committed

Table 5.2 Founding dates of Scottish police forces

Glasgow	1779
Aberdeen	1795
Edinburgh	1805
Paisley	1806
Gorbals	1808
Leith	By 1808
Dundee	1824

in the area – possibly due to the lack of population centres. Philip Jenkins has carried out considerable research into the population of Wales, and states that: 'Even by 1801, there were only twelve [towns with 2,000 people or more], and the largest community in Wales had less than 8,000 people.'[56] However, only two identified cases in a period of 48 years still seems remarkably low, even bearing in mind the low density of population.

Another possible explanation could be that the Welsh were particularly prone to dispensing summary unofficial 'justice'; Fewtrell Clements has suggested from his research into the history of the Denbighshire police that during the first half of the nineteenth century 'shaming was a very common occurrence in Wales'.[57] This *ceffyl pren* or *charivari* could clearly have been used to obviate the need for involvement of outside agencies such as Bow Street.[58]

Referring to a slightly later period, David J. V. Jones remarks that:

> Judges in mid and late-Victorian Wales, for example, grew increasingly suspicious of the empty calendars [...] especially in [...] backward rural communities', and this suggests that certain crimes were either dealt with internally within a community or possibly not regarded as crimes and therefore ignored.[59]

Wales was certainly regarded by contemporaries as something of a closed community; it was known in the nineteenth century as the 'secret land', and in 1842, Captain Napier, head of the newly formed Glamorgan constabulary, remarked upon 'a species of clanship [which] renders the Welshman peculiarly averse to giving evidence against a neighbour'.[60] Although this 'internal' approach to the enforcement of law and order at first seems unlikely to have been a viable option for serious crimes such as murder or manslaughter, Jones suggests that on occasion it appears that even these two types of crime were not reported to the official authorities; he states that official statistics show a marked discrepancy between English and Welsh indictments for both murder and manslaughter, and that this discrepancy was largely the result of failure to report such crimes.[61]

This failure to report crimes to the magistracy may have had an underlying religious reason; Carl Zangerl, in his study of the returns of Justices of the Peace in England and Wales between 1831 and 1887, has calculated that in 1831 clerical magistrates made up 28.8 per cent of the total number of magistrates in Wales and states that these Anglican magistrates were often deeply resented (and probably mistrusted) by Non-conformists in Wales.[62] The social and religious composition of the magistracy was not a haphazard state of affairs; as David Eastwood remarks, 'the politics of the gentry and of magisterial power had a very precise social location', and the Anglican domination among the clerical magistrates can be seen as a deliberate attempt by the ruling elite to ensure that the views of the Established Church held sway with regard to judicial decisions. [63]

David J. V. Jones' research suggests that Welsh magistrates were often loath to involve outside law-enforcement agencies: 'Only in the last resort were Welsh justices prepared to bring in professional policemen from outside.'[64] However, there are records of the magistrates occasionally resorting to such measures – a letter dated 20 October 1800 survives in Home Department records in which the mayor of Haverfordwest, where there had been a serious spate of rick-burning and sending of threatening letters, requests the Secretary of State to send some of 'the Persons known by the name of the Bow Street Runners'.[65] There is no record of whether the request was granted.

By contrast, the magistracy seemed willing enough to involve the military when threatened by insurrection – the case of Dic Penderyn and his role in the Merthyr Rising of 1831, where soldiers from Brecon were called in to prevent 'rioting', is perhaps the most well-known example.[66]

Another reason for the lack of identified cases in Wales during the period under discussion may simply be that the primary sources consulted had a limited interest (and readership) in Wales and therefore often did not report criminal cases from the principality. The national newspapers did, however, often gather and reprint news from local newspapers, and there is no obvious reason why they should not have done the same with regard to Welsh newspapers (language barriers excepted). Despite being sparsely populated, Wales was (at least at the beginning of the period under discussion) well-served with newspapers: Hannah Barker remarks that in Wales and the English Midlands, 'in the 1780s, the concentration of papers was probably as dense in this area as anywhere else outside the capital'.[67]

Finally, the language barrier may have provided another disincentive to employ English-speaking Bow Street personnel; investigations could have proved well-nigh impossible if those questioned either did not understand or refused to answer in English. In 1838 Llandovery Workhouse burned down, apparently as the result of malicious intent, and the authorities applied to the Home Department for a Welsh-speaking Metropolitan Police officer to assist in their enquiries. The

Home Department reply is dated a month later, the delay suggesting that they had had some difficulty complying with this request. The reply contains an affidavit that 'PC 190 John Emry is an intelligent officer who can speak Welsh'.[68] The fact that the Llandovery authorities specifically asked for a Metropolitan Police officer and not for a Bow Street officer could suggest one of two things: either the authorities knew that no Bow Street officer spoke Welsh or that they were not used to applying to Bow Street.

Any or all of the above possible reasons may have been responsible for the lack of recorded cases, but further research beyond the scope of this book is required to more confidently ascribe the lack of recorded cases in Wales to a particular set of causes.

Success rate of Principal Officers

While the level of provincial operation of the Principal Officers has been quantified to some extent within this book, any attempt to measure the level of success in their investigations is fraught with difficulties. The fact that they were used repeatedly throughout the period by a multiplicity of employers including private and public institutions, together with the longevity of a system that was instigated in 1748 and which continued for over ninety years without significant alteration, is perhaps some indication of their perceived success, but this can only be a subjective measure. Taking all of the verdicts recorded in all Old Bailey cases 1792–1839 we arrive at the figures shown in Table 5.3.[69] The comparative figures for all Old Bailey cases involving Principal Officers are shown in Table 5.4.

Table 5.3 Verdicts in all Old Bailey cases involving Principal Officers, 1792–1839

Total number of verdicts	74,673
Number of guilty verdicts	56,058
% of guilty verdicts of total verdicts	75.1%

Table 5.4 'Guilty' verdicts in Old Bailey cases involving Principal Officers, 1792–1839

Total number of verdicts	292
Number of guilty verdicts	235
% of guilty verdicts of total verdicts	80.5%

There is therefore a difference of over 5 per cent in guilty verdicts in OBP cases which involve Principal Officers. The percentage of guilty verdicts for metropolitan cases involving Principal Officers (80.5) is similar to the percentage (83.9) of guilty verdicts in the 62 provincial cases in which the verdict is recorded. The higher percentage of guilty verdicts for cases involving Principal Officers suggests tentatively that the Officers may have been more proficient than any of their contemporary counterparts in obtaining a 'successful' outcome to their investigations through a number of means, including the polished presentation of evidence, although it is recognised that the type of crime investigated has to be borne in mind – murders (the prime offence investigated by Principal Officers) were, and remain, statistically more likely to be solved than a crime such as rape.

It is also true that the criminal justice system of the period generally made it difficult for accused persons to prove their innocence, and this may have been even more of a problem when faced with an experienced and professional prosecution witness in the form of a Principal Officer.[70] Beattie has remarked that:

> The office accounts [of Bow Street] also make it clear they often helped to organise the witnesses who would give evidence for the prosecution. There can be little doubt that in so doing they helped to strengthen the prosecution side in at least some cases, helping to tilt the balance in a courtroom in which defendants had few rights, even further to their disadvantage.[71]

Beattie also speculates that such police intervention in the presentation of prosecuting evidence could have been partially responsible for the rise in the use of defence counsel in Old Bailey cases in the latter decade of the eighteenth century.

Juries (comprised of the very classes of society that predominantly utilised them in the cases recorded for this book) seem to have been generally happy to take the word of Principal Officers at face value. This in turn leads to an admittedly somewhat charitable implication that the Officers were trusted by juries to be telling the truth about their investigations and enquiries, and contradicts the oft-repeated viewpoint of the Officers being widely seen as corrupt and untrustworthy.[72] From the OBP, it is also clear that challenges to the authority of Principal Officers were rare; only in a handful of cases is their integrity or procedural behaviour disputed by defendants or their legal representatives. A rare example can be found in a trial in 1811, in which the defendant, Thomas Northem, was accused of pickpocketing in the Opera House. The defendant's appeal to the judge contained the following words: 'Still I believe there will be enough witnesses called, whose words will go further than a Bow Street Officer's. I believe my Lord, you know that Bow Street Officers is [sic] not very nice in what they say.'[73]

Peter King remarks that Officers could also influence sentencing decisions after the defendant had been found guilty; he states that 'Bow Street Public Officer, John Townsend, for example, claimed that he frequently influenced pardoning decisions by quietly informing the judge about the previous convictions (or lack of them) of the offenders he had just sentenced.'[74]

The degree of trust shown by the juries (and judges) must of course be tempered by the realisation that the Officers involved in the cases were in positions of considerable authority and were viewed as being part of the socio-political fabric that maintained the status quo against the perceived rising tide of the 'dangerous classes'. To question their validity as witnesses for the prosecution was therefore to implicitly question the status quo itself, and as V. A. C. Gatrell comments, the 'criminal justice system [...] quite purposefully upheld propertied hierarchy first and delivered justice second'.[75]

It must also be recognised that the above statistics only refer to cases which reached trial – there must have been many completely unsuccessful investigations in which the Principal Officers were unable to make any arrests. Through their very nature, such cases are impossible to quantify; newspaper reports of investigations occasionally make mention of the fact that the perpetrators remained at large, but newspaper editors quickly lost interest in cases which did not fulfil the needs of a public eager to read the often salacious details of a crime and the subsequent trial.

Conclusion

This chapter has shown that while historians' views of the efficacy of the parish constabulary system have been somewhat modified over recent years, the system was undoubtedly regarded by many contemporaries as a largely inadequate one. The alternatives to the parish constabulary method of local law enforcement were extremely limited, with Associations for the Prosecutions of Felons only providing a very limited scope for victims of provincial crime.[76] The use of Principal Officers throughout Britain by those who could afford to employ their services is not therefore surprising. There were, as have been demonstrated above, several alternatives available to victims of provincial crime – especially if the victim was either wealthy or well-connected, but it is clear that for many such victims, the only viable chance of obtaining a satisfactory outcome to their situation was to employ a Principal Officer, hoping that the concomitant expense was balanced by a successful investigation.

Although Principal Officers operated both within and without the metropolis, much of their activities took place in the provinces. It is impossible to quantify the percentage of metropolitan versus provincial work carried out by each Officer, but it has been demonstrated that much of their time was occupied in the investigation of provincial crime throughout the length and breadth of at least England and (to a markedly lesser extent), Scotland; Wales currently remains somewhat of an enigma. While just over 600 cases over a 48 year period does not at first sight indicate a widespread provincial use of such Officers, it must be stressed again that the number of recorded cases is undoubtedly only a relatively small percentage of actual provincial cases that were investigated by a Principal Officer. The very nature of many of the crimes and the slowness of travel also necessitated their absence from London for not inconsiderable periods of time, and consequently precluded them from taking part in many London-based investigations.

The next chapter discusses the variety of methods utilised by the Principal Officers by means of detailed analyses of specific cases, using these as exemplars by which to demonstrate similarities and differences between their methods and those of other contemporary law-enforcement agencies.

Notes

1 Charles Reith, *A Short History of the British Police* (Oxford: OUP, 1948), p. 4.
2 Stanley Cohen and Andrew Scull (eds), *Social Control and the State: Historical and Comparative Essays* (Oxford: OUP, 1983), pp. 61–2. For succinct accounts of police historiography, see Robert Reiner, *The Politics of the Police*, 3rd edn (Oxford: OUP, 2000) and Cyril D. Robinson, 'Ideology as History: A Look at the Way Some English Police Historians Look at the Police', *Police Studies*, vol. 2, no. 2 (Summer 1979), pp. 35–49. Although dealing primarily with the post-1829 period, David Philips and Robert Storch, *Policing Provincial England 1829–1856: The Politics of Reform*

(London: Leicester University Press, 1999) remains a seminal work on the state of provincial policing prior to the introduction of the County and Borough Police Act of 1856.

3 *Crime and Punishment Police vol. VIII* (IUP Reprints Series): *First Report on the Constabulary Force in England and Wales*, PP 1839 (169) vol. XIX, p. 102. For a general introduction to Anglo-Saxon and mediaeval policing, see Philip Rawlings, *Policing: A Short History* (Cullompton: Willan, 2002).

4 E. Chadwick, 'Preventive Police', *London Review*, vol. 1 (1829), pp. 252–308, at p. 255.

5 *Crime and Punishment Police vol. VIII* (IUP Reprints Series): *First Report on the Constabulary Force in England and Wales*, PP 1839 (169) vol. XIX, p. 116.

6 Alastair Dinsmor, 'Glasgow Police Pioneers', *Journal of the Police History Society*, vol. 15 (2000), pp. 9–11, at p. 9.

7 J. A. Sharpe, *Crime in Early Modern England 1550–1750* (London: Longman, 1984), and John Styles, 'An Eighteenth-Century Magistrate as Detective: Samuel Lister of Little Horton', *Bradford Antiquary*, New Series, Part XLVII (October 1982), pp. 98–117.

8 R. W. England, 'Investigating murders in Northern England, 1800–1824', *Criminal Justice History*, vol. VI (1985), pp. 105–24.

9 Robert Thornhill (ed.), *A Village Constable's Accounts 1791–1839* (Derby: Derbyshire Archaeological and Natural History Society, 1957).

10 *Staffordshire Advertiser*, 17 March 1827. This may of course have been little more than a grateful response to the fact that the Assize calendar was short on this occasion. It is interesting that the newspaper report states that the constable operated in both borough and county.

11 *Staffordshire Advertiser*, 8 January 1831. Constable Jones' 'effective services' three years later in February 1834 extended to the highly unusual and inspired decision to use a female deputy to spy on the activities of a female pickpocket (*Staffordshire Advertiser*, 8 February 1834). Such employment of females in law enforcement was not, however, unique, *The Times* of 29 March 1792 reporting on 'among other eccentricities of the day, a female constable in the Borough of Southwark, who keeps a Lock-up House for persons arrested for debt'.

12 Roger E. Swift, 'The English Urban Magistracy and the Administration of Justice During the Early Nineteenth Century: Wolverhampton, 1815–60', *Midland History*, XVII (1992), pp. 75–93, at p. 7.

13 Stourbridge population figure extrapolated from J. W. Willis-Bund (ed.), *Victoria County History of Worcestershire*, vol. 4 (London: St Catherine Press, 1924).

14 Joseph Hunt, 'Bombelles in Britain: Extracts from the Diary Kept by a French Diplomat, the Marquis de Bombelles, During a Visit to the Midlands, 4 August–10 September 1784', *The Blackcountryman*, vol. 34, no. 1 (Autumn 2001), pp. 45–51, at p. 50.

15 Craig B. Little and Christopher P. Sheffield, 'Frontiers of Criminal Justice: English Private Prosecution Societies and American Vigilantism in the Eighteenth and Nineteenth Centuries', *American Sociological Review*, vol. 48 (February 1983), pp. 796–808, at p. 798.

16 David Eastwood, *Government and Community in the English Provinces 1700–1870* (Basingstoke: Macmillan, 1997), p. 140. Many of these Associations appear to have quickly degenerated into little more than an excuse for an annual social event in the form of a grand dinner, and by the middle of the nineteenth century most had disappeared altogether. The *Crewe Chronicle* of 20 October 1877 details the business of a rare active survivor; it reported on the activities of the Crewe and Church Coppenhall Association for the Prosecution of Felons for that year, stating that 18 cases were brought before the Association. Of these, 16 paid a small fine and two were sent from the Association to the magistrates' court (suggesting that the crimes dealt with were misdemeanours rather than felonies). James Sutton's recent research into the Staffordshire Society for the Apprehension of Felons has found that in the years 1830–34, the Association brought 16 cases to the Assizes, with a further 30 appearing at Quarter Sessions (James Sutton, 'The Staffordshire Society for the Apprehension of Felons', *Staffordshire Studies*, vol. 14 (2002), p. 51). See Chapter 6 for details of the cost of a murder prosecution involving the Stourbridge Association for the Prosecution of Felons.

17 Some research into the activities of particular Associations was carried out in the early twentieth century, while there has been much more detailed recent research carried out by David Philips and R. P. Hastings. See: G. P. Mander, 'The Wolverhampton "Association"', *The Wolverhampton Antiquary*, vol. 11, no. 1 (July 1934), pp. 60–3; David Philips, 'Good Men to Associate and Bad Men to Conspire: Associations for the Prosecution of Felons in England 1760–1860', in D. Hay and F. Snyder (eds), *Policy and Prosecution in Britain, 1750–1850* (Oxford: OUP, 1989), pp. 113–70; R. P. Hastings, 'Private Law-Enforcement Associations', *The Local Historian*, 14, no. 4 (November 1980), pp. 226–31. David Friedman of the University of Chicago Law School has penned an interesting piece on the role of such associations and their preventive value in his article 'Making Sense of English Law Enforcement in the Eighteenth Century', *University of Chicago Law School Roundtable* (Spring/Summer 1995).

18 See Bryan Jerrard, 'Early Policing in Gloucestershire', *Transaction of the Bristol and Gloucestershire Archaeological Society for 1992*, vol. C (1993), pp. 221–40, at p. 231 for further details of this Association employing its own police force.

19 Philips, 'Good Men to Associate and Bad Men to Conspire', p. 118.

20 *Crime and Punishment Police vol. VIII* (IUP Reprints Series): *First Report on the Constabulary Force in England and Wales*, PP 1839 (169) vol. XIX, p. 69. The British Transport Police (born out of the various railway companies' police forces) claim, with some justification, to be the only national

police force in Britain, tracing their origins back to 1830 (http://www.btp.police.uk/History).

21 Shortly after the foundation of the Metropolitan Police there seems to have been a de facto acceptance of the use of plain-clothes Metropolitan officers despite the official insistence that the force was purely preventive in nature; at the trial of Henry Miller for larceny in September 1830, Abraham Fletcher, a Metropolitan Police officer who later became a Principal Officer, stated in his evidence that 'I was there in plain clothes' (OBP, September 1830, trial of Henry Miller, t18300916-195). For a synopsis of the history of plain-clothes officers in the Metropolitan force, see Paul Begg and Keith Skinner, *The Scotland Yard Files: 150 years of the CID* (London: Headline, 1992), p. 198.

22 *Staffordshire Advertiser*, 21 April 1798. From 1812 magistrates employed at the London Police Offices were expected to be trained barristers and therefore would have been much more qualified to deal with legal matters (J. J. Tobias, *Prince of Fences: The Life and Crimes of Ikey Solomons* (London: Valentine Mitchell, 1974), p. 9).

23 Henry Goddard, *Memoirs* (4-volume manuscript, 1875–79), vol. 2, p. 115.

24 This view is reinforced by trial reports provided by the OBP – the evidence given by Principal Officers involved in Metropolitan cases confirms that they were not routinely used in preventive measures such as patrolling the streets.

25 PP 1822, p. 14.

26 Stanley H. Palmer, *Police and Protest in England and Ireland 1780–1850* (London: Longman, 1992), p. 72.

27 At the time of writing, the debate has recently been stoked by the terrorist incidents of July 2005 in London, which have led to calls from the Inspectorate of Constabulary and the Police Superintendents' Association for a more integrated British policing system (see news.bbc.co.uk/1/hi/uk/4253138.stm, 16 September 2005, for a report of the debate).

28 For a detailed and cogent account of the failings of the Major-Generals see Christopher Durston, *Cromwell's Major-Generals: Godly Government during the English Revolution* (Manchester: Manchester University Press, 2001).

29 John Wade, *A Treatise on the Police and Crimes of the Metropolis*, intro. J. J. Tobias (Montclair, NJ: Patterson Smith, 1972 [1829]) p. 358. General Savary succeeded Joseph Fouché as Minister of Police in 1810. The Comte de Villèle was the leader of the French Cabinet and Minister of Finance from 1821.

30 For a concise debate about changes in Georgian and Victorian attitudes to policing in the provinces, see Eastwood, *Government and Community in the English Provinces 1700–1870*, pp. 139–47.

31 PP 1816, p. 175.

32 *Crime and Punishment Police vol. VIII* (IUP Reprints Series): *Constabulary Force in England and Wales*, PP 1839 (169) vol. XIX, pp. 17–23. Vickery may well have read the convict's thoughts in the Report, as the Officer did not die until 1840.

33 David Philips and Robert D. Storch, 'Whigs and Coppers: The Grey Ministry's National Police Scheme, 1832', *Historical Research*, vol. LXVII (1994), pp. 75–90.

34 It remains the fact that in subsequent years, there is still considerable disquiet at the notion of creating a truly national police force, although there has been what Tom Bowden describes as an 'important piecemeal drift towards the creation of a *de facto* if not *de jure* national police force', with the number of police forces continuing to diminish steadily (there are now 43 police forces in the country compared to 131 in 1947 – some of the reduction in the number of police forces being due to the major county boundary reorganisations in 1974) (Tom Bowden, *Beyond the Limits of the Law: A Comparative Study of the Police in Crisis Politics* (Harmondsworth: Penguin, 1978), p. 213). The debate over a national police force continues; a recent report by three serving police officers into the problems of dealing with international money-launderers remarks that 'one option would be a National Police Force that would align itself to European models but all the signs are that such a move does not form part of current government thinking now or in the future' (http://www.polfed.org/magazine/02_2003/02_2003_organised_crime.htm, *Police Magazine*, February 2003). Calls were also made on 15 August 2002 by a member of the Metropolitan Police Authority and James Stalker, ex-Deputy Chief Constable of Greater Manchester Police, for the creation of a British national detective force based on FBI lines (http://www.news.bbc.co.uk/1/hi/england/2195635.stm). The Serious Organised Crime Agency (SOCA), created in 2006, has a UK-wide remit, and with over 4,000 officers and a budget of almost £½ billion per year fulfils some of Stalker's aspirations. Current recruitment publicity for British Transport Police makes great play that it operates throughout Britain. It points out that it is 'the only national police force delivering a comprehensive police service to the general public' (http://www.policecouldyou.co.uk/defaultasp?action-article&ID=236). Figures for 1947 are taken from Clive Emsley, *The English Police: A Political and Social History*, 2nd edn (London: Longman, 1996), p. 169.

35 Sidney Webb and Beatrice Webb, *English Local Government Vol. 1: The Parish and the County* (London: Frank Cass, 1963), p. 342.

36 The counties referred to are those of the pre-1974 major boundary and name changes. Nineteen cases originated either abroad or at an unrecorded location.

37 Hay and Snyder, *Policy and Prosecution in Britain, 1750–1850*, pp. 23–4. Colquhoun had suggested the creation of an office of a Crown Prosecutor in a series of suggestions to the 1798 Finance Committee (*Twenty-eighth Report from the Select Committee on Finance: Police, including Convict Establishments*, June 1798), p. 355.

38 PP 1822, p. 63 – evidence of Matthew Wyatt, Whitechapel magistrate, and Wade, *A Treatise on the Police and Crimes of the Metropolis*, pp. 57–8.

39 See T38/673 for examples which include a chaise to and from Hounslow £1 5s, or 10s coach hire from London to Abridge and return.

40 For a detailed account of the state of road transport in the late eighteenth and early nineteenth centuries, see Sir William Addison, *The Old Roads of England* (London: Batsford, 1980). The mail coach system was instigated on 2 August 1784 by John Palmer, a theatre proprietor of Bath, who developed a system of using fast, light coaches with frequent changes of horse to create what was then the quickest form of mass transport. The only biography of Palmer remains Charles R. Clear, *John Palmer of Bath: Mail Coach Pioneer* (London: Blandford Press, 1955).

41 The case was a series of arson attacks in Godstone, Surrey.

42 HO 52/6/75, ff. 151–54, December 1830, and see also HO 65/2, letter dated 23 February 1831.

43 HO 65/2, letter dated 25 September 1830.

44 Ibid.

45 From Goddard's *Memoirs* it would appear that the Principal Officers did not stint on their lodgings or board when on duty – he often stayed at hotels rather than lesser establishments such as lodging houses, and on one memorable occasion in London, during a state-sponsored undercover investigation of the Duke of Brunswick's activities, Goddard paid 18s for a meal at the Brunswick Hotel, which included a 'pint of Moet's champagne' (*Memoirs*, p. 118).

46 The only detailed publication on the subject remains T. W. Holmes, *The Story of the Admiralty-to-Portsmouth Shutter Telegraph and Semaphore Lines, 1796–1847* (Ilfracombe: Stockwell, 1983).

47 Gerald Newman (ed.), *Britain in the Hanoverian Age 1714–1837* (New York and London: Garland, 1997), p. 433 (Manchester population), p. 75 (Bristol population) and p. 414 (Liverpool population). The Hammonds state that in 1800, 'the five most populous counties in England were Middlesex, Lancashire, the West Riding, Staffordshire, and Warwickshire' (J. L. Hammond and Barbara Hammond, *The Town Labourer 1760–1832: The New Civilisation*, 2nd edn, 2 vols (London: Guild Books, 1949), vol. 1, p. 18).

48 Bristol, although still the fourth most populous town in Britain, was by this time entering a period of economic recession and loss of eminence – George Rudé remarks that 'in spite of its great mercantile wealth, [Bristol] was, at its grass roots, one of the poorest and most disease-ridden cities in the Kingdom' (George Rudé, *Criminal and Victim: Crime and Society in Early Nineteenth-Century England* (Oxford: Clarendon Press, 1985), pp. 94–5).

49 A. G. L. Shaw, *Convicts and Colonies: A Study of Penal Transportation from Great Britain and Ireland to Australia and Other Parts of the British Empire*, 2nd edn (London: Faber, 1971), p. 151. For an investigation into the effects transportation had on convicts, see Barry Godfrey and David J.

Cox, 'The "Last Fleet": Crime, Reformation, and Punishment in Western Australia after 1868', *Australia and New Zealand Journal of Criminology*, vol. 1, no. 2 (Summer 2008), pp. 236–58.

50 Population figures taken from Bamber Gascoigne, *Encyclopaedia of Britain* (Basingstoke: Macmillan, 1993), p. 500.

51 Travel to Scotland from London was rarely accomplished in under three days before the advent of the railway, and even this feat was deemed worthy of contemporary comment. The *Manchester Guardian* exemplified the timescales involved when it reported on 2 September 1826 that a steamboat from London to Leith took 47 hours to cover 495 miles. The paper ingenuously pondered, 'who would have dreamed of such a velocity being obtained?'

52 David G. Barrie, *Police in the Age of Improvement: Police Development and the Civic Tradition in Scotland, 1775–1865* (Cullompton: Willan, 2008), p. 96.

53 Figures taken from Dinsmor, 'Glasgow Police Pioneers', p. 11.

54 The date given in Table 5.2 for Glasgow was of an abortive attempt and the Glasgow Police were refounded successfully in 1800. Dates abstracted from W. G. Carson, 'Policing the Periphery: The Development of Scottish Policing 1795–1900 Part 1', *Australian and New Zealand Journal of Criminology* 17 (1984), pp. 207–32; Alastair Dinsmor, 'Glasgow Police Pioneers'; and John McGowan, 'The Emergence of Modern Civil Police in Scotland: A Case Study of the Police and Systems of Policing in Edinburghshire 1800–1833' (unpublished PhD thesis, Open University, 1996). With regard to Leith, there appears to be some confusion in the various consulted sources, as several state that the Master of the Leith Police was an ex-Bow Street 'Runner' named Denovan. Research carried out as part of this book has, however, failed to locate any Principal Officer with this name, and this suggests that he may have been a member of one of the Bow Street patrols.

55 See David J. V. Jones, *Crime in Nineteenth-Century Wales* (Cardiff: University of Wales Press, 1992) and David J. V. Jones, *Rebecca's Children: A Study of Rural Society, Crime, and Protest* (Oxford: Clarendon Press, 1989). Fewtrell Clements and Richard Ireland are also continuing to add considerably to our knowledge of nineteenth-century Welsh policing and criminal justice history; see Fewtrell Clements, 'The Development and Aims of the Denbighshire Constabulary in the Nineteenth Century' (unpublished PhD thesis, Open University, 2004), and Richard Ireland, '"A Second Ireland"? Crime and Popular Culture in Nineteenth-Century Wales', in Richard McMahon (ed.), *Crime, Law and Popular Culture in Europe, 1500–1900* (Cullompton: Willan, 2008), pp. 239–61.

56 Philip Jenkins, *A History of Modern Wales 1536–1990* (London: Longman, 1992), p. 34.

57 Fewtrell Clements, 'A Divided Empire: Policing in Wales between 1839 and 1856', paper given at the European Centre for the Study of Policing Seminar, Open University, 19 October 2001.

58 The *ceffyl pren* or wooden horse was used in Wales to carry wrongdoers around the village in shame. *Charivari* emanates from the French for noisy racket or disturbance, and was first used in Britain in 1735 (*OED*).

59 David J. V. Jones, *Crime, Protest, Community and Police in Nineteenth-Century Britain* (London: Routledge & Kegan Paul, 1982), pp. 2–3. This lack of cases at Assizes was not limited to Wales; the *Staffordshire Advertiser* of 13 July 1809 carries a report of a speech to the members of the Grand Jury given by one of the Assize judges. In it, he comments somewhat ingenuously that 'the shortness of the calendar impresses upon my mind a high opinion of the police of the county; for when one looks at the extent and population of it, the offences are very small indeed.'

60 David J. V. Jones, in Clive Emsley and James Wallin (eds), *Artisans, Peasants and Proletarians 1760–1860* (London: Croom Helm, 1985), p. 82, and Chief Constable's Report of 28 June 1842, quoted in Jones, *Crime in Nineteenth-Century Wales*, p. 6.

61 Jones, *Crime in Nineteenth-Century Wales*, pp. 65 and 72 *et passim*. For clashes encountered throughout Britain between local custom and national statute, see David Foster and Adrianne Dill Linton, *The Rural Constabulary Act 1839: National Legislation and the Problems of Enforcement (National Statutes and the Local Community)* (London: Bedford Square Press, 1982).

62 Carl H. E. Zangerl, 'The Social Composition of the County Magistracy in England and Wales', *Journal of British Studies*, vol. XI (November 1971), pp. 113–25, at pp. 118–19.

63 Eastwood, *Government and Community in the English Provinces 1700–1870*, p. 96.

64 David J. V. Jones, *Before Rebecca: Popular Protests in Wales 1793–1835* (London: Allen Lane, 1973), p. 180.

65 HO 42/53, quoted in Jones, *Before Rebecca*, p. 180. At least one of the local magistrates in Wales seems to have been impressed by Bow Street's reputation; in the early nineteenth century the local squire and magistrate of the Dyfed village of Brisgaga nicknamed his sessions after the London office, and the village has ever since been officially known as Bow Street.

66 Dic Penderyn (also known as Richard Lewis) was executed after being found guilty of the attempted murder of a soldier during the Merthyr Rising of 1831. The verdict was deeply unpopular and contentious at the time, and attempts to obtain a posthumous pardon for Penderyn continue to the present day – Daffydd Wigley of Plaid Cymru tabled a question in the House of Commons to then Home Secretary, Jack Straw, about such a pardon in May 2000 (*Hansard*, 8 May 2000). For further accounts of the Merthyr Rising, see Gwyn A. Williams, *The Merthyr Rising*, 2nd edn (Cardiff: Croom Helm, 1988) and Christopher Evans,

The Labyrinth of Flames: Work and Social Conflict in Early Industrial Merthyr Tydfil (Cardiff: Paul & Co., 1993).

67 Hannah Barker, *Newspapers, Politics and Public Opinion in Late Eighteenth-Century England* (Oxford: Clarendon Press, 1998), p. 122.

68 HO 64/8 ff. 51–61, letter dated 25 July 1838. For an analysis of how difficulties with languages can continue to hamper police investigations, see Roy D. Ingleton, *Mission Incomprehensible: The Linguistic Barrier to Effective Police Co-operation in Europe* (Clevedon: Multilingual Matters, 1994).

69 This number of guilty verdicts includes special and miscellaneous verdicts such as part guilty, in which the defendant is found guilty of a less serious offence, e.g. manslaughter instead of murder. The actual sentence is also not taken into account; for example, a defendant could be found guilty but recommended to mercy on account of his youth etc. The OBP figures are calculated using the 'Statistics' facility and then using the 'counting by verdict' option at http://www.oldbaileyonline.org/forms/formStats.jsp.

70 For accounts of the role of defence lawyers in the period, see John Langbein, 'Criminal Trials before the Lawyers', *University of Chicago Law Review*, vol. 45, no. 2 (Winter 1978), pp. 263–316, and John Langbein, 'Shaping the Eighteenth-Century Criminal Trial: A View from the Ryder Sources', *University of Chicago Law Review*, vol. 50 no. 1 (Winter 1983), pp. 1–136.

71 John Beattie, *English Detectives in the Late Eighteenth Century*, paper presented at the European Social Science History Conference, The Hague, March 2002.

72 Such an implication of course relies on the presumption that the jury members were themselves impartial and trustworthy. The jury may also have considered the social status of the victim(s) in such cases, but if so they may also have done the same in cases with no Bow Street involvement.

73 OBP, May 1811, trial of Thomas Northem, t18110529-42.

74 Peter King, *Crime, Justice, and Discretion in England 1740–1820* (Oxford: OUP, 2000), p. 315.

75 V. A. C. Gatrell, *The Hanging Tree: Execution and the English People* (Oxford: OUP Paperbacks, 1996), p. 515. For a detailed discussion of the role of various participants in trials such as character witnesses, parish officials, etc., see J. M. Beattie, *Crime and the Courts in England 1660–1800* (Oxford: OUP, 1986), pp. 400–49.

76 Emsley has also found a more informal network of 'country deputies' employed by the Post Office who, among other duties, collected information on crime and disorder in their communities, but these individuals did not possess any constabulary power and they did not act as law-enforcement officials (Clive Emsley, 'The Home Office and Its Sources of Information and Investigation 1791–1801', *English Historical Review*, vol. XCIV (July 1979), pp. 532–61, at p. 537).

Chapter 6

'Domiciliary visits, spies, and all the rest of Fouché's contrivances': six case studies of provincial investigations by Principal Officers

Introduction

Although previous chapters of the book have referred to specific cases when discussing different aspects of the provincial activities of Bow Street personnel, these references are perforce necessarily brief. This chapter therefore concentrates on more detailed research into six particular provincial cases involving Principal Officers in order to illustrate specific areas of their activities and relate these to the wider concerns of the book. The cases (which are presented in chronological order), although by no means paradigms of all of the types of cases investigated or of all the activities of the Officers, are representative of much of their work, and have been selected for the light each throws on particular aspects of the Officers' activities, relating the issues of the individual case to the wider themes and questions addressed by the book.

Case 1: Fraudulent arson attack on the house of Reverend Robert Bingham, Maresfield, Sussex, January 1811

Background

On Sunday, 16 December 1810, the Reverend Robert Bingham, curate of Maresfield, Ashdown Forest, Sussex, alleged that he was riding down the main street towards his home, when he saw a piece of paper on the ground in front of his horse. He picked it up and found that it contained the following threatening letter:

MURDER! FIRE! and REVENGE!

Fifty of us are determined to keep our lands or have revenge. Therefore Parson, Churchwards and Farmer your Barns and Houses shall burn if you take over Lands, your lives two shall pay Your Sheep we will eat – Your Oxen we can mame your Stacks shall blaze and DICK you shall be shuted as you return home from the market or fare. We are united and sworn to stand by one another. Fifty good fellows.[1]

Bingham took the note to his friend and neighbour, Richard Jenner, who was a farmer and thought to be the 'Dick' referred to in the letter.

Bingham first became curate at Maresfield in 1804 and lived in apparent harmony there with his wife and twelve children. As well as being a curate, he ran a small private school for farmers' children. In September 1810 he wrote a letter to the local magistrates suggesting that a Mr Goldspring, keeper of the Hare and Hounds public house in Maresfield, not have his licence granted. Later in the same month, Bingham's stables were burnt, after threatening letters were apparently received. Rewards totalling £100 were offered by Lord Sheffield of Sheffield Park (a personal friend of Bingham), the Union Fire Office (with whom Bingham had insured the stables for a considerable amount) and Bingham. No one was traced in connection with the arson attack, but Bingham received £187 6s 2d from the Union Fire Office in October 1810.

Both Bingham and Jenner were therefore disturbed by the letter, as there was also continuing trouble between the residents of Maresfield and the Ashdown Foresters, described in one contemporary account as 'a set of people who established themselves in the Forest, and lived chiefly on plundering the farmers'.[2] The Foresters had enclosed several parts of Ashdown Forest in order to create smallholdings, thus angering the local farmers who relied on the Forest for pannage and other benefits.[3]

After the contents of the threatening letter were made public, 200 guineas were offered in reward, but no one came forward with information. On the night of 17 January 1811, Reverend Bingham's house and outbuildings were set alight, and many of the contents of the house were apparently consumed by fire. Lord Sheffield immediately contacted Bow Street and on 21 January 1811, Harry Adkins arrived at Bingham's badly damaged house to investigate the arson attack.

Adkins rapidly came to the conclusion, by examining the available evidence, that Bingham had in fact both written the threatening letter and set fire to the house himself in order to claim the £1,050 which he had insured the property for in 1810 with the Union Fire Office. Bingham was accused of burying considerable amounts of his property (including a quantity of silver plate) before and during the fire. He also said that he couldn't get water with which to attempt to extinguish the fire, except from a 75-foot-deep well. However, the jury was told by prosecuting counsel that 'there was a pond of water close by, and also a bucket in the wash-house, and he might have helped himself to water'.[4]

In his evidence to the court, Harry Adkins stated that when he arrived at the burnt-out house, he was asked by Bingham if he had a warrant. He had, and Bingham then demanded a sight of it. Adkins then stated:

> He says, now then I must submit. Immediately upon that, he said, if you will burn that warrant, I will give you all the information you want. I told him it would answer no purpose to burn the warrant, as I could take him without it.[5]

Bingham's trial took place on 26 March 1811 before Chief Baron Archibald McDonald at Horsham General Assizes. He was tried on two separate offences – writing a threatening letter to his neighbour, farmer Richard Jenner, and for arson committed on his own property. After a trial lasting twelve-and-a-half hours, in which Bingham conducted his own defence, he was acquitted of the first charge, after the jury had retired for half an hour. He was then immediately tried with the second offence of arson, and again found not guilty – the jury taking just one minute to consider their verdict.

Employment of particular Principal Officers

Harry Adkins was not employed by Reverend Bingham to investigate the threatening letters and the arson attack on Bingham's property – rather he was employed at the behest of John Baker Holroyd, first Earl of Sheffield (1735–1821), who was the major land and property owner in the area and also an acting County Magistrate at the time. Maresfield does seem to have possessed a Prosecuting Society, but it was not involved in the decision to utilise the services of Bow Street.[6] Lord Sheffield seems to have wanted the matter thoroughly and quickly investigated, but there is circumstantial evidence that Sheffield thought Bingham may have been guilty, as Sheffield's solicitor, Edward Verrel of Lewes, expressed grave doubts about Sheffield defending Bingham.[7]

However, the most obvious reason for employing Harry Adkins was that his brother Joseph was Lord Sheffield's steward at Sheffield Park from 1809 to 1817.[8] Joseph perhaps saw an opportunity to do his brother a favour by mentioning him to his employer, or perhaps Lord Sheffield already knew what his steward's brother did for a living.

Several of the Principal Officers were often seen in the company of such aristocratic and 'fashionable' society as Lord Sheffield. In a sarcastic article of April 1800, *The Times* remarked that 'the Knights of the Order of Bow Street are become such necessary appendages of the *haut ton*, that no grand Fête can go off with éclat without them'.[9] The *haut ton* – literally 'high tone' – was an expression used by many for the most fashionable members of high society in London. Townsend in particular became a familiar figure among such people, being friendly with the Prince Regent and other members of his circle. Henry Angelo, fencing master to King George III, mentions him in his *Reminiscences*, when he spotted him at the Pantheon Masquerades c.1790-95: 'His portly figure soon discovered him to me – my old and very pleasant *slang* friend, Townsend, of Bow Street memory.'[10] Captain Gronow, another member of the *haut ton*, also provides a description of Townsend in his memoirs: 'To the most daring courage he added great dexterity and cunning; and was said, *in propriâ personâ*, to have taken more thieves than all the other Bow Street Public Officers put together'.[11] Consequently, Principal Officers were often asked for by name when their services were required by this group of people and their friends; in his evidence to the 1822 Select Committee, Sir Richard Birnie stated that applications were often received for particular Officers.[12] Similarly, those who utilised the services of Principal Officers were often well aware of the seniority of the Officer that they were employing.

Several of the Principal Officers such as John Vickery, Stephen Lavender and Samuel Taunton became well-known individuals in the press, more often than not being referred to by name in crime reports. In many of the surviving letters to the Home Department requesting the engagement of a Principal Officer, the phrases 'experienced Officer' and 'senior Officer' regularly occur. There appears to have been a certain cachet in employing a well-known Principal Officer, John

Townsend in particular often being sought in metropolitan circles due to his known friendship with and patronage by the Prince Regent.

Such requests seem to have been based either on personal knowledge of the individual Officer concerned (as in the choice of Harry Adkins by Lord Sheffield) or that certain Officers were considered to be specialists in investigating particular types of crime. Sir Richard Birnie remarked in his evidence to the 1822 Select Committee that 'we endeavour to exercise our judgment according to the nature of the offence that the person is qualified for', adding that, if the prospective employer had utilised the services of a particular Officer in the past, the same Officer would be again sent if possible.[13] There is, however, only a limited amount of evidence for any specialist knowledge held by a particular Officer.[14] It has been demonstrated above that Bishop was well-known for his success against poachers, while a letter from J. King in Whitehall to Bow Street Police Office requests the sending of particular personnel (Macmanus, Maynard, Jeallous or Kennedy) to attend King George III on a journey from Windsor to Weymouth.[15] It also appears that Samuel Taunton and George Ruthven were often chosen to undertake journeys to France because they were both familiar with French ways and language.[16]

Anthony Babington remarks (without citing sources) that 'Vickery was constantly employed by the Post Office, both for security and for the investigation of frauds, while Keys was an expert on coining and forgery', but seems to have based this assumption on brief references to cases involving Vickery and Keys mentioned in Fitzgerald's account of the history of Bow Street, which in turn seem to stem from passing remarks made in the 1816 Select Committee *Report*.[17]

There is no reference among the surviving primary records of Bow Street Police Office that definitely indicates that particular Officers were noted for expertise in any specific field of investigation, and this book has not indicated any such clear-cut division of specific types of investigation with particular Officers, though admittedly this may be the result of the inherent difficulties in identifying particular Officers in the sources.

Gender of employers

Many of the private employers of Principal Officers were men of considerable social and economic standing such as Lord Sheffield. There are a few documented cases where Principal Officers were employed directly by or on behalf of women; for example, in January

1817, Daniel Bishop was employed by the Countess of Orkney to recover jewellery stolen from her residence in Taplow, while in August 1835, Goddard investigated a burglary at Lady Harvey's house in Chigwell.[18] In July 1823 Mr Minshull, magistrate at Bow Street, gave a distraught mother from Chichester free use of Ruthven in an attempt to trace her runaway daughter.[19] However, such examples are very much the exception to the rule, and in an age where women were rarely in control of their own finances and had little say in the legal process, the dominance of men as employers of Bow Street's services is perhaps unsurprising.

Social status of accused

It has been suggested above that the social status of the victim of a crime could make a considerable difference to the investigation of the crime with regard to the various options open to the victim. In this case, it is also clear that the social status of the accused could also make a difference to the outcome of a trial. It is apparent that the judge and jury were loathe to find a member of the local elite guilty. The arson case involving Reverend Bingham demonstrates that the social status of the accused could also play an important role in the outcome of the investigation and trial process. While a disinterested onlooker from France could state in 1784 that 'there is no distinction made in legal affairs [in England] and the son of a duke is the equal of the lowest English peasant in a court of law', many of those a little nearer to the actual situation would no doubt have queried the validity of this statement.[20]

An example from *The Times* of 1824 corroborates this contention that in practice, the social status of suspects could make an immediate and dramatic difference to the outcome of investigations. A parish constable was severely reprimanded by Mr Thomas Halls (magistrate at Bow Street) for releasing a suspect who had refused to pay his outstanding cab fare.

The constable stated that he let the suspect walk free (on the strength of the suspect's promise to attend Bow Street court in the morning) because 'he was such a nice respectable-looking gentleman that I thought it was a pity he should be locked up all night and so – and so – I let him go; that's all, your worship.' Mr Halls replied, 'You would not have offered a poor man to have his liberty until the morning, and such a mode of doing your duty, will not do, Mr Constable; we must have something like even-handed justice.'[21]

The Reverend Bingham clearly had influential friends and contacts; several Reverends were called by him as character witnesses, as were his brother, Richard, who was himself a magistrate, and his other brother, Joseph, who held rank as a Post-Captain in the Royal Navy.[22] He also utilised his relationship with Lord Sheffield to its maximum potential, with Sheffield providing Bingham with a good character reference. The trial judge, Archibald MacDonald, clearly took these character references seriously, stating in his summing up of the case to the jury that 'if you entertain serious doubts, you will throw the excellent character he has received from the honourable and respectable witnesses into the gale'.[23] The judge continued, suggesting that Reverend Bingham was a gentleman, and as such, had impeccable moral credentials:

> The character and morals [...] of the Reverend were of such a nature that he did not know, nor could conceive what motive he could have for committing such a dreadful crime [...] he could not surely commit such an act of ingratitude and injustice.[24]

After the 'not guilty' verdicts had been given, Bingham must have hoped that he would be allowed to stay as curate at Maresfield, but this was clearly thought to be inadvisable by his superiors. Lord Sheffield corresponded with the Bishop of Chichester, John Buckner, on Bingham's fate, and the two men jointly refused to accede to Bingham's two brothers' entreaties that Bingham be allowed to continue at Maresfield. Bishop Buckner suggested a curacy in 'some distant county', or a mission, either in the West Indies or North America. Bingham's eventual fate is unknown.[25]

Publicity and reporting of cases

The trial was extremely well-publicised, generating considerable interest in the London press as well as the local newspapers. At least two accounts of the trial were printed for circulation, with one enterprising printer advertising his pamphlet of 32 pages for sale at 2s 6d.[26] The other version was printed on the authority of the Union Insurance company, which was rather unusual in that it was a verbatim and unabridged record of the trial, running to 239 pages.[27]

Accounts of the case also appeared in the London papers well before the trial had begun, much to the chagrin of the presiding judge, who was extremely concerned about the prejudicial nature of much of the reporting. Bow Street was heavily implicated in this respect, as the judge questioned Harry Adkins as to how the London press could have got hold of some of the more private facts about his investigation. Adkins was asked if his examination, i.e. his questioning of Reverend Bingham, was conducted in private. Adkins confirmed that the interview had taken place in private, and was then asked to explain, if this indeed was the situation, how did the facts of the examination reach the newspapers? Adkins replied that:

> It was the usual way, when they had been in the country, on their return to the office, to give Mr Read [Chief Magistrate] an account of what they had done. While he was relating to Mr Read the present case, the Editor of their paper, meaning the *Hue & Cry*, was in the office; and the witness cannot account for its appearance in the papers through any other means.[28]

The judge was highly critical of such behaviour, stating:

> I am extremely sorry that, when this officer made a report of what he had heard and seen of this business to Justice Read, that any editor of a newspaper should have been present, and have taken notes of what was stated by Adkins to the magistrate at Bow Street, and that partial statements should have been inserted in the public newspapers, in order to inflame the public mind; it ought to be severely punished; it has an effect on persons in some of the highest situations in this country; it poisons the minds of juries and witnesses; it is the most pernicious thing that can be done in thwarting the administration of justice; it may be turned to the very worst purposes.[29]

This criticism of the proceedings of Bow Street being reported in the London press was nothing new; *Bell's Weekly Messenger* of 4 April 1798 reported that the Attorney-General aimed to put a stop to the practice following the reporting of a particularly sensitive case – he was clearly not successful in his attempt. The *Manchester Guardian* of 22 May 1830 was able to vindicate its view on the public reporting of police matters when it recounted a case at Lancaster Assizes in which newspaper reports of the proceedings and the verdict of capital sentences issued to two men led to their acquittal. A Wolverhampton police officer, Mr Diggory, read of the case and 'visited Lancaster, for the purposes of making inquiries'. These inquiries proved that the two men under sentence of death were innocent, as the prosecutor of the case was found to be a fraudster.

Conversely, Sir Richard Birnie was known to be in favour of the public reporting of police reports. The *Manchester Guardian* remarked in its edition of 3 January 1824 that:

> Sir Richard, we perceive has been sneeringly echoing – in a case where the publication of a police report has just led to the detention of a thief – the solemn twaddle of Mr Justice Park, about the mischief of publishing police reports. What a mortification it must be to the knight of the common pleas, to be so snubbed by his Bow Street brother![30]

It is interesting to note the furore raised by the prejudicial reporting of this case compared with the similarly prejudicial remarks printed concerning the trial of William Howe (see Case 2 below), which do not seem to have elicited any such disapprobation. The concern voiced by the judge in the case of Reverend Bingham seems to have stemmed as much from his dissatisfaction at having the name of a 'gentleman' besmirched in public as from a concern about the implications of prejudicing a jury.

The investigation into the claims and activities of Reverend Bingham illustrates several aspects of the provincial activities of the Principal Officers. It demonstrates that several of the Officers were known personally to the ruling elite who were their main employers, and that individual Officers seem to have been more in demand than others; it does not, however, support claims for specialism among the Officers. It also suggests that the social status of the accused was just as important as that of the victim, and that despite what appeared to be overwhelming evidence to the contrary, such accused could escape justice.

The contemporary row concerning pre-trial publication of case details seems to have had more to do with the perceived damage to the social standing of the accused than any concern with the outcome of the trial. The next case demonstrates that the social status of the victim could also influence local opinion as to the nature of the investigation and the severity of the punishment inflicted on the perpetrator of the crime.

Case 2: The robbery and murder of Mr Benjamin Robins of Dunsley Hall, Staffordshire, December 1812[31]

Background

Near Dunsley, a hamlet near Kinver on the extreme southern border of Staffordshire, on 18 December 1812, William Howe, a 32-year-old journeyman joiner from Ombersley, Worcestershire, met, walked and conversed for a short while with Benjamin Robins, a gentleman farmer from nearby Dunsley Hall, who was on the way back from the nearby weekly Stourbridge Market. Less than half a mile from Robins' house, at around 5 p.m., Howe dropped behind Robins, drew a primed pistol and without warning shot him in the back at point-blank range, subsequently robbing him of £21 8s and a silver pocket watch. Despite severe injury and the threat of being shot again by Howe with a companion pistol, Robins managed to stagger back to his house, where one of his servants immediately raised the alarm.

Robins seems to have given a fairly detailed description of his attacker and a handbill offering a reward of one hundred pounds above and beyond the statutory government-funded reward was hastily printed and also published in the local newspaper. Robins fought bravely against his injury but expired on the morning of 28 December 1812 at the age of 57.

After two local men were originally arrested and released without charge by the parish constable, William Howe was subsequently suspected and two Principal Officers, Harry Adkins and Samuel Taunton, were called in by local magistrates and the victim's family to investigate the murder and apprehend the culprit.

Howe was finally arrested in London on 13 January 1813 after a lengthy and convoluted investigation involving journeys by Principal Officers of over 400 miles.[32] He was tried for wilful murder at Stafford Lent Assizes on 16 March 1813, and was found guilty after a trial lasting eight-and-a-half hours in which over thirty prosecution witnesses were called.[33] At his trial the evidence showed that Howe was apparently immediately singled out for suspicion by many of the witnesses because he was both a stranger and acting strangely. G. P. Mander remarked in his research into the Wolverhampton Association for the Prosecution of Felons that 'strangers [...] were then much more marked and suspected men than they are now, for there was less social movement, and the unknown and uninvited were fit objects for the inquisitive eye', and this seems to have been the case with Howe.[34] He finally confessed all at the scaffold, but vehemently denied being the murderer of another gentleman farmer, Mr Edward Wiggan, who had been murdered in strikingly similar circumstances on 25 November 1812 near Bridgnorth in Shropshire.

Mr Wiggan was returning from Bridgnorth Market, and had just reached the Eardington turnpike toll house, when he was shot without warning at point-blank range. The murderer ran off when he was challenged by the turnpike-keeper. Despite being investigated by an anonymous Principal Officer, the murder was never solved. Howe, who used at least four aliases, was also suspected of another murder that took place in 1808 in Camden Town, London, where a Mr Joachim Pratt was shot and robbed in very similar circumstances – a watch corresponding to that taken from Mr Pratt was found in Howe's possession, but the case was not pursued further after Howe was arrested for Robins' murder. Howe was hanged at Stafford within 48 hours of the verdict as per the requirements of the 1752 Murder Act and his body was fixed in gibbeting irons and publicly displayed for a short while outside Stafford Gaol. The cadaver was then brought back by open cart to Stourbridge, where on the following day it was gibbeted on a 20-foot-high nail-studded post and exhibited for almost 18 months near the scene of the crime

Decision to utilise the services of Bow Street

Benjamin Robins was a well-to-do gentleman farmer who had several connections with the local elite; one of his brothers, Joseph, was a practising attorney in Stourbridge, while a nephew, William, later sat as a magistrate at Stourbridge.[36] The offering of a £100 reward for his attacker's conviction indicated that he was a man of considerable wealth and local influence at the time of his murder – in short, a paradigm of the type of man who could and who did utilise the services of Bow Street. He could also reasonably have expected his numerous friends in positions of authority to leave no stone unturned in the search for his attacker.

The period during which the murder took place was a particularly unsettled one in England; mainland Europe had recently witnessed a cataclysmic revolution and Britain was subsequently in the middle of the Peninsular War, with the concomitant problems resulting from a long-term conflict. The pages of many of the national newspapers of the time (including *Hue & Cry*) were taken up with lists of deserters who had either broken ranks abroad or, perhaps of more immediate concern to the propertied and relatively well-heeled section of the populace who could afford to read of such events, who had absconded from their barracks in England. The Luddite disorders were in full swing – proclamations threatening immediate transportation (or a worse fate) were issued by the Prince Regent against those found damaging machinery – and staple food prices were rapidly rising beyond the pockets of those most in need, leading to increased tensions in many areas.

In early September 1812, one of the local magistrates, Thomas Biggs, who was a prosperous local farmer like Robins, received the following threatening letter:

Mr. Bigges,

Sir

We right to let you no if you do not a medetley see that the bread is made cheper you may and all your nebern [neighbouring] farmers expect all your houses rickes barns all fiered and bournd down to the ground. You are a gestes [justice] and see all your felley cretyrs starved to death. Pray see for som alterreshon in a mounth or you shall see what shall be the matter.[37]

This letter was followed by another, received on 21 January 1813, by which time Robins' murderer Howe had been apprehended. It was a crude attempt to link Howe's crime with the social unrest felt by much of the local population – in fact he had nothing to do with the protest, as he was not local, coming from Ombersley in Worcestershire (punctuation and clarification of unclear words have been added):

Sir,

Be carefuel what you do with this man as he is not giltey. You may depend all of you shall fowlow the same deth of Robens before longe for all you have gout [got] a fourness[?] [furnace or harness] arected to Bill. Poreg [Porridge] for the Poor I would have you to no the[y] shall live as well as you before it be long. Mind what we say.[38]

Not surprisingly, these letters clearly unnerved Mr. Biggs and his fellow magistrates (who all had farming interests), and *Hue & Cry* reported on 20 March 1813 that the Prince Regent had been notified of the contents of the letters and had consequently been requested to issue a Royal Proclamation stating that the newly created Stourbridge Association for the Prosecution of Felons had issued a reward of one hundred guineas for the capture of the writer(s).[39]

Given this situation, and the murder of Edward Wiggan in nearby Bridgnorth, the attack on Robins undoubtedly unnerved many of the members of the upper echelons of local society and therefore it is not unreasonable to suppose that, as magistrates and farmers, the four Stourbridge worthies who employed the services of the two Principal Officers had a vested interest in ensuring that the perpetrator of the attack upon one of their fellow 'gentlemen farmers' was brought swiftly to justice, and that strenuous efforts be made both to ensure that all the available evidence was gathered and, as importantly, that it was seen to be being gathered.

The limitations (perceived and actual) of the parish constabulary have already been touched on above. With regard to the murder of Benjamin Robins, the parish constable of Stourbridge, Mr Jones, was in fact among the first to be notified of the attack.[40] However, he makes no appearance in the various accounts of Howe's trial, despite the prisoner being delivered into his custody by Adkins and Taunton who brought the prisoner back from London. He must have begun his own investigation into the attack, as two local men, Christopher Smith and Thomas Lines, were arrested on the same day as the attack.[41] However, as they were examined on the same day at Kidderminster (some twelve miles from Stourbridge), this could perhaps indicate that another law-enforcement officer from a different town may have also played a part in their arrest. The speed of their arrest suggests that they were thought to be likely offenders, perhaps because of a known history of violence against others. They were, however, quickly released without charge.

After this misguided arrest, the abilities of Constable Jones appear to have been called into question and a decision reached to ask for help from Bow Street. Constable Jones was the only law-enforcement officer in Stourbridge, which had a population approaching 4,500, and therefore may not have been considered able to devote the requisite amount of time to this particular case. What Constable Jones thought of this is unfortunately lost to posterity; perhaps he was relieved not to have had to chase an armed and ruthless individual, but on the other hand he may not have been happy at the possibility of missing out on a share of the various rewards on offer for the apprehension of Mr Robins' murderer.

The rewards on offer from this case were, in the event, considerable. It is indicative of the many claimants of such rewards that when cross-examined during the trial, Harry Adkins made it clear that he 'expects a share of the £100 reward if the prisoner is convicted'.[42]

This £100 was augmented by the Parliamentary reward of £40 and the *Wolverhampton Chronicle* reported that on 24 December 1812, the principal inhabitants of Kinver (the nearest village to Robins' home) had 'at a numerous and respectable meeting', raised the sum of £50 for the conviction of Robins' attacker (at this time Robins was still alive).[43]

The Principal Officers would have expected to receive at least a share of these rewards and, following the arrest of Howe on 13 January 1813, £50 'was collected for Adkins and Taunton, Principal Officers, as a reward for their vigilance in apprehending Howe' by the principal inhabitants of Stourbridge.[44] This reward was therefore given specifically to the capturers of Howe almost two months before he went to trial on 16 March 1813 at Stafford, but this fact does not appear to have been commented upon by Howe's defence counsel, who could have reasonably argued that this payment somewhat prejudiced the case against his client.

This case exemplifies the fact that Principal Officers often had considerable incentives to perform their duties; the rewards in this particular instance amounted to £240 (roughly equivalent to some £25,000 in present-day terms). Unfortunately, no details survive as to how the various rewards were distributed, but as numerous individuals were involved in Howe's detection and eventual capture, it is most unlikely that the Officers received the full amount (with the exception of the aforementioned £50 given directly to them by the inhabitants of Stourbridge), but they would undoubtedly still have gained a relatively large sum of money for their efforts.

Forensic capability of Principal Officers

The case is extremely important in the history of forensic science and also demonstrates the often innovative approach of Principal Officers. A crucial piece of evidence in the trial was the pistol with which Robins was shot. The pistol was a screw-barrelled flintlock, found secreted with three unfired lead balls in a hayrick a few miles from the scene of the murder. Such pistols did not generally have rifled barrels, firing lead shot rather than bullets, and as such, it was not normally possible to ascertain with certainty that a particular projectile had been fired from a particular weapon, as no specific grooves were left on the projectile by the rifling. The term 'screw-barrelled' refers to an arrangement by which the barrel was unscrewed by means of a key, the single charge applied to the muzzle and the barrel reassembled. This had the advantage that the pistol could be dismantled for storage or concealment and such pistols were consequently favoured by criminals. Percussion-cap pistols did not make a general appearance until the late 1820s, while modern-style bullets encased in a cartridge were developed in the late 1830s. The pistol proved to be the companion piece to one found by Adkins in Howe's trunk in Bishopsgate, along with a lead mould. Adkins noticed that there was a slight flaw in the lead mould, and successfully matched the three lead balls with both the mould and with the lead ball retrieved from Mr Robins' body, thereby proving that the pistol used by Howe in the murder and the hidden weapon were part of the same set.

This action is possibly the earliest recorded use of ballistic forensic detection in the world. Another Principal Officer, Henry Goddard, is often credited with being the first to carry out such forensic firearms analysis, but he did not do so until 1834.[45] Forensic science was in its infancy at this time; after a murder at Bath in January 1828 the chief suspect, Richard Gillam, was arrested, having been found with blood-stained clothing near the scene of the crime – but he stated that the blood was that of a hare given to him earlier, and the prosecution was unable to prove this one way or the other.[46] This situation did not improve for several years; 'before 1850 it was not possible to identify a mark as a blood stain; not until 1895 could human blood be distinguished from animal blood', while fingerprinting was not commonplace until the early years of the twentieth century.[47]

In the same year as the Robins murder case, Stephen Lavender utilised basic forensic examination of a shoe, including matching its shape to a footprint, to prove that a suspect had committed a murder in Chislehurst.[48]

In 1834 a Bow Street Officer investigated the robbery and murder of Francis James Ren in Stow-on-the-Wold. A letter from a local magistrate to the Home Department survives, and it details a considerable amount of forensic detection, including matching a stick known to belong to the suspect to the dents and marks on the victim's head:

> The stick has been compared with the wounds on poor Ren's head and they fit exactly the stick being most singularly shaped at top the point of one wound exactly corresponding with the increasing point of the knob or end of the stick.[49]

The stick was found to have been recently washed and cleaned, as it was still damp, and it was also cracked. Clifford's (the suspect) trousers were 'smeared with what we all believe to be blood down the right knee'. The letter also stated that the road was 'too hard to take an impression' – this probably refers to footprints.

The practice of such methods, however, remained otherwise unusual throughout most of the remainder of the nineteenth century, and the fact that some were regularly carried out by Principal Officers indicates that they were often highly innovative and intelligent during the course of their investigations.

Responsibility for and the role of the prosecution

Although the two Principal Officers played a pivotal role in the detection and arrest of Howe, they were not responsible for his prosecution. This was at the time fundamentally the responsibility of the victim(s), their family or friends. R. W. England states that 'unless obliged to do so because someone initiated a private prosecution, parish officials or local magistrates were not required to investigate crimes.'[50] In a similar vein, the Principal Officers did not bring prosecutions.[51] However, once it was known that a prosecution case was proceeding to trial, it would obviously have been in the Officers' interest to do everything they could to ensure a successful prosecution in order to benefit from any rewards that may have been offered on conviction of an offender. Until 1826, prosecutors could not even be sure of recouping any expenses arising from their efforts to prosecute suspected perpetrators of offences. Acts of Parliament had been passed in 1770 and 1818 which gave limited expenses to certain prosecutors of felonies, but it was not until 1826 that the Criminal Justice Act made such payments the norm rather than the exception.[52] This obviously made it much more difficult for poorer members of society to successfully prosecute a case – as Jeremy Bentham wrote in 1830, 'the lot of the offender depends not on the gravity of his offence but on [...] the party injured'.

With regard to Benjamin Robins' attack, the prosecution and investigation was originally instigated by Robins himself, and continued by his relatives and friends (including local magistrates) after his death. The prosecutors would undoubtedly have benefited from Benjamin's brother Joseph's experience as an attorney, although it is interesting to note that he declined to undertake the role of prosecuting counsel, instead employing two other attorneys, so as not to be vulnerable for a charge of prejudicing the case.[54] However, the prosecutors in this case did far more than simply finance and organise the prosecution. Much of the mundane 'legwork' for the prosecution case was carried out by members of Robins' family. The aforementioned, Joseph Robins, managed to interview a petty offender named Edward Priest in Stafford Gaol, who had shared a cell with Howe while awaiting trial for stealing ducks. Priest stated that Howe had told him that he had committed the murder and also where he had pawned Robins' watch. Joseph Robins managed to give Justice Bayley a letter detailing his findings at the start of Stafford Lent Assizes, and Priest was subsequently allowed to give evidence for the prosecution:

> Joseph Robins of Stourbridge in the county of Worcestershire, Gentleman, maketh oath and saith that since he came to Stafford this morning he hath seen and conversed with Edward Priest the younger, a prisoner now in the custody of the Sheriff of the county of Stafford on a charge of stealing a drake, four tame hens and a game cock, and intended to be tried for such offence at these present assizes. And this deponent hath saith that he verily believes that the said Edward Priest is and will be a very material witness to be produced and examined on the part of the prosecution on the trial of the said William Howe otherwise John Wood at these present assizes for the wilful murder of one Benjamin Robins. Sworn in court 12 March 1813 Jos. Robins before Judge Bayley.[55]

Benjamin Robins' nephew, William, also played a crucial role in the investigation. Howe wrote a letter to his wife who was lodging in Stafford awaiting his trial, in which he informed her that he had hidden a pistol and bullets in a hayrick near Stourbridge. Unfortunately for Howe, the couple had only recently married (probably bigamously), and Howe did not know that his wife could not read. She was forced to ask her landlady to read the letter out loud and thus unwittingly incriminated her husband. The information was passed to William Robins, who found the offending weapon in the hayrick, and it was produced as evidence at the trial.

The case surrounding the murder of Benjamin Robins demonstrates several facets of the provincial activities of Principal Officers. Their capabilities, including their use of basic forensic work, are contrasted with their limitations, and the necessary involvement of those intent upon prosecuting suspects is demonstrated. Local events such as the sending of threatening letters to the Stourbridge magistrates clearly influenced their thinking, both with regard to the decision to avail themselves of Bow Street's services and the later decision to make an example of Howe by having his body gruesomely exhibited at the scene of his crime. The social standing and connections of the victim also played a part in the way in which the case progressed.

The next case illustrates how an influential and wealthy employer (in this instance, a financial institution) could utilise the services of Bow Street in both a preventive and detective capacity, and also how particular activities could be regarded in a different light by distinct social groups.

Case 3: The plundering of the *Adamant*, Newhaven, Sussex, December 1815

Background

On 27 December 1815, *The Times* carried a report of the shipwreck of the *Adamant* from Malta. The ship was previously a Royal Navy vessel, *HMS Thrasher*, and as such was intrinsically valuable for her copper-bottomed hull. She had foundered in bad weather off the Sussex coast near Newhaven, carrying a considerable amount of cargo, underwritten by the insurers, Lloyd's of London, for £100,000.[56]

Not surprisingly, news of the wreck spread rapidly throughout the locality. *The Times* reported that 'the cargo and vessel were besieged by the inhabitants for miles round the country, and considered fair game for plunder'.[57] It was further reported that even the local military force, rather than attempting to prevent the plundering, decided to help themselves – five soldiers 'joined in the general scramble for plunder' and 'tapped a pipe of wine and carried away the wine in bushels'.[58]

Lloyd's were understandably perturbed by the illegal behaviour of the locals and therefore 'determined to endeavour to stop the system of plundering wrecks, and to make an example of the ringleaders'.[59] Consequently, two experienced Principal Officers were directly employed by the Committee of Underwriters at Lloyd's to prevent the continuance of the plundering and to recover what stolen cargo they could. They subsequently visited over 200 properties in the area. *The Times* reported that on being told that they had carried out an illegal activity:

the owners and occupiers [...] appeared astonished that they should be considered to have done wrong, considering it an undisputed and ancient right of the inhabitants near the spot where a wreck takes place, to appropriate whatever of the cargo and vessel they could save from the sea.[60]

Among numerous finds, the Officers recovered herring barrels stuffed with opium from the cellar of the Pelham Arms in Seaford near Newhaven and apprehended a marine stores dealer who was carrying a sack full of copper sheathing from the ship's keel. *The Times* reported that 'the part of the cargo of the wreck, principally saved by the officers, consisted of nutgalls [used for dyeing], quicksilver, goat skins, otto of roses [rose-water], yellow birch for making carpet brooms, and a variety of other articles'.[61]

Use of Principal Officers in a preventive role

When used as a detective force, the Principal Officers can be seen as somewhat analogous to the later CID, but they also carried out duties more akin to those latterly performed by Special Branch, most notably preventive 'policing' and spying in order to discourage sedition or planned rioting. There is the obvious caveat that detective and preventive policing cannot always be easily separated into mutually exclusive activities, the two often overlapping.

Although in this particular case of plundering the Officers were employed after the event, the report in *The Times* makes it clear that Lloyd's of London were as anxious to prevent the continuance of such behaviour as to reclaim the stolen goods and property.[62] The Principal Officers were not primarily employed as a preventive force, being overwhelmingly reactive and detective by design; a handful of Officers could not realistically be expected to form a preventive corps to police the entire nation. However, from the outset, both Fieldings recognised that an effective detective force could possess a degree of preventive capability, in that fear of being detected could act as a powerful preventive to would-be malefactors.[63]

This preventive aspect of the Principal Officers' role relied heavily on publicity; it was no use preventing a particular crime if details of the successful prevention were not subsequently widely circulated in order to dissuade people from attempting a similar felony. *Hue & Cry*, as has been shown above, was not slow to promote all aspects of the work of the Officers, and there are several instances in which it stresses the preventive and deterrent nature of their employment, its editor obviously convinced of the value of such publicity:

> The Police of the metropolis is very active in tracking offenders uttering counterfeit silver coins; and several persons have been lately apprehended.[64]

> Thieving has grown to such an extent all over the Kingdom, as to call much upon the activity of the Police, who happily for the community, are routing them everywhere, exposing them to public view, and bringing them to punishment.[65]

Such non-specific reports of the successes of Bow Street in preventing the continuance of illegal activities illustrate the point that such publicity was perceived to fulfil a dual role: that of reassuring those in authority that the law-enforcement system was effective and vigilant, and acting as a warning to would-be perpetrators that such behaviour would be discovered and punished. Jeremy Black states with regard to such editorial insertions that 'those who might break the law, either deliberately or inadvertently could be warned of the consequences. Newspapers clearly thought these warnings of value.'[66] However, there is the obvious caveat that it is simply not known to what extent those suspected of being capable of carrying out such criminal activities would have been influenced by such publicity – especially that promoted by a newspaper such as *Hue & Cry* which had a very limited circulation. The real value of such warnings may have been more in reassuring those at risk from such depredations that measures were being undertaken rather than their effectiveness as a deterrent to potential lawbreakers.

Employment of Principal Officers by private institutions

Chapter 4 has shown that Principal Officers were often employed by the government to assist Customs Officers and other public bodies. This case illustrates that the Principal Officers were also employed by private institutions as well as by individuals or local magistrates. Lloyd's of London evolved from the 1680s coffee house of Edward Lloyd as an insurance company specialising in the underwriting of shipping, and by the nineteenth century had become one of the leading private companies in England.

The company employed insurance agents throughout the country, but these agents often complained when investigating cases of plundering that they were not receiving sufficient help from local authorities. The agents on occasion clearly tried to prevent plundering by appearing at the wreck site in person and appealing directly to the plunderers; similarly, on one occasion in 1838 on the Wirral peninsula, it was reported that:

> when a Lloyd's agent tried to stop them plundering [...] the wreckers replied: 'We are not taking anything. I suppose every man has a right to take what is here, one as much another'.[67]

The plundering of the *Adamant* was on such a scale that it appears that Lloyd's wanted to create fear of retribution among the perpetrators of such an offence and consequently employed the services of Vickery and Bishop. The use of the Officers in this case appears to have at least partially fulfilled the insurers' wishes; after learning that anyone found in possession of plundered goods would face prosecution and a severe punishment, much of the 'booty' was subsequently handed in to the Officers. The plundering involved considerable numbers of local inhabitants, including members of the military, but not apparently anyone from other than what were then considered to be the 'lower orders' of society. The inhabitants involved in the plundering were clearly intimidated by the presence of the Principal Officers and the efforts of the insurance company. There was obviously a conflict of identities with regard to class and locale with the interference in local affairs by people hired from London at the behest of the insurers. Prior to the proliferation of insurance companies and the creation of the London Police Offices with their groups of professional, full-time police officers, there was no one, apart from the local parish constable, to enforce the law in such a given situation. The parish constable may well have been reluctant to try and prevent such a popular activity, especially as he lived in the local community.

'Social' crime

The act of plundering, although, as is illustrated by this case, considered by many of those who participated in it to be nothing more than taking sensible advantage of someone else's unfortunate situation, had in fact been illegal for a considerable time. An Act was passed in 1753 'for enforcing the laws against persons who shall steal or detain shipwrecked goods; and for the relief of persons suffering losses thereby', and contained the following preamble:

Whereas notwithstanding the good and salutary laws now in being against plundering and destroying vessels in distress, and against taking away shipwrecked, lost or stranded goods, many wicked enormities have been committed, to the disgrace of the nation, and to the grievous damage of merchants and mariners of our own and other countries.[68]

As such, it was clearly an attempt to strengthen existing laws on plundering. The legal penalties for plundering were extremely harsh: death without benefit of clergy, while petty larceny was punishable by six months' imprisonment. JPs were to issue search warrants and assaults on JPs or officers of the law were punishable by seven years' transportation. The Act does not differentiate between plundering and wrecking, although these activities could be quite separate; the deliberate wrecking of ships by luring them on to rocks by means of false signals often had far more serious consequences with regard to loss of life than removing property from a ship that had been wrecked through accidental causes.

Such breaches of these regulations were by no means confined to the Newhaven area – contemporary sources carry numerous accounts of plundering. In a letter circulated to his subordinates in January 1817, the Bishop of St David's exhorted them to preach against:

The cruel and unchristianlike enormity of plundering wrecks; and that, for the future, they will preach to them on this subject once a quarter, or at least twice a year [...] the practice is wholly repugnant to every principle, spiritual and practical, of the benevolent religion they profess.[69]

David Jones remarks of one case that 'on 19 December 1833, when the *Brothers* was lost on the sands [of Cardigan Bay], its cargo of hides and cotton had totally disappeared before customs officers arrived.'[70] Many of the participants in plundering considered, both explicitly and implicitly, that their activities were sanctioned by tradition and past practice, and therefore such activities could not suddenly become illegal.

Such crimes have come to be known as 'social' crimes – a term first coined by Eric Hobsbawm in the late 1950s, and although, as

John Lea remarks, 'the concept of social crime [...] is quite broad and at times even opaque', with regard to plundering the overwhelming characteristic was what has been termed 'positive popular sanction' as opposed to political, economic or social protest.[71] The rapid changes resulting from the effects of the burgeoning Industrial Revolution – from rural to urban society, from agricultural subsistence to proto-mass production – led to changes in attitudes to plundering and other social crimes such as poaching, smuggling and gleaning – such behaviour was increasingly no longer to be tolerated by those in positions of authority.

These changes in the attitudes of those in power to such crimes were reflected in increasing legislation and stiffer penalties for those caught breaching the newly rewritten 'rules of the game'. The increased policing of such crimes – including the creation of the National Coast Guard in 1821, the use of Bow Street and Revenue Officers in smuggling cases and the increasingly severe Game Laws – was the result of what Stanley Cohen and Andrew Scull have referred to in *Social Control and the State* as a period 'when the whole apparatus of the State dealing with the criminal law, police and punishment underwent a revolution as substantial as the Industrial Revolution that Britain was experiencing at the same time'.[72]

Participants in the activity of plundering were, they argued, merely continuing ancient customs and rights of salvage rather than consciously engaging in an illegal activity. George Rudé described such actions as 'survival crime', but it was not always just the poorest orders of society that took part in such activity.[73]

The *Earl of Wemyss* Leith packet foundered on Brancaster Sands during horrendous gales on the evening of 1 September 1833. Due to the incompetence of the captain and crew (all of whom survived unscathed), eleven women and children were drowned in their cabins. Their bodies were recovered, but their baggage and personal possessions were stripped from them; circumstantial evidence suggests that this occurred whilst some were still alive. Jewellery and other personal items to the value of £2–3,000 were alleged to have gone missing. The local Lord of the Manor was Mr Law Simms (a former Excise officer); his son-in-law, Joseph Newman Reeve, rode down to the shore as Simms' official representative and claimed 'Right of Wreck' over anything cast up on the shore from the wreck.

Whoever held the 'Right of Wreck' for a particular area of coastline (normally the lord of the manor which included such coastline) had 'rights over the contents of a wreck, which in law they were free to plunder and steal, without any consideration or regard for the rightful owner'.[74] Consequently, 'Right of Wreck' was an exceptionally lucrative and jealously guarded perquisite. Reeve clearly also seemed to have considered that anything remaining on the ship also came within his remit, as he also allegedly stripped the bodies of the deceased of their property while they were still on board the stricken vessel.[75]

A public enquiry was opened on 28 September 1833.[76] The magistrates were told that after the storm had wreaked its havoc:

> The captain and crew with the surviving passengers instantly left the vessel and went up to the village of Brancaster. No steps whatever were then taken to extricate the deceased passengers […]. The son-in-law of the Lord of the Manor, […] Mr Newman Reeve, went on board the vessel the moment he was enabled to do so and it appears from his own statement that he stripped the bodies of the property which was found on them. The baggage and many boxes belonging to the passengers were taken by the populace and opened by them.[77]

The enquiry led to the subsequent trial of Newman Reeve on 26 March 1834, where he was represented by a very successful and well-known advocate, Sir James Scarlett (later to become Attorney-General). The prosecution case collapsed, despite numerous witnesses claiming that the populace of Brancaster had behaved disgracefully and illegally. The head of the Coast Guard in the area, Commander McHardy, wrote that

> a disgraceful occurrence in my opinion took place on the part of a person in a respectable situation in life (a representative of the Lord of the Manor) by his claiming and taking from the dead bodies, while on board the vessel, their ornaments and money from a mistaken idea of his authority.[78]

Melbourne, despite his inherent dislike of Bow Street, ordered George Ruthven to investigate the circumstances of the case. At the trial Ruthven was questioned and stated that he had searched Brancaster Hall, home of Law Simms, and had found several hundred pounds in gold. Scarlett pressed Ruthven on the matter of his warrant, and Ruthven admitted that the warrant only stated that he was allowed to look for goods, not money, and that therefore the money found was inadmissible as evidence.[79]

The judge, clearly a supporter of the 'Right of Wreck', summed up:

> I don't know what your impression, gentlemen of the jury, will be but such is my opinion: It does not appear to me that there is the slightest evidence upon which Mr. Reeve is to be branded with infamy or to support his character by calling witnesses [...]. The evidence has failed utterly to sustain the charge. There is no reason why Mr. Reeve should not be restored to society without the slightest stain upon him.[80]

After this glowing testimonial, it is perhaps unsurprising that Reeve was almost immediately found 'not guilty'.[81]

Case 4: Poaching and murder on the estate of Colonel Berkeley, Gloucestershire, January 1816

Background

On the night of 18 January 1816, following a series of large-scale poaching incidents on Colonel Berkeley's estate at Berkeley in Gloucestershire, his gamekeeper, William Ingram, was patrolling the estate with a number of assistants. They came across a large gang of poachers, who it was later reported had taken a collective oath to kill anyone who prevented them from poaching.[83] A pitched battle between gamekeepers and poachers took place, which resulted in Ingram being shot dead, another keeper losing an eye, yet another being shot in the knee and several others being seriously wounded.[84]

John Stafford gave a brief account of the case in his evidence to the 1822 Select Committee:

> Vickery, who was a very intelligent officer, was sent down upon that occasion, and from his exertions, and the assistance he met with in the neighbourhood, he was enabled to bring the whole gang, or pretty nearly so, to justice; it consisted of about twenty, there were thirteen [...] of them, I think, tried and convicted for murder.[85]

On 1 February 1816, 16 of the poachers were committed for trial at Gloucester Assizes and lodged in Gloucester Gaol. The trial took place on 29 July 1816, and two members of the poaching gang, John Penny and John Allen, were subsequently found guilty of the murder of William Ingram and hanged. Those involved even in the more serious attacks on gamekeepers were aware of popular feelings of sympathy for poachers; the *Gloucester Journal* reported that John Penny, when being arrested and dragged through the streets of Bristol by Vickery, was heard to appeal loudly to passers-by to free him, stating 'I was only taken for poaching', conveniently forgetting to mention that he had also been arrested for murder.[86]

Dangerous nature of investigations by Principal Officers

By the beginning of the nineteenth century, organised poaching such as that which occurred on Colonel Berkeley's estate was widely considered (especially by its victims and its victims' employers) to be on the increase; David Jones remarks that 'in the second quarter of the century poaching was widely regarded as one of the fastest growing crimes in Britain', and consequently, throughout the first decades of the century, anti-poaching laws became increasingly severe.[87] Ellenborough's Act of 1803 imposed an automatic death penalty if armed poachers resisted lawful arrest (including arrest by a gamekeeper), and in 1817 the penalty for unarmed night-time poaching was raised to seven years' transportation.[88] Many poachers therefore had little to lose if they were challenged by gamekeepers or other law-enforcement officers, including Bow Street personnel. In 1819, a Bow Street Conductor of Patrol, Francis Holyland, was badly beaten by Bedfordshire poachers after he had entered a public house in order to arrest the ringleader of their extremely large and profitable gang. The *Annual Register* reported that:

> He was assisted by two of Lady Jane de Grey's keepers 'who to their credit, stood by him until Field was taken. The officer was much assaulted and had his warrant torn from him, when he drew his cutlass, and by a spirited and well-timed play, he carried Field off'.[89]

Holyland had previously been injured when capturing another of the poaching gang, a Mr Usher, who according to the *Annual Register* was 'a very stout, bony man, six feet one inch high; he defended himself with a spade, till the officer wrest it from him, who was much hurt by the blows he received'.[90]

The Officers were well aware of the inherent dangers, and Daniel Bishop in his evidence to the 1823 Select Committee on the Game

Laws provided some insight into the methods used to detect poaching gangs. He stated that on numerous occasions 'I have been sent down to different places in the country to look after poachers, where depredations have been committed on gentlemen's game-keepers.'[91] He remarked that his initial investigations were often focused on the local hostelries used by the suspected poachers, where he could obtain information from publicans by threatening them with the loss of their licence if they did not cooperate with him. He was obviously successful with such a ploy – he claimed that in the previous four months, he had been responsible for the transportation of 21 men on poaching charges.

Undercover work of Principal Officers

The Officers' preferred method of detection and subsequent arrest seems to have been to infiltrate the poaching gangs by posing as itinerant and out-of-work labourers who had fallen on hard times and were looking for easy money. They seem to have been readily accepted in this ruse, as Bishop commented that in most of the places he had visited, there had not been sufficient employment for general labourers, and that in one of the villages he had stayed in and arrested numerous suspects, 'the whole of the village from which they were taken, were poachers; the constable of the village, the shoemaker, and other inhabitants of the village'.[92]

This undercover work was roundly criticised by political agitators such as Cobbett, who indignantly commented that Principal Officers knew how to 'worm themselves into the confidence of poachers in order to ensure their detection and punishment!'[93] One of the longest periods of undercover activity by a Principal Officer seems to have taken place in Downham Market, Norfolk, in 1815–16, when a Principal Officer was reported to have infiltrated a poaching gang by posing as an unemployed gentleman's servant. He stayed in the vicinity for several months, and eventually succeeded in arresting numerous gang members.[94] Many of the provincial cases involving Bow Street personnel could be similarly long drawn-out affairs, necessitating an investigation that lasted several weeks or even months. In July 1812, following the murder of a mill-owner in Huddersfield, an anonymous Principal Officer spent nearly a month in the area, infiltrating Luddite societies and eventually assisting in the arrest of some fifty men for various degrees of rioting and sedition.[95]

Respective roles of gamekeepers and Principal Officers

Despite there often being considerable involvement of Principal Officers with the detection and arrest of poaching gangs, the vast majority of poaching incidents throughout Britain were dealt with directly by gamekeepers. Bow Street seems to have generally been involved only in the more serious cases of organised poaching (again with an implicitly preventive motive in order to dissuade others from pursuing the practice) as opposed to the opportunistic exploits of individual poachers, as well as investigating the murder or attempted murder of gamekeepers and their assistants.

The first line of defence in game preservation was the gamekeeper, who by this period played an important part in local law enforcement with regard to the Game Laws. Peter King has argued that 'with their extensive rights to search labourers' cottages for game or poaching equipment the gamekeepers represented a powerful form of private policing'; these rights dated back to 1670, when they were 'given power to search houses for guns, bows or sporting dogs (in houses less than £100 freehold, £150 leasehold for 99 years or less, excepting houses of heirs apparent of squires and others of a "higher degree")'.[96]

Munsche has gone so far as to argue that:

> The gamekeeper, in short, was a policeman. Indeed, aside from excise officers, he was the closest thing to a professional law-enforcement official to be found in rural England before the middle of the nineteenth century.[97]

While this claim is highly questionable, there was certainly a considerable number of gamekeepers throughout Britain; after the introduction of Game Licences in 1784, the figures approached 4,000. However, they had a very limited remit in terms of authority, being servants of the upper classes, and were obviously inexperienced in the type of detective work carried out by Bow Street officials. It appears that while their employers considered them adequate for the mundane (though still dangerous) job of immediate preservation of game, for the more difficult job of tracing perpetrators after they had escaped from the clutches of the gamekeeper and his assistants, Bow Street was occasionally considered to be a more viable alternative.[98] Indeed, as has been shown above, Bow Street was often the only alternative, as in many cases the local constable or watchman was himself involved in poaching, or at the very least unwilling to implicate the fellow inhabitants of his residence either through sympathy with their grievances or fear of reprisals. Poaching cases such as the one above also demonstrate the lengths that the Principal Officers often went to in order to satisfactorily pursue a case; their undercover detective work was unique during the period in England and Wales.

Poaching was a major concern to the landed gentry throughout the period under discussion; it was seen as an attack both on their possessions and on their social status. As a result, strenuous and often costly efforts were made to control or eradicate the activities of both opportunistic individuals and organised groups of poachers. Bow Street seems to have been mainly involved in detecting the latter, having little preventive role apart from increasing the fear of being caught. The case discussed above demonstrates that Principal Officers were often placed in situations of great and immediate personal danger, and that they frequently exhibited a great deal of courage and resourcefulness in tracking down and arresting perpetrators, including a large degree of undercover work.

Case 5: The abduction of Miss Ellen Turner to the continent by Edward Gibbon Wakefield, March 1826

Background

On 7 March 1826, Edward Gibbon Wakefield abducted Miss Ellen Turner, the only child and heiress of William Turner and described as 'an uncommonly fine woman', after enticing her from her family home at Shrigley Park, Cheshire.[99] He deceived her into believing that her father had incurred debts of £60,000, but that these would be paid off by Wakefield's rich uncle on condition that she marry Wakefield. Miss Turner, who was only 15 at the time, appears to have dutifully acquiesced with Wakefield's wishes and, with the help of one of Wakefield's servants, Edward Thevenot, and two of Wakefield's relatives, the couple were taken to Gretna Green where a marriage ceremony took place. The newly married couple then travelled down to London, and thence to Dover, where they caught a boat to Calais.

In the meantime, the alarm had been raised and Mr Turner's solicitor, Thomas Grimsditch, hurried down to London in pursuit of the fleeing couple. In the capital, Mr Grimsditch applied to Bow Street and received a warrant for Wakefield's arrest. It appears that

Mr Grimsditch was aided by Mr Robert Turner and Mr Critchley, two of Miss Turner's uncles.

Mr Grimsditch employed James Ellis, a Principal Officer, to help with the capture of Wakefield. The suspect and Miss Turner were eventually traced to Calais, where Wakefield finally surrendered to Ellis, Grimsditch and the French authorities. At Lancaster Assizes on 23 March 1827, Wakefield, along with his two relatives and his manservant, was tried for conspiracy and abduction. The case generated a considerable amount of interest in both the local and national press, and Wakefield's actions were satirised in pamphlets such as *Une Nouvelle Manière d'attraper une Femme, or A Bold Stroke for a Wife, exemplified in Mr. Wakefield's 'New Art of Love'*, published at the time of the trial, in which the 32-year-old Wakefield was referred to as 'the new Adonis'.[100] A purportedly verbatim account of the trial, running to 303 pages, also appeared shortly after the event.[101]

After the trial, the jury retired for 45 minutes and returned a 'guilty' verdict. Wakefield subsequently served a three-year jail sentence for his crime, while the forced marriage was annulled by an Act of Parliament. Wakefield served his sentence at Newgate Gaol, and after his release in May 1830, he wrote an influential book on punishment and the harsh regime in gaol entitled *Facts relating to the Punishment of Death in the metropolis*. He travelled extensively and became a well-respected public figure in his later life, being heavily involved in the colonisation of New Zealand and eventually becoming an MP there.

Use of Principal Officers abroad

The above case serves to demonstrate that Principal Officers were occasionally called upon to carry out investigations and other duties outside mainland Britain. Although this use abroad does not appear frequently (15 cases out of a total of 601), it is clear that foreign travel was by no means unknown to the Principal Officers, and as has been demonstrated above, several of the Officers were quite familiar with at least one foreign language and continental ways.[102]

It was recognised at the time that such foreign travel was a component of the work of Principal Officers; John Wade remarks in his *Treatise* that Bow Street's 'officers are frequently despatched into the country, to Scotland and Ireland, and even to the Continent, for the apprehension of offenders'.[103] Similarly, even in a work of fiction, the foreign activities of the Officers are recognised; in *Delaware; or The Ruined Family*, first published in 1833, a fictitious Principal Officer is despatched to France to investigate a fraud.[104]

Cases in which the offence had taken place in London but which either involved foreign nationals or the perpetrators fled to the continent are not the subject of this book, but it is clear that such instances were by no means uncommon; the large robbery of £35,000 from Rundell & Bridges has already been mentioned (see Chapter 2), and similarly, during the scandal over the Queen's Plate Committee in October 1820, Vickery spent several weeks investigating the matter in France, this time without success.[105]

Interaction between Bow Street personnel and continental police

The vast majority of this service abroad seems to have taken place in France – perhaps unsurprisingly considering its relative proximity to Great Britain. For their work abroad to be effective, i.e. for the Officers to apprehend and extradite suspect(s) from France or any other foreign country, there must have been a degree of effective cooperation between the British and continental law-enforcement agencies. Once a person had been taken into foreign custody, the situation became more difficult; a note on the back of a letter dated 23 August 1820 appealing for a warrant to extradite a suspect from jail in Antwerp states that 'no warrant which can be issued in this kingdom will authorise the taking of Liddard [*the suspect*]'.[106] A trial of 1824 does suggest, however, that some types of warrant were considered legally binding on the Continent; William Salmon, a Principal Officer, remarks in his evidence that 'I had a common warrant and went to the Hague, but finding my warrant of no use, I returned, and went again in a few days with a Judge's warrant'.[107] This case also illustrates that it was considered quite unexceptional for an Officer to travel between Britain and the continent in the course of an investigation, the Officer making light of his two return journeys.

Cooperation between Britain and France was obviously made more difficult during the Napoleonic wars, there being no official diplomatic relations with France; there are no recorded cases in which Bow Street officials were active in France until 1817. However, during the brief respite offered by the Treaty of Amiens, when England and France were at peace between 27 March 1802 and 17 May 1803, there is a recorded case in which Bow Street cooperated with the French authorities: a group of Frenchmen suspected of being forgers were delivered into the hands of French government officials.[108] At the time, there were no formal extradition treaties between Britain and any continental country, but in practice, despite a certain degree of complexity, it does not appear to have been insurmountably difficult to retrieve a suspect who had fled to the continent.

In Wakefield's case, correspondence seems to have taken place at the highest level, with Prime Minister Canning sending a letter to the French government asking for the release of Wakefield into the hands of Bow Street. An account of the case states that Wakefield at first refused to believe the validity of both the warrant held jointly by Mr Grimsditch and James Ellis and the despatch signed by the English Prime Minister, stating that they 'were on the wrong side of the water for that'.[109] Any doubt in his mind was apparently soon dispelled by the sight of Monsieur Duraine from the Calais Police Office, who was also present 'for the purpose of assisting in taking her from him if he refused'.[110] It is interesting that *The Times* reported that Sir Richard Birnie was keen to despatch another Officer to France to assist Ellis; no reason for this is given, but as Ellis had only been appointed as a Principal Officer less than three years previously, and would have still been relatively inexperienced, Birnie may have wished him to have the assistance of a more knowledgeable colleague while abroad.[111] In the event, *The Times* reported that:

At midnight of the day on which the application [for a Principal Officer] was made, Taunton, another officer, arrived from a country journey; and he, being well acquainted with France and its language was ordered to follow the parties to Calais with all speed.[112]

In this case there was clearly a considerable amount of liaison and cooperation between Bow Street, the English government and the French local authorities. Such cooperation, while relatively uncommon due to the difficulties and time-based limitations of communication and travel, seems to have taken place on a fairly regular basis throughout the period under discussion.

As early as 1786, John Townsend travelled to Dunkirk in order to 'fetch over four that were [subsequently] hanged. I went for [was employed by] Mr Taylor, a Hamburg merchant'.[113]

Several contemporary accounts indicate that the relationship between English and French law-enforcement agencies could be mutually beneficial; *The Times* reported in November 1815 that following the murder of four Revenue Officers at Deal in August of that year, 'several of the best-informed [Bow Street] officers were employed to endeavour to discover the murderers', and that Taunton 'with the assistance of the Dutch and French police, traced out [the] suspicious circumstances'.[114] Pringle argues that the Principal Officers operated on the continent without the cooperation or knowledge of the continental police, but this seems unlikely, as their cooperation would have made pursuit and arrest abroad much easier. Pringle also admits that there is evidence to support the idea of cooperation between the forces; he states that 'an unsigned report on the police of the metropolis in the Pelham Papers, British Museum, add. Mss. 33,122, f. 79, dated 1802, says that "before the war the Chief Magistrate at Bow Street held a correspondence with the principal police officer in Paris"'.[115]

Similarly, five years later, Vickery was involved in a bankruptcy case in which £20,000 mysteriously disappeared, the suspect fleeing to the continent. Vickery finally tracked the suspect down after a five-month chase abroad, culminating with him stopping the suspect with the help of the French Police at the French–Dutch border.[116] In August 1838, Bow Street personnel were sent to Boulogne to collect a suspect held by the French authorities on a charge of murder.[117] It was not Bow Street's exclusive prerogative to liaise with foreign police officials; on 11 August 1821 the *Manchester Guardian* reported details of a large forgery in London that had been perpetrated on the Prussian government. Two Marlborough Street Principal Officers were involved in solving the case after liaising with Inspector Augustus William Eckort of the Prussian Police. This may also have been the case that Ruthven was involved in which resulted in his subsequent gaining of a pension from the Prussian government.

The abduction of Ellen Turner by Wakefield illustrates the fact that the activities of Principal Officers were not exclusively confined to mainland Britain. Although not common, cases either arising abroad, or involving foreign travel, were certainly not unknown during the period under discussion. From the limited evidence available, it is clear that several of the Principal Officers were experienced in such matters, even to the extent of speaking a foreign language, which also suggests that they were reasonably well educated. This level of international *savoir vivre* suggests that these Officers were well travelled and experienced men, and provides a contrast to later portrayals of them as little better than bumbling amateurs, unaware of the world outside their 'patch'.

The evidence of Bow Street's involvement in foreign cases also suggests that, despite the often considerable difficulties in travel and communication with the continent during the period under discussion, successful outcomes from such investigations were possible, due mainly to the mutual cooperation between English and continental law-enforcement bodies. Further investigation into international cooperation between such agencies (including King's Messengers) would be of great benefit in clarifying the situation during the first decades of the nineteenth century.

Case 6: Attempted prevention of a prizefighting bout, Hanslope, June 1830

Background

In June 1830 attempts were made to prevent a bare-knuckle prizefight occurring on the Duke of Grafton's estate at Hanslope on the borders of Northamptonshire and Buckinghamshire. The main reason for attempting to prevent the fight was not to regulate the conduct of the participants and onlookers in what was an illegal activity (and had been since the 1760s). Rather the Duke was concerned that it was to be held within the grounds of his forestry estate and that considerable damage would occur to his valuable timber stocks. Similarly, the Crown Commissioner was at pains to ensure that the fight was not held on nearby Crown Estate land.

There appears to have been no general objection from the local elite to the fight being held in an alternative location, despite its technical illegality; as Albert Borowitz remarks:

> Bareknuckle boxing shared certain characteristics with two of the other ruling pleasures of Regency England, gambling and whoring: it was carried on in open violation of criminal laws, and its celebrants paid no respect to the class distinctions that were generally recognised by the rigidly stratified society of the period.[118]

Indeed, *The Times* remarked that 'several noblemen and gentlemen were on the ground during the fight [...] and Mr Jackson, the retired magistrate, superintended the arrangements of the "sport"'.[119]

Bow Street officer George Leadbitter was employed by the Duke of Grafton's son, Earl Euston, to assist the Crown Commissioner and the local parish constable, Thomas Evans, in either preventing the fight or at least moving its location to common ground where no damage to private property was likely to ensue. The constable was subsequently outwitted by the simple expedient of enticing him into the local public house, where he was distracted by the respective charms of the landlord's daughter and unlimited free beer. Leadbitter, seemingly made of sterner stuff, did not manage to prevent the fight taking place, but he did succeed in stopping it being held either on Crown land or on the Duke of Grafton's estate. Both Leadbitter and Evans stayed to watch the fight, which took place on common land on 2 June 1830, but this had unforeseen consequences. The fight, between Simon Byrne, the Irish champion, and Alexander (Sandy) Mackay, a Glaswegian, was a particularly brutal affair that lasted almost an hour and ended with Mackay being beaten senseless and unconscious. He later died of his injuries and Byrne was subsequently tried for manslaughter at Buckingham Assizes.

Leadbitter gave the following evidence at the trial held on 22 July 1830:

> I am a police officer at Bow Street, and know the prisoner, and saw him fighting with a person who was called Sandy Mackay on the 2nd June in the neighbourhood of Hanslope. I was sent down by Lord Euston to assist the Commissioner of Crown lands in preventing the fight taking place on Crown lands. I saw the middle part of the fight [...] I have known Byrne two years. He is a kind and humane man.[120]

The judge, in his summing up, observed that:

> It did not appear to have been an unfair fight; it was, in all probability, conducted as these fights usually are; but they are all illegal, and if death ensues at one of them, the person giving the blow which produced the death was guilty of murder.[121]

The jury was obviously as reluctant as Leadbitter and Constable Evans were to apportion blame on Byrne – it retired for just two minutes before returning a verdict of 'not guilty'.[122] There was obviously a conspiracy of silence among the boxing fraternity known as 'the Fancy'. The tragic result of the fight had widespread consequences – a newspaper in Glasgow reported that a man was murdered and 141 prisoners remanded following rioting in the city after arguments had broken out about the respective merits of the pugilists.[123]

Double standards

In this case, the Bow Street Officer was clearly employed to assuage the personal worries of a rich and influential member of the aristocracy over possible damage to his property. The illegality of the fight, no matter where its location, seems to have been of secondary importance to the Duke of Grafton, the representative of the Crown and the Bow Street Officer.

George Leadbitter's failure to attempt to stop the fight can also be viewed on a more pragmatic level – one man, even a Bow Street Officer who was 'a big man of imposing appearance', was unlikely to be able to persuade a crowd of several hundreds to forego their eagerly awaited entertainment.[124] Several of the Principal Officers seem to have been large men – the *Foot Patrol Register 1821–29* gives the height of several future Principal Officers.[125] Leadbitter is described as being five feet eleven and a half inches tall, Richard Gardner six feet one inch tall and Francis Keys six feet tall. Although height clearly cannot be equated directly with physical prowess, such stature would probably have helped the Officers maintain an imposing air when necessary. The minimum height requirement for Metropolitan Police constables in 1829 was five feet seven inches.

Bare-knuckle prizefighting had for many years occupied a position in society similar to that of duelling; it was illegal, but still took place on a regular basis, often with the connivance of the local law-enforcement authorities. It was extremely popular among all classes of society in the mid-eighteenth century, fell into a period of disrepute during the last decades of the century and underwent something of a revival during the Regency (the Prince Regent was, in his early days, a great lover of the sport). Contemporary reports of the prizefight under discussion show that 'M'Kay [*sic*] was backed by "swells of the first water", Byrne by "gentlemen of rank and respectability"', and no attempt was made to arrest either of the protagonists before the fight began.[126]

The social position of many of the backers and spectators of prizefights often ensured that there were no serious repercussions from such people being seen at such events – as Brailsford remarks, 'no mere spectator at a prizefight was ever prosecuted'.[127]

Indeed, members of the local gentry and aristocracy often took an active role at such events; on 7 January 1824, Colonel Berkeley (one of the protagonists in the Berkeley poaching case above) acted as referee in a prizefight between John Langan and Tom Spring at Worcester racecourse.[128] It was seen as a virtuous and noble entertainment by several commentators, including Cobbett, who remarked in 1805 that:

> Boxing matches give rise to assemblages of the people; they tend to make the people bold: they produce a communication of

notions of hardihood; they serve to remind men of the importance of bodily strength; they, each in its sphere, occasion a transient relaxation from labour; they tend in short, to keep alive even among the lowest of the people some idea of independence.[129]

Prizefights could range in scope from a hastily arranged fight in order to publicly settle a private grievance at which the onlookers bet on the outcome, to pre-arranged and well-organised bouts involving several pugilists, with the purses often being several hundreds of guineas.[130] Several prizefighters became household names, courted by royalty and the aristocracy, often to the annoyance of local magistrates who had to attempt to prevent the bouts taking place within their jurisdiction. Notices prohibiting the holding of such contests were published by magistrates in often vain attempts to dissuade the viewing public from attending:

> Whereas a boxing match, between Mendoza and Ward, has been announced in several public papers for next Wednesday the 15th instant, I am directed by the Mayor of Dover (under whose jurisdiction this place is) to take the necessary steps to prevent the same; this is therefore to give notice, that the said meetings, or any other of the kind, will not be suffered to take place, within this parish. – Francis Cobb, Deputy.[131]

Provincial police could occasionally intervene effectively to prevent such fights taking place; the *Staffordshire Advertiser* of 16 April 1836 reported that a prizefight was stopped at Scott Arms, Walsall, by the Superintendent of Walsall Police disguising his officers in smocks, enabling them to pass among the crowd as agricultural labourers. Bow Street officials seem to have been called out on numerous occasions to prevent such prizefights. *The Times* reported in 1804 that:

> It has been known for some time that a battle was to be fought between Pittoon, the Jew, and Wood, the coachman, for a subscription prize of fifty guineas. The vigilance of the magistrates around the metropolis has lately been so great to prevent scenes of this kind from taking place. [...] Several other battles were about to be fought, but the arrival of Bow Street Public Officers prevented them, to the great regret of the amateurs.[132]

Similarly, in 1800, Daniel Mendoza, one of the most celebrated pugilists, unusual in that he wrote and published his *Memoirs*, appeared before Sir Richard Ford, after being arrested at Bethnal Green to prevent him taking part in a scheduled bout. He was asked the whereabouts of his prospective opponent, Belcher, and replied insouciantly:

> On his inquiry where Belcher was, I declared I knew not, and that consequently the ingenuity of the police officers must be exercised in tracing him out. On being asked whether I had challenged Belcher, I replied I had not, that he had challenged not only me, but everyone else. 'Indeed', replied Sir Richard, 'then how happens it that he has not challenged me?' To this question, I answered 'Because you cannot fight, Sir Richard; indeed I know no better reason'.[133]

Leadbitter's evidence in Byrne's trial shows that he was well-acquainted with the prizefighter and that he considered him a good man. Byrne himself was not dissuaded from continuing his pugilistic career despite his arrest, and met his own demise in 1833 when, after the longest recorded bareknuckle fight in history (99 rounds over 3 hours and 16 minutes), he was killed by his opponent in the ring.[134] After a series of such fatalities, the aristocracy and the upper classes gradually lost interest in such bloody displays of pugilism.

Following an increase in the number of prizefights in the period 1813–22, the number began to decline due to the loss of aristocratic patronage, and it has been argued that the lowering of the class of patrons and therefore backers led to fights where the gamblers 'were likely to insist that boxers continued to struggle on when their cause was well and truly beyond redemption'.[135]

Despite this lessening of interest from influential backers, bareknuckle fighting continued well into the middle of the nineteenth century, with a former Principal Officer being indirectly involved in one of the major fights of the 1840s.[136]

Use of Bow Street personnel other than Principal Officers in provincial cases

This case illustrates that provincial cases, or 'country duties' as such employment was often called, did not exclusively involve Principal Officers. At the time of the fight, George Leadbitter appears to have been employed in the Patrol (probably as a Conductor) – he was not formally appointed as a Principal Officer until 5 April 1831, having been appointed as a Patrol Constable on 14 February 1824.[137] As stated above, the use of patrol officials rather than Principal Officers seems to have been due to one of two reasons: either all the Principal Officers were occupied or the Patrol official was sent out on probation for a period of time before being promoted.

When asked by the 1816 Select Committee about the selection process of Principal Officers, Sir Richard Birnie replied that:

> They are selected by long observation of their general character; some of them have been conductors of the patrol, or in some such employ within the view of the Magistrates, for a length of time; they have in some instances been otherwise recommended, but not within my time; but always with characters that the Magistrates thought would answer the purposes of the public.[138]

John Stafford, Chief Clerk at Bow Street, expanded upon the selection process in his evidence to the same Committee:

> When a man solicits employment at Bow street, he is placed at first upon the patrol; and after having being there for some time, and his conduct being approved of, he may succeed to the appointment of Conductor, or perhaps be selected for an Officer.[139]

If Leadbitter was used in a probationary capacity in this case, such a task seems to have been something of a baptism of fire. There are several cases in which Patrol Conductors or Constables accompanied Principal Officers – usually situations in which a significant amount of manpower was required, e.g. riots etc. – but it seems to have been fairly unusual to send out an unaccompanied Patrol official on his own to a major case. However, it must be stated that it is often extremely difficult to differentiate Principal Officers from Patrol members; sources often merely state that a Bow Street Police Officer was involved and on further investigation the Officer turns out to be a member of the Patrol. All the cases recorded do, to the best of my knowledge, involve Principal Officers rather than other Bow Street officials, except where specifically stated.

Much research remains to be carried out with regard to the provincial activities of Patrol Conductors and members of the Horse Patrol, who operated outside the metropolis. It would appear that in certain cases, the use of such personnel was seen as a probationary measure to evaluate the particular man's suitability for promotion to the post of Principal Officer. With such a relatively large number of personnel in the various Patrols and only a very limited number of Principal Officer posts, competition among the other personnel must have been fierce. The chance to show one's capabilities in a provincial investigation would have been an excellent opportunity for such personnel to impress their superiors.

Conclusion

This chapter has investigated, through means of a small selection from the myriad of cases involving Principal Officers, many of the ways in which they were utilised throughout the period under discussion. It has demonstrated that they were employed in a wide spectrum of activities, ranging from the mundane to the unusual, and that they were invariably employed by those who had the necessary financial means so to do. The chapter has also shown that there could be many different reasons for seeking their help and services: complicated investigations thought to be beyond the capabilities of the local law-enforcement bodies, undercover work that could not be carried out by parish constables known to the suspects, specialised detective work and work of a preventive nature. The dangerous aspect of much of their work has also been discussed, as has their often innovative and ground-breaking use of basic forensic analysis.

The often high levels of professionalism and use of personal initiative have also been discussed, as have the inevitable limitations created by reliance on such a small body of men. Their employment has also been related to many of the wider issues of early nineteenth-century law enforcement and the concomitant problems of prosecution at a time when no system of public prosecution existed. The double standards practised by many of those in positions of authority have also been highlighted; the social status of the employer(s), victims and accused clearly played an important role in decisions to prosecute and the resultant punishment.

Their interaction and cooperation with other law enforcement bodies has been shown to be vital for their successful completion of their investigations, and this cooperation has been demonstrated to extend on occasions across the Channel. Above all, the chapter has shown that they were clearly considered by many of their contemporaries, albeit primarily those who could afford to make use of their services, to be an important and often effective tool in the detection and prevention of crime throughout the nation and beyond.

The next chapter discusses their continued usage after the creation of the Metropolitan Police, arguing that they were not disbanded because they were seen to still serve a useful purpose.

Notes

1 Anon., *The Trial of the Reverend Robert Bingham, Curate of Maresfield, Tuesday March 26th 1811* (Lewes: Sussex Press, 1811), p. 10.
2 Ibid., p. 16.
3 Pannage was the ancient right of grazing pigs on common land.
4 Anon., *The Trial of the Reverend Robert Bingham, taken in shorthand by Mr Adams, by order of the Directors of The Union Fire Office, London* (London: J. M. Richardson, 1811), pp. 128–9.
5 Ibid., p. 159.
6 W. H. Johnson, *Previous Offences: Sussex Crimes and Punishments in the Past* (Seaford: S. B. Publications, 1997), p. 25.
7 East Sussex Record Office AMS 6403.
8 SPK Estate Management Accounts E11/1 Correspondence of Joseph Adkins 1809–1817.
9 *The Times*, 4 April 1800. Quoted in Christopher Hibbert (ed.), *Captain Gronow: His Reminiscences of Regency and Victorian Life 1810–60* (London: Kyle Cathie Ltd, 1991), p. 110.
10 Henry Angelo, *Reminiscences of Henry Angelo*, 2 vols (London: Henry Colburn and Richard Bentley, 1830), vol. 2, pp. 332–3.
11 Quoted in Hibbert, *Captain Gronow: His Reminiscences of Regency and Victorian Life 1810–60*, p. 110.
12 PP 1822, p. 15.
13 PP 1822, p. 16.
14 Due to the nature of the sources, it has unfortunately proved impossible to carry out a valid analysis of the cases in order to see if there was any statistically significant degree of specialisation among the Officers; there are too many variables to contend with to provide any meaningful data for recognised statistical tests.
15 HO 65/1, letter dated 15 August 1795.
16 For Ruthven's and Taunton's familiarity with France, see the *Guardian*, 24 October 1822: 'Ruthven [...] said he had seen and played at the game of roulette in France', and in *The Times*, 23 March 1826, Taunton was described as 'being well acquainted with France and its language'.
17 Anthony Babington, *A House in Bow Street: Crime and the Magistracy, London 1740–1881*, 2nd edn (London: Macdonald, 1999), p. 188.

Fitzgerald mentions two cases, one involving Vickery when employed by the Post Office and the other involving Keys breaking a coining ring (P. Fitzgerald, *Chronicle of Bow Street Police Office: with an account of the Magistrates, 'Runners' and Police*, 2 vols (London: Chapman & Hall, 1888), vol. 1, pp. 111–18), and this seems to be one of the main sources from which subsequent commentators have claimed specialisms for individual Officers.

18 *The Times*, 6 January 1817 and 12 August 1835.

19 *The Times*, 28 July 1823.

20 Marc de Bombelles, quoted in Joseph Hunt, 'Bombelles in Britain: extracts from the diary kept by a French diplomat, the Marquis de Bombelles, during a visit to the Midlands, 4 August – 10 September 1784' *The Blackcountryman*, vol. 34, no. 4 (Autumn 2001), pp. 45–51, at p. 50.

21 *The Times*, 18 February 1824.

22 Reverend Richard Bingham later became a canon at Chichester, but in 1813 was imprisoned for six months at Winchester for fraudulently obtaining a licence for a public house in his capacity as magistrate for Hampshire (East Sussex Record Office: Notes on Bingham case AMS 6403 and PRO 30/45/1/11 f. 127). A Post-Captain was a captain whose name had been posted in the Royal Navy seniority lists, usually in command of a ship and therefore considered to be of more senior rank than a normal captain.

23 Anon., *The Trial of the Reverend Robert Bingham, taken in shorthand by Mr Adams*, p. 123.

24 Anon., *The Trial of the Reverend Robert Bingham, Curate of Maresfield, Tuesday March 26th 1811*, p. 17.

25 East Sussex Record Office: Notes on Bingham case AMS 6403.

26 Johnson, *Previous Offences: Sussex Crimes and Punishments in the Past*, p. 29.

27 Anon., *The Trial of the Reverend Robert Bingham, taken in shorthand by Mr Adams*.

28 Anon., *The Trial of the Reverend Robert Bingham, Curate of Maresfield, Tuesday March 26th 1811*, p. 21.

29 Anon., *The Trial of the Reverend Robert Bingham, taken in shorthand by Mr Adams, by order of the Directors of The Union Fire Office, London*, p. 226.

30 Justice Park was the Chief Magistrate at the Court of Common Pleas, one of the superior courts of civil law.

31 For a detailed analysis of this case, see David J. Cox, *The Dunsley Murder of 1812: A Study in Early Nineteenth-Century Crime Detection, Justice and Punishment* (Kingswinford: Dulston Press, 2003).

32 The Officers travelled from Stourbridge to Ombersley where they gathered evidence against Howe and learned that he had left his employment on the day before he attacked Mr Robins. They then travelled to Coventry after learning that Howe had pawned Robins' watch there. They then

travelled back to Stourbridge to report their finding and finally caught up with Howe in London.

33 For a contemporary account of the trial, see Anon., *The Trial of William Howe, alias John Wood, for the Wilful Murder of Mr. Benjamin Robins of Dunsley, near Stourbridge on the 18th of December 1813* [sic] (Stourbridge: J. Heming, 1813).

34 G. P. Mander, 'The Wolverhampton "Association"', *The Wolverhampton Antiquary*, vol. 2, no. 1 (July 1934), pp. 60–3, at p. 61.

35 Such gibbets were often heavily nail-studded to prevent friends or relatives of the gibbeted criminal removing the body. T 38/673 contains a record of expenses paid to Patrol Constables for watching the gibbet on Wimbledon Common for several nights 'to prevent the same from being cut down'. In a rather macabre postscript to the Howe gibbeting, the *Stourbridge & Dudley Messenger* of 9 September 1814, under the strapline 'ROBBERY EXTRAORDINARY' carried a report that Howe's skeleton had been stolen from the gibbet – by then it may well have become disarticulated and therefore easier to remove.

36 For a case involving William Robins in his magisterial capacity, see David Cox, 'The Strange Case of Eliza Price', *Journal of the Police History Society*, no. 17 (2002), pp. 9–12.

37 *Hue & Cry*, 6 February 1813 (spelling is original).

38 Ibid. (spelling is again original).

39 This Association was not the first to be founded in Stourbridge; *Aris's Birmingham Gazette* of 16 December 1765 records that 'the principal inhabitants of Stourbridge have entered into an Annual Subscription for seven years for the rigorous prosecution of the perpetrators, as well as compounders, of all felonies.' The period 1765–66 saw considerable unrest in the region with numerous food riots – for a brief account of such riots see David Cox, 'Civil Unrest in the Black Country 1766–1816', *Family and Local History Year Book*, 9th edn (Nether Poppleton: Robert Blatchford Publishing, 2005), pp. 30–3. The Stourbridge Association had clearly been allowed to lapse in the intervening years, and the idea was only rejuvenated during a time of considerable unrest. A document detailing the prosecution costs of the Howe case survives (many thanks to James Morgan for providing me with a copy) and it shows how expensive the prosecution process could be; the total cost was £757 8s 10d, of which the County of Stafford paid £106 16s, and Robins' family paid £100 (presumably the reward offered and subsequently paid to the Bow Street officers for Howe's arrest). The printing costs for the various notices and handbills amounted to £29 12s 6d.

40 This is a different Constable Jones to the Constable of Stafford referred to earlier in this book.

41 P. H. Foley, *Report of The Trial of William Howe at Stafford Lent Assizes 1813* (no publication details given), p. 81.

42 Anon., *The Trial of William Howe*, p. 21.

43 *Wolverhampton Chronicle*, 30 December 1812.

44 *Staffordshire Advertiser*, 6 February 1813.

45 Henry Goddard, *Memoirs* (4-volume manuscript, 1875–79), vol. 3, p. 207. James E. Hamby in his article, 'The History of Firearm and Toolmark Identification', *Association of Firearm and Tool Mark Examiners Journal*, vol. 31, no. 3 (Summer 1999), gives Goddard's discovery as the first recorded example of ballistic forensics in the world, but this is incorrect, though admittedly Goddard went one step further by also locating the ripped-up newspaper that the criminal used for the wadding around the projectile thereby proving beyond doubt that this was indeed the weapon used in the attack.

46 *Annual Register*, vol. 70 (1828), pp. 49–54.

47 Stanley H. Palmer, *Police and Protest in England and Ireland 1780–1850* (London: Longman, 1992), p. 533.

48 *The Times*, 2 June 1813. Philip Rawlings, *Policing: A Short History* (Cullompton: Willan, 2002), p. 79, contains similar examples from the eighteenth century, while G. P. R. James, *Delaware; or the Ruined Family*, 3 vols (Edinburgh: G. P. R. James, 1833), one of the English-speaking world's first detective novels, includes the examination of forensic evidence by a fictional Principal Officer, Cousins. The analysis included footprints, fingerprints and other forensic examination, with the results announced in a style of which Sherlock Holmes himself would have been proud: 'The fellow, whoever he is, wanted part of the third finger of his left hand' (vol. 2, p. 255). For a debate on the contemporary relationship between crime and fiction, see Ian A. Bell, *Literature and Crime in Augustan England* (London: Routledge, 1991).

49 HO 44/127 f. 176, letter from C. Pole to Samuel March Phillips concerning murder of Francis James Ren 10 March 1834, also containing details of evidence in enclosure HO 44/127/178.

50 R. W. England, 'Investigating Murders in Northern England, 1800–1824', *Criminal Justice History*, vol. 6 (1985), pp. 105–24, at p. 113.

51 John Beattie, *English Detectives in the Late Eighteenth Century*, paper presented at the European Social Science History Conference, The Hague, March 2002.

52 For further details of prosecutors' reimbursement in the eighteenth century, see J. M. Beattie, *Crime and the Courts in England 1660–1800* (Oxford: OUP, 1986), pp. 42–8; for the early nineteenth century, see George Rudé, *Criminal and Victim: Crime and Society in Early Nineteenth-Century England* (Oxford: Clarendon Press, 1985).

53 Jeremy Bentham, *The Rationale of Punishment* (London: Robert Heward, 1830), p. 247, quoted in Peter King, *Crime, Justice, and Discretion in England 1740–1820* (Oxford: OUP, 2000), p. 315.

54 Anon., *The Trial of William Howe*, p. 5.

55 ASSI 2/29.

56 Such a large insurance figure was not unique – it has been estimated that in total 'private underwriters had covered risks worth £140 million in 1809' – while the *Scaleby Castle*, sailing from Bombay to London in 1801, was insured for a total of £148,700 (H. A. L. Cockerell and Edwin Green, *The British Insurance Business 1547–1970* (London: Heinemann Educational, 1976), pp. 6 and 13).

57 *The Times*, 27 December 1815.

58 Ibid., 27 December 1815.

59 Ibid.

60 Ibid. It is unclear what part, if any, the sailors from the *Adamant* took in the salvage/plundering operation, but they would certainly have had a vested interest in recovering goods, as Rainer Behre's research has suggested that 'only if the ship was salvaged could the sailors claim their wages' (Rainer Behre, *Shipwrecks and the Body: 18th and 19th Century Encounters with Death and Survival at Sea*, paper delivered at the *Controlling Bodies – The Regulation of Conduct 1650–2000 Conference*, University of Glamorgan, July 2002).

61 *The Times*, 27 December 1815.

62 This case illustrates that plundering on such a large scale often took many days, if not weeks – the cargo must have been considerable, as the Principal Officers managed to catch several perpetrators 'in the act', despite having arrived several days after the ship foundered.

63 Beattie's research into the earliest decades of Bow Street's activities suggests that such a preventive role was originally consciously undertaken: 'In 1765–7, Fielding's accounts reveal, for example, that the Bow Street men were sent out on surveillance in order to prevent crime and disorder' (Beattie, *English Detectives in the Late Eighteenth Century*, unpaginated). This role passed to the various Patrols in the ensuing years, and by the first decade of the nineteenth century, the Principal Officers took very little part in such activity.

64 *Hue & Cry*, 29 September 1811.

65 Ibid., 6 November 1813.

66 Jeremy Black, *The English Press 1621–1861* (Stroud: Sutton, 2001), p. 54.

67 John Rule and Roger Wells, *Crime, Protest and Popular Politics in Southern England 1740–1850* (London: Hambledon Press, 1997).

68 Danby Pickering, *The Statutes at Large from the 23rd to the 26th year of King George II*, Statute 26 Geo II c19 (London and Cambridge: Joseph Bentham, 1765).

69 *The Times*, 6 January 1817.

70 David J. V. Jones, *Rebecca's Children: A Study of Rural Society, Crime and Protest* (Oxford: Clarendon Press, 1989), p. 167.

71 John Lea, 'Social Crime Revisited', *Theoretical Criminology*, vol. 3, no. 3 (August 1999), pp. 307–25.

72 Stanley Cohen and Andrew Scull (eds), *Social Control and the State: Historical and Comparative Essays* (Oxford: OUP, 1983), p. 62.

73   Rudé, *Criminal and Victim*, p. 89.

74   Richard Larn and Bridget Larn, *Shipwreck Index of the British Isles*, vol. 2 (London: Lloyd's Register of Shipping, 1995), Introduction, p. ix.

75   Bernard Philips, 'Shipwreck at Brancaster', published on the Internet at http://www.northcoastal.freeserve.co.uk/shipwreck.htm.

76   The enquiry resulted from a petition from the relatives of those who perished being sent to Lord Melbourne, the Home Secretary, asking him to use his 'utmost endeavours to assist us in procuring a thorough investigation of the sad affair for the purpose of bringing to justice those who may be found guilty of any neglect of duty with a view to prevent so frightful an occurrence in the future' (HO 44/26 ff. 164).

77   http://www.northcoastal.freeserve.co.uk/wreck3.htm.

78   http://www.northcoastal.freeserve.co.uk/wreck4.htm.

79   http://www.northcoastal.freeserve.co.uk/wreck5.htm.

80   http://www.northcoastal.freeserve.co.uk/wreck6.htm.

81   Rudé, *Criminal and Victim*, p. 89.

82   For general accounts of the history of poaching, see Harry Hopkins, *The Long Affray: The Poaching Wars 1760–1914* (London: Secker & Warburg, 1985), P. B. Munsche, *Gentlemen and Poachers: The English Game Laws 1671–1831* (Cambridge: CUP, 1981) and Charles Chenevix Trench, *The Poacher and the Squire: A History of Poaching and Game Preservation in England* (London: Longmans, 1967). For more specific investigations into the connection between poaching and rural discontent, see John E. Archer, *By a Flash and a Scare: Incendiarism, Animal Maiming and Poaching in East Anglia 1815–70* (Oxford: Clarendon Press, 1990); and Michael J. Carter, *Peasants and Poachers: A Study in Rural Disorder in Norfolk* (Woodbridge: Boydell Press, 1980). For a poacher's viewpoint from the 1840s, see Garth Christian (ed.), *A Victorian Poacher: James Hawker's Journal* (Oxford: OUP, 1978).

83   *Notes and Queries*, 7th Series III (1887), pp. 221–2.

84   *Annual Register*, vol. 58 (1816) p. 9.

85   PP 1822, p. 37.

86   *Gloucester Journal*, 6 February 1816, quoted in Hopkins, *The Long Affray*, p. 59. The same John Penny of Littleton had been previously accused of poaching pheasants at Cromhall and of being a rogue and vagabond on 12 January 1814. He was committed to Horsley House of Correction (Irene Wyatt (ed.), *Calendar of Summary Convictions at Petty Sessions 1781–1837*, Gloucestershire Record Series vol. 22 (Gloucester: Bristol and Gloucestershire Archaeological Society, 2008), p. 103).

87   David J. V. Jones, 'The Poacher: A Study in Victorian Crime and Punishment', *Historical Journal*, vol. XXII (1974), pp. 825–60, at p. 825.

88   Trench, *The Poacher and the Squire*, p. 148.

89   *Annual Register*, vol. 60 (1818), p. 153. This is one of the few cases in which a less senior member of Bow Street was in charge of a poaching investigation.

90 *Annual Register*, vol. 60 (1818), p. 154.

91 PP 1823, p. 29.

92 Ibid., p. 31. The wholesale involvement of the village resulted in Bishop and his assistants (probably local gamekeepers) having to resort to the use of firearms to make subsequent arrests.

93 Quoted in Hopkins, *The Long Affray*, p. 93.

94 Carter, *Peasants and Poachers*, pp. 6–8.

95 *Staffordshire Advertiser*, 11 July 1812.

96 King, *Crime, Justice, and Discretion in England 1740–1820*, p. 64, and J. F. Stephen, *A History of the Criminal Law of England*, 3 vols (London: Macmillan, 1883), vol. 3, p. 280.

97 P. B. Munsche, 'The Gamekeeper and English Rural Society', *Journal of British Studies*, vol. XX, no. 2 (Spring 1981), pp. 82–105, at p. 83.

98 With reference to the mundane and uncomfortable aspect of many gamekeepers' duties, Munsche quotes a letter held at Bedfordshire Record Office (W1/6157) from one Thomas Delahay, a gamekeeper who complained to his employer that he 'laid ought Maney cold Nights in your Woods and Plantations Wen the Rest of your Servants Ware a Bed, and By doing so I have Decayed my Concitration for the Percivation of your Game' (Munsche, 'The Gamekeeper and English Rural Society', p. 92, note 37).

99 Anon., *The trial of Edward Gibbon Wakefield*, 2nd edn (London: Edward Duncombe, 1827), p. 11. This was the second wealthy heiress that Wakefield had pursued; in 1816 he had wooed Miss Eliza Pattle and she had given him her hand (and a £70,000 marriage settlement).

100 Anon., *Une Nouvelle Manière d'attrapper une Femme, or A Bold Stroke for a Wife, exemplified in Mr. Wakefield's 'New Art of Love'* (London: Anon., 1827), p. 6. For a detailed modern account of the abduction, see Abby Ashby and Audrey Jones, *The Shrigley Abduction: A Tale of Anguish, Deceit and Violation of the Domestic Hearth* (Stroud: Sutton, 2003).

101 Anon., *The trial of Edward Gibbon Wakefield, William Wakefield and Frances Wakefield, indicted with one Edward Thevenot, a servant, for a conspiracy and for the abduction of Miss Ellen Turner* (London: John Murray, 1827). In neither this nor the other 16-page account of the trial does any evidence given by Ellis appear. This seems somewhat unusual at first sight, but as Wakefield was captured in the presence of Ellis, Mr Grimsditch (a solicitor) and the French authorities, perhaps Ellis's evidence was not considered necessary.

102 Circumstantial evidence suggests that Daniel Bishop was one of the Officers who had spent some time in France – in his evidence to the 1813 Game Laws Select Committee he was asked: 'Were there many pheasants when you were in France?' and he replied, 'No, principally hares' (PP 1823, p. 32).

103 John Wade, *A Treatise on the Police and Crimes of the Metropolis*, intro, J. J. Tobias (Montclair, NJ: Patterson Smith, 1972 [original 1829]), p. 39.

104 James, *Delaware; or the Ruined Family*, vol. 3, pp. 99–102.

105 The Queen's Plate Committee was originally set up to support the cause of Queen Caroline, widow of King George III. A public subscription was created to provide her with financial support, but the scheme was badly administered, with accusations of corruption rumbling on into the 1830s (see *Bell's Weekly Messenger*, no. 1838, 26 June 1831 for a detailed explanation by the Treasurer of the Committee, Mr Alderman Wood, of what had happened to the funds raised).

106 HO 61/1.

107 OBP, April 1824, trial of John Frederick Elick and Elizabeth Harriot Crees, t18240407-2.

108 *Staffordshire Advertiser*, 18 January 1803.

109 Anon., *The trial of Edward Gibbon Wakefield, William Wakefield and Frances Wakefield, indicted with one Edward Thevenot, a servant, for a conspiracy and for the abduction of Miss Ellen Turner* (London: John Murray, 1827), p. 131.

110 Ibid., p. 134.

111 *The Times*, 23 March 1826.

112 Ibid.

113 PP 1816, quoted in Henry Goddard, *Memoirs of a Bow Street Runner*, intro. and ed. P. Pringle (London: Museum Press, 1956), Editor's note, p. 108. Cooperation worked both ways: the *Annual Register* of 1803 announced that on 4 January 'a person arrived in London, to communicate a shocking transaction to the English Police, in order to procure assistance in tracing out the perpetrators [of the murder of five people], in case they should have crossed the Channel'.

114 *The Times*, 15 November 1815. Goddard, *Memoirs of a Bow Street Runner*, Editor's note, p. 108.

115 Goddard, *Memoirs of a Bow Street Runner*, Editor's note, p. 108.

116 *The Times*, 20 April 1820.

117 HO 60/3, correspondence dated 1 August 1838.

118 Albert Borowitz, *The Thurtell-Hunt Murder Case: Dark Mirror to Regency England* (Baton Rouge, LA: Louisiana State University Press, 1987), p. 6.

119 *The Times*, 5 June 1830.

120 Ibid., 24 July 1830.

121 Ibid. A contemporary letter to the Home Department suggested that the coroner who certified the cause of death of Mackay had messed up the arrest warrants for Byrne and his backer, being 'in a state of intoxication and unable to perform the duties of his office' (HO 44/20 ff. 274–9, Letter from Mr George Moore dated 9 June 1830 re warrants issued for arrest of Simon Byrne). His verdict was therefore questionable, leading to much speculation as to the reasons for Mackay's demise.

122 The *Manchester Guardian* of 31 July 1830 reported that the 'not guilty' verdict was 'received by loud acclamation' in the courtroom.

123 The *Glasgow Chronicle*, quoted in *The Times*, 11 July 1830. Mackay, a native of Glasgow, was a favourite son of the city, and the Glaswegian press began circulating a rumour that he had lost the fight (and his life) after being drugged.

124 George Dilnot, *Triumphs of Detection* (London: Geoffrey Bles, 1929), p. 38.

125 MEPO 4/508.

126 Denis Brailsford, *Bareknuckles: A Social History of Prizefighting* (Cambridge: Lutterworth Press, 1998), p. 86.

127 Ibid., p. 46. The *Caledonian Mercury*, 9 January 1834 scathingly referred to Bow Street personnel as 'the most sedentary, unrunning, lethargic men in the universe' when dealing with prizefights.

128 John Ford, *Prizefighting: The Age of Regency Boximania* (Newton Abbott: David & Charles, 1971), p. 23.

129 J. M. Cobbett and J. P. Cobbett, *Selection from Cobbett's Political Works*, 6 vols (London: Ann Cobbett, 1835), vol. 2, p. 16. For a general history of boxing, see Tony Gee, *Up to Scratch: Bareknuckle Fighting and Heroes of the Prize-ring* (Harpenden: Queen Anne's Press, 1998), and Brailsford, *Bareknuckles: A Social History of Prizefighting*. The latter is generally the more perceptive book, with Brailsford commenting that 'as an illegal sport, it has much to suggest on policing and law-enforcement' (p. xii). Randy Roberts, in his paper, 'Eighteenth-Century Boxing', *Journal of Sport History*, vol. 4, no. 3 (Fall 1977), pp. 246–59, gives an interesting view that 'pugilism also had a tranquilising effect on eighteenth-century English society' – he suggests that the vast crowds who often attended such matches could vent their anger and frustration by proxy by identifying with one or other of the contenders.

130 An example of the former can be found in the *Annual Register*, vol. 53 (1811) – the fight was the result of a quarrel rather than a professional pre-arranged fight. Charles Beale, a farmer, and Stringer Tonks, a basket maker, agreed to settle their differences by fighting – the resultant contest leaving Beale dead from a blow under his ear. The *Annual Register* exclaims that 'the constable of the parish was a stakeholder' in the fight, indicating that such fights were not only held with the full knowledge of the local law-enforcement agent, but that such agents were not averse to wagering on the outcome. For an account of the large sums that were often involved in organised bouts, see Daniel Mendoza, *The Memoirs of the Life of Daniel Mendoza*, ed. by Paul Magriel (London: Batsford, 1951 [reprint of 1816 original]).

131 Letter reproduced in Mendoza, *The Memoirs of the Life of Daniel Mendoza*, p. 80.

132 *The Times*, 17 August 1804. Many of these bouts seem to have been policed by the less senior ranks of Bow Street, as they often required sufficient manpower to disperse the crowds.

133 Mendoza, *The Memoirs of the Life of Daniel Mendoza*, p. 103.
134 For a contemporary report of this fight, see *National Gazette and Literary Register*, Philadelphia, no. 1928, vol. XII.
135 Gee, *Up to Scratch*, p. 111. For the increase during 1813–22, see Ford, *Prizefighting*. *The Times* of 29 July 1830 reported that scurrilous rumours that King George IV was about to become a patron of the prize-ring again were circulating in an attempt to discredit him.
136 In December 1842, the 'Tipton Slasher', William Perry, later to become World Champion, participated in a series of fights with Charles Freeman, the 'American Giant', in Kent. Freeman's training camp was set up at the Duke of York public house near Barnet. This hostelry was kept by Francis Keys, a former Principal Officer. For further information regarding these fights, see David J. Cox, 'The Tipton Slasher and the American Giant', *The Blackcountryman*, vol. 36, no. 2 (Spring 2003), pp. 9–12.
137 HO 60/2, Letter appointing Leadbitter as Principal Officer, and MEPO 4/508 Foot patrol register, 1821–29, appointment of Leadbitter as Patrol Constable.
138 PP 1816, p. 7.
139 Ibid., p. 42.

Chapter 7

'More expert in tracing and detecting crime': the post-1829 situation

Introduction

This chapter discusses the reasons for the continued existence of the Principal Officers in the decade following the creation of the Metropolitan Police in 1829.

Continued employment of Principal Officers after 1829

Despite the continuing unease with which Bow Street was viewed by several influential politicians, including Peel and Melbourne, the introduction of the Metropolitan Police Act in 1829 did not signal the immediate demise of the Principal Officers.[1] Although all of the various other constituents of the Bow Street personnel were either disbanded or placed under the control of the Metropolitan Police Commissioners by late 1836, Bow Street, along with the other London Police Offices, retained its complement of Principal Officers, who were still directly responsible to the magistrates and not the Commissioners, until 1839.[2]

The reasons for this anomaly remain somewhat unclear. It is certain that from the time the idea of the Metropolitan Police was first mooted by Peel that he considered it to be a solely preventive force, with no detective element, and that he also viewed it as a force that would operate purely within the bounds of the metropolis.[3] There was no official provision until 1842 for a detective element within the Metropolitan Police or for the deployment of Metropolitan Police officers outside the metropolis.[4] As John Beattie remarks, 'the

Metropolitan Police Act of 1829, which, although forward-looking in some ways, reached back to an older ideal of policing in its total dependence on the prevention of crime by surveillance'.[5]

The net effect was that the Principal Officers of the London Police Offices in general and Bow Street Police Office in particular remained the only detective forces available for use throughout England and Wales.[6]

As the Metropolitan Police was still a relatively new force, it is not surprising that it was acknowledged by many contemporaries to be lacking in experience of detection of crime when compared to the Police Offices. Samuel March Phillips (Under-Secretary of State for the Home Department) admitted in his evidence to the 1837 Committee that

> the officers attached to the police offices would be more expert in the detection of crime than the common Metropolitan Police officers; they are more practised in that particular business, more experienced in looking for and searching out proofs, and therefore more expert in tracing and detecting crime, than the common Metropolitan Police officer.[7]

In a similar vein, some four years earlier, in his evidence to the 1833 Committee on the Metropolitan Police, Mr Hardwick, a magistrate at Lambeth Police Office, had stated that 'the Metropolitan Police are efficient in the preventive part of their duties. In the detective part they are, and ever will be, deficient – from the nature of their regulation and their discipline.'[8]

This book suggests that, far from being increasingly isolated and under-used following the creation of the Metropolitan Police, the Principal Officers were utilised rather more in the post-1829 period than in the pre-Metropolitan Police era.[9] In the ten-year period 1820–29, the number of reported provincial cases was 130, while in the period 1830–39, the number rose to 206, an increase of almost 60 per cent.

Frederick Roe, Chief Magistrate at Bow Street, was questioned in some depth about this increase in the 1837 *Report of the Select Committee on the Metropolis Police Offices*, and he makes it clear that he believed that there was a definite growth in the provincial usage of his Principal Officers. He was specifically asked, 'Are they much engaged upon special services in the country?', and he replied 'Very much'.[10] He was further questioned: 'Have they been, since the establishment of the Metropolitan Police [and] are they employed as they were before?' He stated in reply that 'I was not at Bow Street before, but I should say they have been more employed for the last three years, than the first year I was at Bow Street [1832].'[11]

The most obvious reason for this increase would at first sight appear to be an assumed reduction of involvement of the Principal Officers in London-based cases following the creation of the Metropolitan Police, therefore leading to the associated police work being carried out by Metropolitan Police officers. This would logically have had the concomitant effect of freeing up some of the time of Principal Officers to be employed on provincial investigations. However, in fact the usage of Principal Officers did not noticeably lessen in the capital following the advent of the Metropolitan Police; it instead rose. The OBP record 52 metropolitan cases involving Principal Officers in the period 1830–39. The types of case (predominantly larceny (63.5 per cent) and fraud (25 per cent) reflect the earlier metropolitan usage of Principal Officers detailed in Chapter 4. Similarly, the types of metropolitan employer mirror the earlier composition of such employers discussed in Chapter 3: 67.32 per cent were private individuals, 19.2 per cent were institutions while one case of threatening behaviour by an insane man was instigated by the Home Department.

It would therefore seem that despite the introduction of the Metropolitan Police, many inhabitants who could afford to utilise the services of Bow Street continued so to do – indeed, despite the increasing number of Metropolitan Police officers available, the Principal Officers remained in favour. This favour seems to have extended to the Royal family – until 1838 the Principal Officers were the only law-enforcement officers allowed within Buckingham Palace.[12]

The increase in provincial cases in the period 1830–39 suggests that the introduction of the Municipal Corporations Act of 1835 (5 & 6 Will. IV c. 76), which enabled a total of 148 listed boroughs to create their own police forces, was not a significant issue in provincial decisions whether or not to utilise the services of Principal Officers. The Act of 1835 signally failed to usher in a new era of 'modern' policing to England and Wales, and the Royal Commission on the Municipal Corporations Act of 1835 found that the state of many of the boroughs' police forces was still woefully inadequate:

> At Bristol, a notoriously ineffective police cannot be improved, chiefly in consequence of the jealousy with which the Corporation is regarded by the inhabitants. At Hull, in consequence of the

disunion between the governing body and the inhabitants, chiefly arising out of a dispute about the tolls and duties, only seven persons attended to suppress a riot, out of 5,000 who had been sworn in as special constables, and on another similar occasion none attended. At Coventry, serious riots and disturbances frequently occur, and the officers of police, being usually selected from one political party, are often active in fomenting them.[13]

The Municipal Corporations Act of 1835 only affected the 148 listed boroughs; it was not until the introduction of the Rural Constabulary Act of 1839 (2 & 3 Vic. c.93) that counties and unincorporated boroughs were formally encouraged (but not compelled) to create their own police forces. By the beginning of the same year Scotland possessed some twenty police forces of varying size and quality.[14] It must be borne in mind that it was not until the 1856 County and Borough Police Act that all towns and boroughs within England and Wales were formally required to create police forces.[15]

Between 1829 and 1839 the Principal Officers were still available for use within the provinces, including those areas where newly created police forces were operating. Such police forces through their very nature generally lacked experienced and professional officers, and it is clear that the Commissioners of the Metropolitan Police were often relied on to provide guidance and advice to several of the newly created borough forces; David Wall's research has found that the Commissioners regularly sent out advisers on a fixed fee of ten shillings per day plus travel and accommodation expenses in much the same way that Bow Street had operated for almost ninety years.[16]

In a similar manner, the Principal Officers continued to be called upon by individuals and institutions to investigate crimes that were thought to be beyond the capabilities of the provincial police. The Bow Street Officers were not the only police officers from the metropolis to be sent to the provinces after the creation of the Metropolitan Police. Principal Officers from the other London Police Offices continued occasionally to be deployed in the same manner; for example, James Lea of Lambeth Police Office was the chief investigator of a series of arson attacks in Dunmow, Essex, in November 1838.[17]

Metropolitan Police officers were used sporadically for some provincial investigations, but this was very much the exception rather than the rule. Samuel March Phillips flatly denied that any were sent out in a detective capacity in his evidence to the 1837 Select

Committee. When asked: 'Is it not the fact, now, that the constables of the police force are very extensively used and usefully employed in the detection of felonies, both in town and country?' Phillips replied that 'they are not sent into the country for that purpose'. In the face of further suggestions that Metropolitan Police officers were occasionally sent out on the instructions of the Commissioners, he expressed surprise, stating that 'I am not aware of such a thing. It is understood by the Commissioners that they are not to be sent, in cases of offences committed in the country, without a direction from the Secretary of State.'[18]

The overwhelming majority of the provincial usage of Metropolitan Police in this ten-year period was of a preventive nature in the form of public order and riot suppression rather than in a detective capacity. Begg and Skinner state that 'in 1838, a total of 647 Metropolitan Police constables were sent to various parts of Britain to help prevent public disorder', and also record that a Metropolitan Police sergeant and eleven constables were utilised in the maintenance of public order during a Chartist election campaign in Huddersfield in 1837.[19]

There are very few recorded examples of Metropolitan Police officers being used in a detective capability in the provinces. Philip Rawlings records that Sergeant James Otway of the Metropolitan Police was utilised in a murder enquiry in the Uxbridge area in 1837, while an 1839 Select Committe *Report* on the Constabulary Force in England and Wales states that an experienced Metropolitan Police officer was sent to investigate a murder at Stow-on-the-Wold in Gloucestershire in 1834.[20]

However, even these two examples may not have been the sole preserve of the Metropolitan Police. The investigation cited by Rawlings was in fact led by Joseph Shackell, a Principal Officer. Sergeant Otway aided the Principal Officer and a parish constable in the investigation of the murder of a farmer on Ruislip Common. With regard to the murder at Stow-on-the-Wold, this was most probably the robbery and murder of Francis James Ren in March 1834 referred to in Chapter 6. The murder generated a reward of £200, and according to *The Times* was investigated by an anonymous Bow Street Officer.[21]

Relationship between Bow Street and the Metropolitan Police 1829–39

The degree of cooperation between Bow Street and the Metropolitan Police in the abovementioned cases was unusual; in general there was often barely concealed animosity between the two bodies, which continued unchecked and unabated post-1829 and certainly extended to the attitude of some senior Bow Street officials to the Metropolitan Police.

Frederick Roe, who became Chief Magistrate at Bow Street in 1832 after leaving Marlborough Street Police Office, seems to have possessed a particular animosity and an almost pathological enmity to Peel's new force. He caustically commented that 'the [Metropolitan] police force is like gas-light; it is a very useful outdoor force, but it is not fit for the detection of thieves', while also promoting the qualities of his Principal Officers: 'I am happy to say I have got the officers at Bow Street very perfect now, and they are all intelligent men.'[22]

Despite such pronouncements, with the benefit of hindsight it is clear that Bow Street, its magistrates and its personnel were fighting a rearguard action for survival against increasing calls for a new form of policing from the mid-1820s onwards. Those who wished to see the end of the existing system were quick to seize upon opportunities such as the 'Blood-Money Scandal' and the Warwick Bank incident to discredit Bow Street and the other Police Offices, and were often indiscriminate in their use of what they considered to be evidence of widespread corruption. This contemporary 'mud-slinging', together with what often amounted to little more than unsubstantiated and garbled accounts of individual cases of corruption, also seems to have coloured many historians' viewpoints up to the present day.

This animosity and the lack of cooperation between Bow Street and the Metropolitan Police is highlighted in both the 1837 Select Committee *Report* and the 1837/8 Select Committee *Report* into the Metropolitan Police Offices.[23] Samuel March Phillips stated in his evidence to the 1837 Committee that the magistrates were unlikely or unwilling to grant warrants to Metropolitan Police constables rather than their own men, because the magistrate

> knows the capacities and powers of the officer, who may have been a long time acting under his orders, and prefers him as best for the purpose; and if the magistrates retain the power of employing constables attached to their office, they will have a preference, and will employ them.[24]

There was, however, some limited movement post-1829 between the Metropolitan Police and Bow Street – three Metropolitan Police officers appear to have been 'promoted' to Bow Street as Principal Officers in the following ten years. Henry Fall, the first of these, was described as 'a man of respectable connexions and high character', being appointed on 24 January 1832 at the suggestion of Sir Richard Birnie (indicating that Birnie kept a weather-eye on the progress of individuals within the Metropolitan Police), while Abraham Fletcher joined in December 1833 from the Metropolitan Police. Joseph Shackell, who was originally appointed as a gaoler in February 1834 after serving in the Metropolitan Police (as a Sergeant in A Division), also became a Principal Officer in May 1836.[25] In 1839, when the Principal Officers were disbanded, he was invited to rejoin the Metropolitan Police as an Inspector with the promise of quick promotion.[26] In 1844, as an Inspector, he became the second head of the Detective Branch, after Nicholas Pearce, himself a former Bow Street Patrol member, was promoted to Superintendent.[27]

Conclusion

By 1838, despite the best efforts of Bow Street magistrates such as Sir Frederick Roe, it was increasingly apparent to everyone involved that the Principal Officers' days as police officers responsible only to their magistrates and acting independently of the remit of the Metropolitan Police Commissioners were numbered. The Select Committee's recommendations, published in 1838, included the following:

> Your Committee cannot see any reason to doubt that out of all the body of 3,000 and upwards of constables of the Metropolitan Police, a sufficient number will be found who are fully equal to the performance of all the duties which can be required of them by the Magistrates; and they adopt the suggestion of two of these Magistrates, and approved of by the Commissioners; viz that the Office Constables should be restricted wholly to the performance of in-door duties, acting merely in attendance upon the magistrates, as ushers or officers of court. There will not, as now, be portions of the criminal business passing through the hands of officers disconnected with the Metropolitan Police, whereby the information which relates to those cases is withdrawn from the general current of information passing to the central establishment.[28]

On 17 August 1839 'An Act for further improving the Police in and near the metropolis (c. XLVII Victoria 2), came into force, followed a week later by 'An Act for regulating the Police Courts in the metropolis (c. LXXI, Victoria 2)'. Neither of these Acts have any specific clause referring to the disbandment of Principal Officers – the only reference is an oblique one to the fact that clerks at the offices could now only be sworn in as constables with authority in the courts and its precincts and with administrative and protective duties only – but then again, there appears never to have been any written legal framework for their formation or duties since their creation in 1748.

The ninety-year period of their existence therefore reached an abrupt and final demise. There appears to have been surprisingly little comment in the press about this somewhat inglorious end; little mention of the situation seems to have reached the pages of *The Times* or the other London newspapers. It was, however, fairly quickly acknowledged that preventive policing alone was unsatisfactory; in August 1842 a Detective Branch of the Metropolitan Police was created in order to deal with serious crimes within the capital.

However, while the disbandment of the Principal Officers in August 1839 may have ended their employment, their legacy continued in several ways, and it is to this aspect of their history that the final chapter of this book turns.

Notes

1 The original force of the Metropolitan Police in 1829 was 1,011 men, consisting of 8 Superintendents, 20 Inspectors, 88 Sergeants and 895 Constables (Martin Fido and Keith Skinner, *The Official Encyclopedia of Scotland Yard* (London: Virgin, 1999), p. 184).

2 The Night Patrol and the Day Patrol (Dismounted Horse Patrol) were put under the authority of the Commissioners of the Metropolitan Police by the Act 10 Geo. IV c. 45 in September 1829. The Horse Patrol was placed under Metropolitan Police authority on 13 August 1836 by Act 6 & 7 Will. IV c.50. Act 3 & 4 Vic. c.84 (1840) provided superannuation for former members of Horse and Foot patrols to receive pensions from the state.

3 Although, as David Ascoli remarks, the Metropolitan Police Bill of 15 April 1829 included the sentence: 'It is no longer possible to leave all the responsibility in connection with the detection of offenders, or the prevention of crimes, in the hands of the parochial authorities', it is clear that detection in this sense meant either catching perpetrators in the act or rounding up the 'usual suspects', rather than the active detection of crimes that had previously occurred (David Ascoli, 'Introduction', *The Queen's Peace: the Origins and Development of the Metropolitan Police 1829–1979* (London: Hamish Hamilton, 1979)).

4   A small detective force of eight men was created in 1842 (out of a total force of some 4,400 men). The number of detectives was not increased until 1864, when it rose to 15. For a succinct account of the early years and the development of the CID, see Alan R. Pike, 'A Brief History of the CID of the London Metropolitan Police', *Police Studies*, vol. 1, no. 2 (June 1978), pp. 22–30. It has been demonstrated that some Metropolitan Police officers did act in a detective capacity prior to the creation of the Detective Department. The case of Sergeant William Popay, who was dismissed in 1833 for exceeding his duties when in plain clothes in his efforts to infiltrate the Camberwell branch of the National Political Union of the Working Classes, is well-known and illustrates the fact that such subterfuge was not officially condoned (though there is circumstantial evidence that Popay's efforts were connived at by the Home Department). For a brief account of Popay's activities, see Fido and Skinner, *The Official Encyclopedia of Scotland Yard*, pp. 210–11.

5   J. M. Beattie, *Policing and Punishment in London 1660–1750: Urban Crime and the Limits of Terror* (Oxford: OUP, 2001), p. 422.

6   It has been discussed above that the situation was somewhat different in Scotland, and also that the other Police Offices seem to have rarely sent Officers outside the metropolis or surrounding area.

7   PP 1837, p. 10.

8   PP 1833, p. 95.

9   It does, however, have to be borne in mind that in general, many of the newspapers utilised for this research expanded in size during the latter part of the period and were therefore able to carry more news. This subsequently could have affected the number of cases reported in such sources. The figures could also be inflated due to the inclusion of cases mentioned in Henry Goddard's *Memoirs* (4-volume manuscript, 1875–79); several of these cases are not recorded in the other utilised sources.

10 PP 1837, p. 23.

11 Ibid. Roe refers to the fact that the provincial usage of the Principal Officers was previously only recorded on a simple card-based system, but that he had recently improved upon this method. Unfortunately, none of the cards or Roe's records survive, although both T 38/673 Treasury: Departmental Accounts, Public Office, Bow Street 1793–1816 and T 38/674 Treasury: Departmental Accounts, Public Office, Bow Street 1816–35 contain a few hurriedly written notes pertaining to provincial cases, written on scraps of paper by Principal Officers, primarily for the purposes of claiming expenses.

12 Paul Begg and Keith Skinner, *The Scotland Yard Files: 150 years of the CID* (London: Headline, 1992), p. 8.

13 Reproduced from http://www.leeds.ac.uk/law/staff/lawdw/cyberpolice/pol0.htm.

14 Figure calculated from Martin Stallion and David S. Wall, *The British Police: Police Forces and Chief Officers 1829–2000* (Bramshill: Police History Society, 2000).

15 For a concise account of the development of provincial policing in the early Victorian period, see Clive Emsley, *The English Police: A Political and Social History* (London: Longman, 1996), pp. 32–42, and for an overview of the period from 1829 to the present day, see David S. Wall, 'The Organisation of Police 1829–2000', in Stallion and Wall, *The British Police*, pp. 1–31.

16 David S. Wall, 'The Organisation of Police 1829–2000', p. 5. Wall has also found evidence to suggest that many such forces wished to employ ex-Metropolitan officers as Chief Constables, but he stresses that not all county forces were created on Metropolitan lines, many being controlled by locally elected representative committees rather than by magistrates.

17 HO 64/8 f. 78.

18 PP 1837, p. 10.

19 Begg and Skinner, *The Scotland Yard Files*, pp. 46–7.

20 *The Times*, 17 March 1834. This may have been the murder of Francis James Ren, which was also investigated by a Principal Officer (see Chapter 6).

21 Ibid.

22 Quoted by Sir Peter Laurie in PP 1837/8, p. 191, and by Frederick Roe, PP 1837, p. 23.

23 PP 1837; PP 1837/8.

24 PP 1837, p. 9.

25 HO 60/2 Police Court Entry Book 1830–35, letter dated 24 January 1832, and letter dated 13 February 1834.

26 HO 60/3 Police Court Entry Book 1836–39, letter dated 30 September 1839.

27 Fido and Skinner, *The Official Encyclopedia of Scotland Yard*, p. 67. The authors describe Pearce as a 'former Bow Street Runner', but in fact he never rose to the rank of Principal Officer.

28 PP 1837/8, pp. 5–6.

Chapter 8

'Rescuing from a historical cul-de-sac': the legacy of the Bow Street Principal Officers

Introduction

This book has hopefully brought to light several previously under-researched aspects of the work of Principal Officers from 1792 to 1839, who combined innovative detective work and a degree of professionalism with 'a certain share of low cunning', and who undoubtedly deserve a more prominent position in the history of British policing.[1] The book has demonstrated that the work and activities of the Principal Officers needs rescuing from what John Beattie has so aptly described as, 'the neglect, if not from the contempt, of history'.[2] It has attempted to clarify the functioning and operation of both the Office in general and the work of the Principal Officers in particular during the period 1792 to 1839, sweeping away much of the often inaccurate assertions and hearsay that have been previously accepted as historical fact.

Summary of findings

The book set out to answer the following questions about the Principal Officers:

- Who were they?
- What was their role and how did it differ from the other Bow Street personnel?
- By whom where they employed?

- How were they employed?
- Where were they employed?
- How did they operate while they were employed?

In order to answer these questions the book has accurately identified all of the Principal Officers who served between 1792 and 1839 and has also separated their activities, duties and misdemeanours from those of their less senior colleagues.

The Appendix enables future scholars to quickly establish whether or not a particular individual was a serving Principal Officer at any given time in the period. It has also demonstrated that the Principal Officers generally served for a considerable period of time, allowing them to gain invaluable experience and skills that other contemporary law-enforcement officials were unlikely to have reaped during their short terms of office.

Bow Street's manpower was divided into a complex series of forces, and it has been demonstrated in Chapter 2 that the Principal Officers played a unique and discrete role in the panoply of law-enforcement officials employed by the Office.

Such definitive identification of the Principal Officers and separation of their history from the less senior ranks of Bow Street will hopefully assist future researchers in avoiding the conflation and confusion of the respective identities and roles of Bow Street personnel that has marred previous accounts of the history of the Police Office.

Chapter 2 has defined the operations and management of the Bow Street Office and delineated how the Principal Officers fitted into this system. It has argued that despite the undoubted presence of a few 'rotten apples' within the Bow Street ranks, the majority of the Principal Officers seem to have been somewhat unfairly tainted with the whiff of corruption; with perhaps one exception, the Officers do not seem to have conformed to their later caricatures as self-serving speculators, eager to profit illegally from their positions.

Chapter 3 has clearly delineated the types of employer of Principal Officers in both the provinces and the metropolis, and has shown that the Officers were predominantly employed in all locations by members of the socio-economic or political elite. It has shown that poor victims of crime did not normally have access to the expertise and experience of Bow Street's most senior personnel and that ability to pay and/or social status appear to have been the principal determinants as to whether or not the Officers were employed. It has also demonstrated that the Officers were widely used by private individuals, private institutions and the Home Department, and were often regarded as the only suitable choice of investigative officials.

Chapter 4 has shown that the Principal Officers were used in the investigation of a wide variety of provincial crimes, ranging from relatively petty offences to more serious felonies, and that once again, ability to pay was the main determinant in their employment. It has also been demonstrated that the Officers were employed in the investigation of far more types of provincial crimes than they were utilised for in the metropolis. While the Officers were used throughout the country in the investigation of more serious felonies such as murder, it is apparent that due to their proximity they were employed to investigate lesser crimes (in terms of financial loss) in the metropolis compared to their provincial employment. The constraints of travel time and expense clearly influenced the decisions of the victims of such crimes. The book has also shown that because of the unique nature of the Principal Officers' employment, provincial employers were willing to use them on often complex and serious criminal investigations that required reserves of both experience and commitment.

Chapter 5 has demonstrated the limitations of the provincial alternatives available to victims of crime, and also shows that the Principal Officers were employed throughout Great Britain and beyond. Although by no means a comprehensive survey of all the provincial cases investigated by the Officers, the book suggests that the Officers were more likely to be utilised outside the capital and that they were considered by those who could afford to make use of their services to be a useful, efficient and in several ways unique body of men who could draw upon considerable experience, skills and expertise.

Their often innovative investigative methods have been shown throughout Chapter 6 by means of a series of examples, each highlighting at least one aspect of their work. The Officers have been shown to be daring, brave and resourceful individuals with often highly developed detective skills, quite capable of carrying out detailed and complex investigations, involving both a considerable range of skills and tenacity that the vast majority of contemporary law-enforcement officials could not have hoped to master.

Chapter 7 has shown why the Principal Officers did not immediately suffer the same fate as their less senior colleagues in the various other forces based at the Police Offices, and in fact were utilised rather more frequently (both in the provinces and in the capital) in the decade following the creation of the Metropolitan Police. It has argued that they were simply too valuable a commodity to dispose of, despite the obvious and occasionally very public antagonism between the Police Office magistrates and the Metropolitan Police.

The Principal Officers were undoubtedly brave, resourceful, intelligent and employed a great variety of talents in order to carry out their work. However, this book is not intended to be a paean to the Principal Officers. It has also recognised and demonstrated that there was much at fault with a system of policing in which law-enforcement officials were employed by an extremely small sector of the population who could afford to pay handsomely for their services, that there were inherent dangers in such a close working relationship between the executive and the judiciary as that which existed between magistrate and Principal Officer, and that such a limited body of men could make very little practical impact on the policing of the country as a whole. The book has also investigated the accusations of corruption at Bow Street, but has shown that much of the resultant criticism unfairly targeted the Principal Officers, most of whom appear to have been reasonably (and perhaps surprisingly) honest in their professional lives.

Although the Principal Officers' employment and their system of policing came to an end in 1839, they have left a legacy that survives in several different ways. At a superficial level, they have become little more than a folk-memory – the term 'Bow Street Runners' to many people evokes a hazy notion of corrupt thieftakers who operated exclusively in London and who took bribes and rewards. In the twenty-first century, however, the phrase remains well-known enough to be used for a black-powder firearms contest, a horse-riding contest, and a whole sub-genre of historical fiction.[3]

The legacy of Bow Street and its Principal Officers with regard to the history of policing is, however, considerably more substantial. The book has proved that, far from the general perception of them being confined to the metropolis, Principal Officers were utilised on a regular basis throughout Great Britain and occasionally on the continent, and it has also demonstrated that they were involved in the investigation of a wide variety of provincial criminal activities. It has demonstrated by means of exemplary case studies that the Principal Officers laid many of the foundations of the effective detection of crimes, and while it has been shown that they were perhaps not quite 'the only detective force in the whole kingdom' as has been claimed in the past, the book has conclusively demonstrated that they were the only such body of experienced men available on a national basis that could be called in by provincial victims or magistrates for cases which proved to be beyond the capability or skill of local law-enforcement bodies.[4]

For the ninety-plus years of its existence the Bow Street Office was often at the forefront of developments in law enforcement, including the promulgation of information about crimes that had taken place in the form of the publication of *Hue & Cry*, the creation of the first professional and salaried detective police force in England and Wales, and innovative detective practices including forensic analysis, undercover work and detailed criminal investigation, all of which have subsequently become part of the bedrock of modern policing and which were largely unknown before the creation of the Principal Officers.

The undercover nature of the Principal Officer's job was often crucial in the detection and capture of suspects, and this subterfuge, although not unique to the Officers, is one of their attributes that sets them apart from the vast majority of other contemporary law-enforcement officials.[5] The adjective 'detective' does not occur in English dictionaries until 1843, following the creation of the Detective Branch of the Metropolitan Police in August 1842, but it has been demonstrated above that many of the Principal Officers were practising detective activities well before this time, and that such activities were regarded as valuable additions to law-enforcement duties.[6] The Principal Officers demonstrated the importance of and need for a detective element to policing, and their innovative and often daring approach to criminal investigations also helped define the role of the detective in the popular psyche.

The creation of the Metropolitan Police, as John Beattie has remarked, 'reached back to an older ideal of policing in its total dependence on the prevention of crime by surveillance'. However, the Commissioners were quick to realise that this style of exclusively preventive police work was neither effective nor practical, creating a Detective Branch based fundamentally on the work of Bow Street's Principal Officers within three years of the creation of the Metropolitan Police.[7]

Historians such as John Styles have further questioned the once widely held assumptions of the Metropolitan Police and its imitators as being innovative by dint of being new, salaried, professional, state-appointed and organised. He argues that many of these adjectives could be equally applied to several of the existing law-enforcement agencies, including Bow Street and the other Police Offices.[8]

He also points out that 'earlier police reformers, like Sir John Fielding in the third quarter of the eighteenth century, had seen prevention as being a matter both of pro-active surveillance *and* deterrence through effective detection', and that 'the development of paid policing and police forces in England was happening long before the setting up of the Metropolitan force in 1829, while professionalisation, central direction and national standardisation remained weak long after that date'.[9]

Conclusion

This book has demonstrated that Bow Street and its contingent of Principal Officers in particular played an important role in the construction of a recognisably 'modern' police force, and were not simply a historical 'cul-de-sac' with no influence on later developments in policing.

While the creation of the Metropolitan Police undoubtedly set an example that was subsequently copied by many county and borough police forces, this book contends that Bow Street, and especially its contingent of Principal Officers, was in many ways more advanced and modern in its operations, acting as a precursor of the Detective Branch, CID, the Flying Squad, Special Branch and even Interpol.[10] Many of the practices instigated by Principal Officers remain fundamental to detective investigation today: the close examination of evidence at the scene of the crime, the interviewing of suspects and witnesses, the undercover nature of their investigations, and the publication of descriptions of both missing goods and suspects.[11] Over a period of almost a century the Principal Officers formulated and improved upon their methods of detective investigation, until the best of them had become experienced and professional investigators, known and praised by many of their contemporaries for their tenacity, innovation and skill in investigating serious crimes in the provinces.[12]

The book has also highlighted the fact that much further research remains to be carried out with regard to many other aspects of early nineteenth-century policing history; the other Police Offices have been largely ignored by historians, while the activities of other law-enforcement officials such as the King's Messengers remain largely an undocumented mystery.

Similarly, the role of the less senior ranks remains to be fully documented and researched; it is hoped that this book has gone some way to stimulating interest in Bow Street Police Office as a whole, and that others will be able to take up the baton with regard to the various Bow Street patrols. Such research would undoubtedly help the work of Bow Street as a whole and the work of the Principal Officers in particular to be fully contextualised with regard to the wider history of policing.

As to the earlier years of the Bow Street Office, from its founding in 1748 to the creation of the other London Police Offices in 1792, the publication of John Beattie's forthcoming research will undoubtedly greatly increase our knowledge of the subject and is therefore eagerly anticipated.

Notes

1 Rev J. Richardson, *Recollections: Political, Literary, Dramatic, and Miscellaneous of the last half-century*, 2 vols (London: C. Mitchell, undated c.1860), vol. 1, p. 58.

2 John Beattie, *English Detectives in the Late Eighteenth Century*, paper presented at the European Social Science History Conference, The Hague, March 2002.

3 See http://www.britishpistolclub.org for details of the firearms contest; http://www.britisheventing.com for details of the eventing contest; and http://www.fantasticfiction.co.uk for details of author T. F. Banks' publications based on the adventures of a fictionalised Bow Street 'Runner'.

4 Leonard W. Cowie, 'The Bow Street "Runners"', *British Heritage*, vol. 1, no. 4 (June/July 1980), pp. 46–57, at p. 52.

5 Their closest analogous contemporaries were probably US Federal marshals, who often worked undercover and engaged in detective activities akin to those of Bow Street from their formation in 1789 – for a detailed account of their work, see Frederick S. Calhoun, *The Lawmen: United States Marshals and Their Deputies, 1789–1989* (Harmondsworth: Penguin, 1991).

6 C. T. Onions (ed.), *The Shorter Oxford English Dictionary on Historical Principles*, 2 vols (Oxford: OUP, 1973), p. 532.

7 J. M. Beattie, *Policing and Punishment in London 1660–1750: Urban Crime and the Limits of Terror* (Oxford: OUP, 2001), p. 422.

8 John Styles, 'The Emergence of the Police: Explaining Police Reform in Eighteenth and Nineteenth Century England', *British Journal of Criminology*, vol. 27, no. 1 (1987), pp. 15–22, at pp. 16–17.

9 Ibid., pp. 17 and 18. National standardisation has still not been achieved with regard to the police forces of England and Wales; the current debate on the proposed merger of the 43 police forces into a dozen larger forces has highlighted many of the differences between existing forces. A striking example is that of the 43 forces, only 13 have a dedicated Murder Squad (ex-Chief Constable Dennis O'Connor, speaking on Radio Four's *PM* programme, 21 December 2005).

10 The Detective Branch of the Metropolitan Police was created 15 August 1842; the Criminal Investigation Department (CID) was created 8 April 1878; the Flying Squad was founded as the Mobile Patrol Experiment in 1919; the Special Branch was created 17 March 1883 as the Special Irish Branch; and Interpol was founded in 1923 (dates taken from Martin Fido and Keith Skinner, *The Official Encyclopedia of Scotland Yard* (London: Virgin, 1999)).

11 The practice instigated in *Hue & Cry* of naming and describing suspects has a direct parallel today in initiatives such as West Midlands Police's 'Operation Strikeout', in which individuals wanted in connection with serious crimes are named and pictured on the Internet.

12 A few of the Principal Officers, notably Goddard and Ballard, capitalised on this experience after their forced redundancy and became successful private investigators.

Appendix

Service record of Bow Street Principal Officers 1792–1839

This appendix only deals with the careers of individuals as Principal Officers – many of the men listed below served a long apprenticeship at Bow Street or the other Police Offices as Patrol members or Conductors of Patrol.

Name	Years of service	Notes
Adkins, Harry	1810–20	Became Governor of Warwick Gaol 1820
Adkins, William	1802–10	Became Governor of Cold Bath Fields House of Correction 1810
Anthony, William	1800–10	Served in Royal retinue 1796–99
Ballard, William	1835–39	Became private detective in 1839, died in 1876
Bishop, Daniel	1816–31	
Carpmeal, Thomas	1792*–1808	Died 1808
Delafontaine, John	1792*–94	
Dowsett, Thomas	1798–99	Served in Royal retinue 1800–37
Edwards, Henry	1798–99	Served in Royal retinue 1800–12

Ellis, James	1823–36	
Fall, Henry	1832–39	
Fletcher, Abraham	1833–39	
Fugion, Edward	1796–98	Died 1798
Gardner, Richard	1831–39	
Goddard, Henry	1834–39	Became Chief Constable at Northants 1840–49, then Principal Door Keeper, House of Lords, 1850–83, died 1883
Kennedy, Christopher	1792*–95	Died 1795
Keys, Francis	1835–39	Became landlord of public house after retirement
Lavender, Stephen	1807–21	Became Deputy Superintendent at Manchester Police 1821, died 1833
Leadbitter, George	1831–39	
McManus, Patrick	1808–16	
Miller, John	1792*–1807	
Morant, Moses	1792*–94	
Pearks, John	1802–18	Died 1818
Rivett, John	1794–1811	Served in Royal retinue 1811–37 after suffering mental breakdown
Ruthven, George Thomas	1818–39	Became landlord of public house after retirement, died 1844
Salmon, William	1820–34	
Sayer, John	1795–1832	Died 1832
Shackell, Joseph	1836–39	Died 1839
Smith, James J.	1821–36	Retired through ill-health 1836
Stevens, Samuel	1831–35	
Taunton, Samuel Hercules	1811–35	
Taylor, Joseph	1792*–98	
Townsend, John	1800–32	Died 1832
Vickery, John	1811–22	Became Governor of Cold Bath Fields House of Correction 1822

*It must also be noted that as the starting date of the Appendix is 1792, those men whose starting dates are given as that year may have served as Principal Officers for several years prior to this date.

Glossary

Dismounted Horse Patrol – This non-uniformed force was also known as the Day Patrol, as it was created in 1822 to patrol in daylight around the area between the jurisdiction of the Foot Patrol (Westminster) and the Horse Patrol (the outer environs of the metropolis). This force (by 1828 consisting of 89 Patrol Constables, 8 Sub-inspectors and 4 Inspectors, divided into 4 divisions) was transferred to the authority of the Metropolitan Police in 1829.

Foot Patrol – Also known as the Night Patrol, this non-uniformed force was firmly established by Sir Sampson Wright, Bow Street Magistrate, in 1790, and by 1828 consisted of 1 Inspector and 82 Patrol Constables split into 17 patrols, each led by a Patrol Conductor. It patrolled the four to five-mile diameter of the City of Westminster at night on regular 'beats'. Two members of this force remained on call at Bow Street Office to respond to crimes or disturbances reported by the public, and they could call upon Principal Officers (if available) for advice and assistance. This force was disbanded in 1829 with the coming of the Metropolitan Police.

Horse Patrol – This force was created in 1805 by Sir Richard Ford in order to patrol the major roads (all of which were turnpiked) leading into the metropolis. These patrols were the first uniformed police force in London, with scarlet waistcoats and blue trousers, and normally operated at a distance of between 10 and 15 miles from central London. The Horse Patrol, which in 1828 consisted of 2 Inspectors together with 54 Patrol men in 4 divisions, each with a

Deputy Inspector, was not disbanded following the creation of the Metropolitan Police in 1829, and continued to operate under Bow Street's jurisdiction until August 1836, when it was placed under the direct control of the Metropolitan Police. Members of the Horse Patrol were not responsible to the Principal Officers and seem to have had relatively little contact with them.

Principal Officer – The most senior rank of police officer employed at Bow Street Police Office or the other London Police Offices. They were sworn in as constables of Westminster, and for much of the period under discussion also had constabulary powers in the four counties surrounding the metropolis and a radius of ten miles around royal residences. Principal Officers were never uniformed and did not at any time patrol the streets of London, spending a large proportion of their employment involved on investigations in the provinces. Such officers usually served as Patrol Constables and Patrol Conductors for a considerable length of time at either Bow Street or the other London Police Offices, learning their trade before being promoted to the rank of Principal Officer. The position of Principal Officer was the highest executive rank (i.e. with regard to constabulary powers) achievable at the Police Offices – the next promotion (only apparently once achieved) was to the position of Magistrate. Throughout the period under discussion there were never more than eleven Principal Officers employed at Bow Street at one time. It is difficult to provide a direct comparison of their status with the structure of present-day police forces, as their roles were significantly different, but it probably roughly equates to that of a Chief Inspector.

Patrol Conductor – The rank below that of Principal Officer. Patrol Conductors were responsible for the immediate supervision of Patrol Constables and were directly responsible to the Magistrates of the Police Offices – they were not responsible to Principal Officers. Patrol Conductors had the same constabulary powers as those of Principal Officers, but rarely operated outside the immediate environs of the metropolis.

Patrol Constable – The most junior rank of executive Bow Street employees, constables were directly responsible to Patrol Conductors and performed the more mundane duties such as patrolling the streets and dealing with everyday petty offences. They had the same constabulary powers as Principal Officers, but their activities were again largely confined to the inner metropolis.

Police (or Public) Office – An office in London consisting of a Chief Magistrate and two other magistrates (all stipendiary magistrates), three clerks and other officials, including the Principal Officers, Patrol Conductors and Patrol Constables. The office was responsible for the policing of a specific district within the metropolis. Bow Street was the original Police Office, being created in 1748, and was followed in 1792 by seven other Police Offices – see Chapter 2, note 18 for names and locations. Such offices were also occasionally referred to as Police Offices – the term is interchangeable.

Runner – Originally a general term for any employee of an institution engaged on messenger duty, the term was subsequently applied somewhat indiscriminately to various employees at Bow Street from *c.*1755. The term seems to have become synonymous with the Principal Officers by the late eighteenth century, but as it implied a lowly status, was never used by any of the various executive personnel based at Bow Street, who invariably referred to themselves as Principal or Senior Officers or, more commonly, simply Officers.

Tipstaff – The only badge of office carried by the Principal Officers, the tipstaff was a small metal or wooden tube, often hollow and capped with a crown, which sometimes unscrewed to allow storage of a magistrate's warrant. This implement is believed to be the source for the expression 'to crown someone', as it is apocryphally stated that the Principal Officer would arrest a suspect by tapping them on the shoulder with the tipstaff. Several such tipstaffs are kept at the Metropolitan Police Museum.

Bibliography

Primary sources

TNA documents

ASSI 2/29	Crown and Gaol books, Staffordshire Lent Assizes 1813
ASSI 5 133/16	Indictments Staffordshire Lent Assizes 1813
ASSI 10	Miscellaneous documents Oxford Circuit 1732–1890
HO 27/9	Criminal Registers Series II 1813
HO 41	Home Office: Disturbances Entry Books 1815–1916
HO 42	Home Office: Domestic Correspondence, George III 1782–1820
HO 43	Home Office: Domestic Entry Books 1782–1898
HO 44	Home Office: Domestic Correspondence 1773–1861
HO 52	Home Office: Counties Correspondence 1820–50
HO 58	Home Office: Police Accounts 1813–26
HO 59	Home Office: Police Courts and Magistrates In-letters and Returns 1820–59
HO 60	Home Office: Police Court Entry books 1821–65
HO 61/1	Home Office: Metropolitan Police Correspondence 1820–29
HO 62	Home Office: Daily Reports from Metropolitan Police Offices 1828–39
HO 64	Home Office: Criminal (Rewards and Pardons) Correspondence and Secret Service Reports 1820–40
HO 65	Home Office: Police Entry Books Series I 1795–1921
HO 73	Home Office: Various Commissions: Records and Correspondence 1786–1949
HO 75	Hue & Cry and Police Gazette 1828–45
HO 130	Miscellaneous Criminal books 1798–1831

MEPO 1/2–33   Office of the Commissioner, Letter Books 1829–39
MEPO 1/49   Police Letter Book from Bow Street Public Office to Home
               Office 1830–38
MEPO 1/50   Police Letter Book from Home Office to Bow Street Public
               Office 1830–39
MEPO 2/25   Bow Street Horse Patrol (Mounted) Register 1827–45
MEPO 4/508   Bow Street Foot Patrol Register 1821–29
PC 1/40/129   Privy Council: Domestic, Military, Trade and Legal Papers:
               Public Office, Bow Street [London]: three accounts, 1797
PRO 30/45   Joseph Hatton: Collection of Home Office Criminal Papers
               1779–1854
PROB 11   Prerogative Court of Canterbury and Related Probate
               Jurisdictions: Will Registers 1384–1858
T 38/671   Treasury: Departmental Accounts, Public Office, Bow Street
               1756–59
T 38/672   Treasury: Departmental Accounts, Public Office, Bow Street
               1800–07
T 38/673   Treasury: Departmental Accounts, Public Office, Bow Street
               1793–1816
T 38/674   Treasury: Departmental Accounts, Public Office, Bow Street
               1816–35
T 54/52   Treasury: Entry book of Warrants etc. 1811–14

Parliamentary Papers

Reports from Committees of the House of Commons vol. XIII Finance Reports XXIII to XXXVI 1803, containing *Twenty-eighth Report from the Select Committee on Finance: Police, including Convict Establishments 1798.*

Crime and Punishment Police vol. I (IUP Reprints Series):
Report from the Select Committee on the Nightly Watch of the Metropolis, PP 1812 (127) vol. II
Report from the Committee on the State of Police of the Metropolis, PP 1816 (510) vol. V
Extracts from the Evidence of Reverend Thomas Thirlwall, PP 1817 (231) vol. XVII

Crime and Punishment Police vol. II (IUP Reprints Series):
1st Report from the Committee on the state of Police of the Metropolis, PP 1817 (233) vol. VII
2nd Report from the Committee on the state of Police of the Metropolis, PP 1817 (484) vol. VII

Crime and Punishment Police vol. III (IUP Reprints Series):
3rd Report from the Committee on the State of Police of the Metropolis, PP 1818 (423) vol. VIII

Report from the Committee on the State of Police of the Metropolis, PP 1822 (440) vol. IV

Crime and Punishment Police vol. IV (IUP Reprints Series):
Report from the Select Committee on the Police of the Metropolis, PP 1828 (533) vol. VI

Crime and Punishment Police vol. V (IUP Reprints Series):
Report from the Select Committee on the Police of the Metropolis, PP 1833 (675) vol. XIII
Petition of Frederick Young and William Popay, PP 1833 (627) vol. XIII
Conduct of the Police on 13th May 1833 at Coldbath Fields, PP 1833 (718) vol. XIII

Crime and Punishment Police vol. VI (IUP Reprints Series):
Report from the Committee on the state of Police of the Metropolis, PP 1834 (600) vol. XVI

Crime and Punishment Police vol. VII (IUP Reprints Series):
Metropolis Police Offices, PP 1837 (451) vol. XII
Metropolis Police Offices, PP 1837–38 (578) vol. XV

Crime and Punishment Police vol. VIII (IUP Reprints Series):
First Report on the Constabulary Force in England and Wales, PP 1839 (169) vol. XIX

Crime and Punishment Prisons vol. XI (IUP Reprints Series):
Report relating to the Petitions of Messrs Lovett and Collins (Warwick Gaol), PP 1839 (462) vol. XXXVIII

Report from the Select Committee on the Laws relating to Game, PP 1823 (107) IV 260

Bank of England Archives

Court Minute Books Index 1780–1899
Freshfields' Papers:
F2   Forged and Other Imitation Bank Notes 1812–1905
F24   Bank Dollars and Tokens 1804–16
F25   Prison Correspondence 1781–1844

Printed material and manuscripts

Allen, Lucas Benjamin, *Brief Considerations on the Present State of the police of the Metropolis: with a few suggestions towards its improvement* (London: Joseph Butterworth, 1821).

Annals of Sporting, vol. 11 (January–June 1827) (London: Sherwood & Co., 1827).

Anon., *Bow Street Foot Patrole 1821–1829* (London: Metropolitan Police Museum, undated).

Anon., *Richmond – Scenes from the life of a Bow Street Runner*, introduction by E. F. Bleiler (New York: Dover Publications, 1976 [reprint of 1827 original]).

Anon., *The Annual Register or a View of History, Politics and Literature*, vol. 34 (1792)–vol. 81 (1839) inclusive (London: Craddock & Joy, Dodsley and others, 1793–1840).

Anon., *The Bow Street Opera in three Acts: written on the plan of The Beggars Opera* (London: T. Mariner and others, 1773).

Anon., *The trial of Edward Gibbon Wakefield, William Wakefield and Frances Wakefield, indicted with one Edward Thevenot, a servant, for a conspiracy and for the abduction of Miss Ellen Turner* (London: John Murray, 1827).

Anon., *The trial of Edward Gibbon Wakefield*, 2nd edn (London: Edward Duncombe, 1827).

Anon., *The Trial of the Reverend Robert Bingham, Curate of Maresfield, Tuesday March 26th 1811* (Lewes: Sussex Press, 1811).

Anon., *The Trial of the Reverend Robert Bingham, taken in shorthand by Mr Adams, by order of the Directors of The Union Fire Office, London* (London: J. M. Richardson, 1811).

Anon., *The Trial of William Howe, alias John Wood, for the Wilful Murder of Mr. Benjamin Robins of Dunsley, near Stourbridge on the 18th of December 1813* [*sic*] (Stourbridge: J. Heming, 1813).

Anon., *Une Nouvelle Manière d'attrapper une Femme, or A Bold Stroke for a Wife, exemplified in Mr. Wakefield's 'New Art of Love'* (London: Anon., 1827).

Anon. (Canon John Brown), *Another Estimate of the Manners and Principles of the Present Times* (London: G. Kearsly, 1769).

Anon. (Sir John Fielding?), *Forgery Unmasked, or, Genuine Memoirs of the two unfortunate brothers, Robert and Daniel Perreau, and Mrs Rudd* (London: A. Grant, 1775).

Anon. (Samuel Hercules Taunton), 'A Reminiscence of a Bow Street Officer', *Harpers New Monthly Magazine*, vol. 5, no. 28 (September 1852), pp. 483–94.

Angelo, Henry, *Reminiscences of Henry Angelo*, 2 vols (London: Henry Colburn and Richard Bentley, 1830).

Aston, Joseph, *A Picture of Manchester* (Manchester: J. Aston, 1816).

Bamford, Samuel, *Passages in the Life of a Radical* (Oxford: OUP, 1964).

Blizard, Sir William, *Desultory Reflections on Police, with an essay on the means of preventing crimes and amending criminals* (London: Anon., 1785).

Burns, Richard, *Justice of the Peace and Parish Officer*, 23rd edn, ed. George Chetwynd, 5 vols (London: Longman and others, 1820).

Chadwick, E., 'Preventive Police', *London Review*, vol. 1 (1829), pp. 252–308.

Christian, Garth (ed.), *A Victorian Poacher: James Hawker's Journal* (Oxford: OUP, 1978).

Colquhoun, Patrick, *A Treatise on the Police of the Metropolis*, 6th edition (London: Joseph Mawman, 1800).

Cottu, M., *On the Administration of Criminal Justice in England; and the Spirit of the English Government*, trans. Anon. (London: R. Stevens and C. Reader, 1822).

Dickens, Charles, *Household Words*, no. 18 (Saturday, 27 July 1850).

Egan, Pierce, *Every Gentleman's Manual: A Lecture on the Art of Self-Defence, and A Review of the Prize-Ring for the last Century and upwards* (London: Sherwood & Bowyer, 1845).

Fielding, Henry, *An enquiry into the causes of the late increase of robbers and related writings*, ed. Malvin R. Zirker (Oxford: Clarendon Press, 1988).

Fielding, Henry, *A journey from this world to the next and The journey of a voyage to Lisbon*, eds Ian A. Bell and Andrew Varney (Oxford: OUP, 1997).

Fielding, John, *A plan for preventing robberies within twenty miles of London, with an account of the rise and establishment of the real THIEFTAKERS* (London: A. Millar, 1755).

Fielding, Sir J. Jr and others, *The New London Spy; or a modern twenty-four hour ramble through the Great British Metropolis* (London: Alex Hogg, 1816).

Gilpin, Charles, *A Plea for the Gibbet by the editor of the Scottish Congregational Magazine, with a reply by a member of the Society formed to promote the Abolition of Capital Punishment* (London: Charles Gilpin, 1848).

Glasse, Samuel, *The Magistrates Assistant: or a summary of those laws which immediately respect the conduct of the Justice of the Peace, by a County Magistrate* (Gloucester: R. Raikes, 1784).

Goddard, Henry, *Memoirs* (4-vol. manuscript dated 1875–79).

Haly, W. T., *The Opinions of Sir Robert Peel expressed in Parliament and in Public* (London: Whittaker & Co, 1843).

Hibbert, Christopher (ed.), *Captain Gronow: His Reminiscences of Regency and Victorian Life 1810–60* (London: Kyle Cathie Ltd, 1991).

Holdsworth, W. A., *The Handy Book of Parish Law* (Devises: Wiltshire Family History Society reprint, 1995 [original published 1859]).

Howe, William, *The Whole Four Trials of the Thief Takers and their Confederates* (London: William Howe, 1816).

Howell, T. J., *Howell's State Trials*, vol. XXIV (1794) (London: Longman, 1818).

Hunt, Joseph (ed.), 'Bombelles in Britain: the Diary Kept by a French Diplomat During a Visit to Midlands England 1784', trans. L. E. Page (Birmingham: unpublished, 2000).

James, G. P. R., *Delaware; or the Ruined Family*, 3 vols (Edinburgh: G. P. R. James, 1833).

Journal of the House of Commons, vol. 32, reprinted 1803 (10 May 1768–25 September 1770), 'Report of the Committee of Inquiry concerning Burglary and Robbery dated 10 April 1770', pp. 878–81.

Mainwaring, G. B., *Observations on the Present State of the Police of the Metropolis* (London: John Murray, 1821).

Mendoza, Daniel, *The Art of Boxing* (London: Anon., 1789).

Mendoza, Daniel, *The Memoirs of the Life of Daniel Mendoza*, ed. Paul Magriel (London: Batsford, 1951 [reprint of 1816 original]).

Monthly Review or Literary Journal, vol. LXXXI (September–December 1816) (London: J. Porter, 1816).

Parliamentary Debates XXIX (London: Hansard, 1792).

Parliamentary Debates 22 (17 March 1812–4 May 1813) (London: Hansard, 1813).

Parker, Charles Stuart (ed.), *Sir Robert Peel: from his private correspondence*, 3 vols (London: John Murray, 1891).

Parker, Thomas Netherton, *Justice's Book of Thomas Netherton Parker, 1805–1813* (Shropshire Archives 1060/168).

Pickering, Danby, *The Statutes at Large from the 23rd to the 26th year of King George II* (London and Cambridge: Joseph Bentham, 1765).

Place, Francis, *The Autobiography of Francis Place*, ed. Mary Thale (London: CUP, 1972).

Potter MacQueen, T., *The State of the Nation, at the Close of 1830* (London: James Ridgway, 1831).

Prince, J. H., *A letter to James Read, Principal Magistrate at the Public Office, Bow Street* (London: J. H. Prince, 1808).

Pryme, George, *Autobiographical Recollections*, ed. Alicia Payne (Cambridge: Deighton Bell & Co., 1870).

Rattenbury, John, *Memoirs of a Smuggler* (London: Renshaw & Kirkman, 1839).

Register of Burials in the Parish of Enville in the County of Stafford 1813–1863 (Stafford Record Office).

Register of Felons in Stafford Gaol 1810–1816 (Stafford Record Office).

Richardson, Rev. J., *Recollections: Political, Literary, Dramatic, and Miscellaneous of the last half-century*, 2 vols (London: C. Mitchell, undated, *c*.1860).

Ritson, Joseph, *In the Office of Constable* (London: Whieldon & Butterworth, 1791).

Roberts, Charles, *Abstract of accounts laid before the Stourbridge Association for the Prosecution of Felons at their meeting held on 29 November 1814* (no details).

Sayer, Edward, *Observations on the Police or Civil Government of Westminster with a proposal for reform* (London: Debrett, 1784).

Southey, Robert, *Southey's Common Place Book (Fourth Series): Original Memoranda etc.* (London: Longman, Brown, Green & Longman, 1851).

Stafford Gaol Quarter Sessions Calendar of Prisoners 1800–1813 (Stafford: Stafford Record Office).

Tayler, William, *Diary of William Tayler, Footman 1837*, ed. Dorothy Wise (London: Westminster City Archives, 1998).

Thornhill, Robert (ed.), *A Village Constable's Accounts (1791–1839)* (Derby: Derbyshire Archaeological and Natural History Society, 1957).

Wade, John, *A treatise on the police and crimes of the Metropolis*, intro. J. J. Tobias (Montclair, NJ: Patterson Smith, 1972 [original published 1829]).

Wade, John, *The Black book or Corruption Unmasked* (London: John Fairburn, 1820).

Westminster Review, vol. XI (July 1829).

Westminster Review, vol. XII (October 1829).

Newspapers (apart from those consulted online)

Bedford, Buckingham and Hertford Gazette, all issues January 1809–March 1809.

British Freeholder and Saturday Evening Journal, all available issues February 1820–December 1820.

Hue & Cry and Police Gazette, all available issues, 1773–1839.

Manchester Guardian, May 1821–September 1839.

Staffordshire Advertiser, January 1795–September 1839.

The Times, January 1792–September 1839.

Wolverhampton Chronicle, December 1812–April 1813.

Online sources

British Library Nineteenth-Century Newspapers Online at: http://www.bl.uk/reshelp/findhelprestype/news/newspdigproj/database/index.html.

Old Bailey Proceedings Online 1674–1913 at: http://www.oldbaileyonline.org.

Secondary sources

Books

Adam, Hargrave L., *The Police Encyclopaedia*, 8 vols (London: Waverley, undated).

Addison, Sir William, *The Old Roads of England* (London: Batsford, 1980).

Andrew, Donna T. and Randall McGowen, *The Perreaus and Mrs. Rudd: Forgery and Betrayal in Eighteenth-Century London* (Berkeley, CA: University of California Press, 2001).

Archer, John E., *By a Flash and a Scare: Incendiarism, Animal Maiming and Poaching in East Anglia 1815–70* (Oxford: Clarendon Press, 1990).

Armitage, Gilbert, *The History of the Bow Street Runners 1729–1829* (London: Wishart & Co., 1932).

Ascoli, David, *The Queen's Peace: The Origins and Development of the Metropolitan Police 1829–1979* (London: Hamish Hamilton, 1979).

Ashby, Abby and Audrey Jones, *The Shrigley Abduction: A Tale of Anguish, Deceit and Violation of the Domestic Hearth* (Stroud: Sutton, 2003).

Axon, William E. A. (ed.), *Annals of Manchester* (Manchester: John Heywood, 1886).

Aylward, James De Vine, *The House of Angelo: A Dynasty of Swordsmen* (London: Batchworth Press, 1953).

Babington, Anthony, *Military Intervention in Britain: From the Gordon Riots to the Gibraltar Incident* (London: Routledge, 1990).

Babington, Anthony, *A House in Bow Street: Crime and the Magistracy, London 1740–1881*, 2nd edn (London: Macdonald, 1999).

Barker, Hannah, *Newspapers, Politics and Public Opinion in Late Eighteenth-Century England* (Oxford: Clarendon Press, 1998).

Barker, Hannah, *Newspapers, Politics and English Society 1695–1855* (Harlow: Pearson Educational, 2000).

Barnsby, George J., *The Working Class Movement in the Black Country 1750 to 1867* (Wolverhampton: Integrated Publishing Services, 1977).

Barrett, A. and C. Harrison, *Crime and Punishment in England* (London: UCL Press, 1999).

Barrie, David G., *Police in the Age of Improvement: Police Development and the Civic Tradition in Scotland, 1775–1865* (Cullompton: Willan, 2008).

Bates, Allen, *Directory of Stage Coach Services 1836* (Newton Abbot: David & Charles, 1969).

Battestin, Michael and Ruthe Battestin, *Henry Fielding – A Life* (London: Routledge, 1989).

Bayley, David, *Patterns of Policing: A Comparative International Analysis* (New Brunswick, NJ: Rutgers University Press, 1985).

Beattie, J. M., *Crime and the Courts in England 1660–1800* (Oxford: OUP, 1986).

Beattie, J. M., *Policing and Punishment in London 1660–1750: Urban Crime and the Limits of Terror* (Oxford: OUP, 2001).

Begg, Paul and Keith Skinner, *The Scotland Yard Files: 150 years of the CID* (London: Headline, 1992).

Bell, Ian A., *Literature and Crime in Augustan England* (London: Routledge, 1991).

Bentham, Jeremy, *The Rationale of Punishment* (London: Robert Heward, 1830).

Bentley, David, *English Criminal Justice in the Nineteenth Century* (London: Hambledon Press, 1998).

Berlière, Jean-Marc, *Le Monde des Polices en France XIXe–XXe siècles* (Paris: Éditions Complexe, 1996).

Birkett, Lord, *The New Newgate Calendar* (London: Folio Society, 1960).

Black, Jeremy, *The English Press 1621–1861* (Stroud: Sutton, 2001).

Bondeson, Jan, *The London Monster: Terror on the Streets in 1790* (Stroud: Tempus, 2000).

Borowitz, Albert, The Thurtell-Hunt Murder Case: Dark Mirror to Regency England (Baton Rouge, LA: Louisiana State University Press, 1987).

Bowden, Tom, Beyond the Limits of the Law: A Comparative Study of the Police in Crisis Politics (Harmondsworth: Penguin, 1978).

Boyce, George and others (eds), *Newspaper History from the Seventeenth Century to the Present Day* (London: Constable, 1978).

Brailsford, Denis, *Bareknuckles: A Social History of Prizefighting* (Cambridge: Lutterworth Press, 1998).

Brake, Laurel, Bill Bell and David Finkelstein (eds), *Nineteenth-Century Media and the Construction of Ideas* (Basingstoke: Palgrave, 2000).

Brett, Dennis T., *The Police of England and Wales: A Bibliography*, 3rd edn (Bramshill: Police Staff College, 1979).

Brett, Edward M., *The British Auxiliary Legion in the First Carlist War, 1835–8* (Dublin: Four Courts Press, 2005).

Bridgeman, Ian and Clive Emsley, *A Guide to the Archives of the Police Forces of England and Wales*, Police History Society Monograph No. 2 (1989).

Briggs, Asa, *The Age of Improvement* (London: Longmans, Green & Co, 1959).

Brogden, M., *The Police: Autonomy and Consent* (London: Academic Press, 1982).

Brooke, Alan and David Brandon, *Tyburn: London's Fatal Tree* (Thrupp: Sutton, 2004).

Browne, Douglas G., *The Rise of Scotland Yard – A History of the Metropolitan Police* (London: Harrap, 1956).

Brumwell, Stephen and W. A. Speck, *Cassell's Companion to Eighteenth-Century Britain* (London: Cassell, 2001).

Buchanan, Charles, *Bow Street Runners* (Saffron Walden: Young Anglia Press, 1992).

Butler, Frank, *A History of Boxing in Britain: A Survey of the Noble Art from Its Origins to the Present Day* (London: Arthur Barker, 1972).

Calhoun, Frederick S., *The Lawmen: United States Marshals and their Deputies, 1789–1989* (Harmondsworth: Penguin, 1991).

Cameron, Alan, *Bank of Scotland 1695–1995: A Very Singular Institution* (Edinburgh: Mainstream Publishing, 1995).

Campbell, Frances E., *Stewponey Countryside* (Stourbridge: Mark & Moody, 1979).

Carter, Michael J., *Peasants and Poachers: A Study in Rural Disorder in Norfolk* (Woodbridge: Boydell Press, 1980).

Charlesworth, A. (ed.), *An Atlas of Rural Protest in Britain 1548–1900* (London: Croom Helm, 1983).

Clark, Erland Fenn, *Truncheons: Their Romance and Reality* (London: Herbert Jenkins, 1935).

Clarkson, C. T. and J. Hall Richardson, *Police!* (London: Field & Tuer, 1889).

Clarkson, C.T. and J. Hall Richardson, *The Rogues Gallery* (London: Field & Tuer, 1890).

Coatman, John, *Police* (London: OUP, 1959).

Cobb, Belton, *The First Detectives and the Early Career of Richard Mayne* (London: Faber & Faber, 1957).

Cobbett, J. M. and J. P. Cobbett, *Selection from Cobbett's Political Works*, 6 vols (London: Ann Cobbett, 1835).

Cochrane, Don, *Black Country Criminal Ancestors 1787–1868* (Halesowen: M. J. Cochrane, 2003).

Cockburn, J. S. (ed.), *Crime in England 1550–1800* (London: Methuen, 1977).

Cockerell, H. A. L. and Edwin Green, *The British Insurance Business 1547–1970* (London: Heinemann Educational, 1976).

Cockin, Tim, *The Staffordshire Encyclopaedia* (Stoke-on-Trent: Malthouse Press, 2000).

Cohen, Stanley and Andrew Scull (eds), *Social Control and the State: Historical and Comparative Essays* (Oxford: OUP, 1983).

Cole, Hubert, *Things for the Surgeon: A History of the Resurrection Men* (London: Heinemann, 1964).

Colledge, J. J., Ships of the Royal Navy: An Historical Index: Volume I Major Ships (Newton Abbot: David & Charles, 1969).

Connolly, S. J. (ed.), *Kingdoms United?* (Dublin: Four Courts Press, 1998).

Cooper, David D., *The Lesson of the Scaffold* (London: Allen Lane, 1974).

Cornish, W. R. and others, *Crime and Law in Nineteenth-Century Britain: Commentaries on BPPs* (Dublin: IUP, 1978).

Cox, David J., *The Dunsley Murder of 1812: A Study in Early Nineteenth-Century Crime Detection, Justice and Punishment* (Kingswinford: Dulston Press, 2003).

Cox, David J., *Foul Deeds and Suspicious Deaths in Shrewsbury and Around Shropshire* (Barnsley: Wharncliffe, 2008).

Cox, David J. and Barry Godfrey (eds), *Cinderellas and Packhorses: A History of the Shropshire Magistracy* (Logaston: Logaston Press, 2005).

Cox, David J. and Michael Pearson, *Foul Deeds and Suspicious Deaths Around the Black Country* (Barnsley: Wharncliffe, 2006).

Critchley, T. A., *A History of Police in England and Wales* (London: Constable, 1978).

Currie, C. R. J. and C. P. Lewis, *A Guide to English County Histories* (Stroud: Sutton, 1997).

Dagall, H., *Creating a Good Impression: 300 Years of the Stamp Office and Stamp Duties* (London: Stamp Office, 1994).

Darvall, Frank Ogley, *Popular Disturbances and Public Order in Regency England* (London: OUP, 1969).

Derry, John W., *Politics in the Age of Fox, Pitt and Liverpool* (Basingstoke: Palgrave, 2001).

Dilnot, George, *The Story of Scotland Yard: Its History and Associations* (London: Geoffrey Bles, 1926).

Dilnot, George, *Triumphs of Detection* (London: Geoffrey Bles, 1929).

Donajgrodski, A. P. (ed.), *Social Control in the Nineteenth Century* (London: Croom Helm, 1977).

Drabble, Margaret (ed.), *The Oxford Companion to English Literature*, 6th edn (Oxford: OUP, 2000).

Drake, Michael and Ruth Finnegan, *Studying Family and Community History 19th and 20th Centuries: vol. 4 Sources and Methods: A Hand Book*, 2nd edn (Cambridge: CUP in association with OU, 1997).

Dudden, F. Holmes, *Henry Fielding, His Life, Works, and Times*, 2 vols (Oxford: Clarendon Press, 1952).

Duff, P. and N. Hutton (eds), *Criminal Justice in Scotland* (Aldershot: Ashgate, 1999).

Duman, D., *The Judicial Bench in England 1727–1875: The Reshaping of a Professional Elite* (London: Royal Historical Society, 1982).

Dunbabin, J. P. D., *Rural Discontent in Nineteenth-century Britain* (London: Faber & Faber, 1974).

Dunkley, Peter, *The Crisis of the Old Poor Law in England 1795–1834: An Interpretive Essay* (New York: Garland, 1982).

Durston, Christopher, *Cromwell's Major-Generals: Godly Government during the English Revolution* (Manchester: Manchester University Press, 2001).

Eastwood, David, *Governing Rural England: Tradition and Transformation in Local Government 1780–1840* (Oxford: Clarendon, 1994).

Eastwood, David, *Government and Community in the English Provinces 1700–1870* (Basingstoke: Macmillan, 1997).

Elrington, C. R. (ed.), *Victoria County History of Staffordshire*, vol. VI (London: University of London Institute of Historical Research, 1979).

Emsley, Clive, *Policing and its Context 1750–1870* (London: Macmillan, 1983).

Emsley, Clive, *The English Police: A Political and Social History*, 2nd edn (London: Longman, 1996).

Emsley, Clive, *Gendarmes and the State in Nineteenth-Century Europe* (Oxford: OUP, 1999).

Emsley, Clive, *Crime and Society in England 1750–1900*, 3rd edn (London: Longman, 2004).

Emsley, Clive, *Hard Men: The English and Violence Since 1750* (London: Hambledon & London, 2005).

Emsley, Clive, *Crime, Police, and Penal Policy: European Experiences 1750–1940* (Oxford: OUP, 2007).

Emsley, Clive, *The Great British Bobby: A History of British Policing from 1829 to the Present* (London: Quercus, 2009).

Emsley, Clive and Haia Shpayer-Makov (eds), *Police Detectives in History, 1750–1950* (Aldershot: Ashgate, 2005).

Emsley, Clive and James Wallin (eds), *Artisans, Peasants and Proletarians 1760–1860* (London: Croom Helm, 1985).

Evans, Christopher, *The Labyrinth of Flames: Work and Social Conflict in Early Industrial Merthyr Tydfil* (Cardiff: Paul & Co., 1993).

Evans, E. J., *The Great Reform Act of 1832* (London: Routledge, 1992).

Farringdon, Karen, *A History of Punishment and Torture* (London: Chancellor Press, 1999).

Fido, Martin and Keith Skinner, *The Official Encyclopedia of Scotland Yard* (London: Virgin, 1999).

Fijnaut, Cyrille and Gary T. Marx, *The Normalisation of Undercover Policing in the West: Historical and Contemporary Perspectives* (The Hague: Kluwer, 1995).

Fitzgerald, Mike and others, *Intervention, Regulation and Surveillance* (Milton Keynes: Open University Press, 1981).

Fitzgerald, P., *Chronicle of Bow Street Police Office: With an Account of the Magistrates, 'Runners' and Police*, 2 vols (London: Chapman & Hall, 1888 [reprinted as a one volume book with an introduction by Anthony Babington and index: Montclair, NJ: Patterson Smith, 1972]).

Fleischer, Nat and Sam Andre, *A Pictorial History of Boxing* (London: Hamlyn, 1979).

Foley, P. H. (ed.), *Report of the Trial of William Howe at Stafford Lent Assizes 1813* (no publication details).

Ford, John, *Prizefighting: The Age of Regency Boximania* (Newton Abbott: David & Charles, 1971).

Forrester, Andrew, *The Revelations of a Private Detective* (London: Ward & Lock, 1863).

Foss, Edward, *Biographia Juridica: A Biographical Dictionary of the Judges of England 1066–870* (London: John Murray, 1870).

Foster, David and Adrianne Dill Linton, *The Rural Constabulary Act 1839: National Legislation and the Problems of Enforcement (National Statutes and the Local Community)* (London: Bedford Square Press, 1982).

Foucault, Michel, *Discipline and Punish: the Birth of the Prison*, trans. Alan Sheridan (London: Penguin, 1991).

Fritz, Paul and David Williams, *The Triumph of Culture: 18th Century Perspectives* (Toronto: A. M. Hakkert, 1972).

Fryde, E. B. and others (eds), *Hand Book of British Chronology*, 3rd ed (London: Royal Historical Society, 1986).

Gardiner, Juliet and Neil Wenborn, (eds), *The History Today Companion to British History* (London: Collins & Brown, 1995).

Garland, David, *Punishment and Modern Society: A Study in Social Theory* (Oxford: OUP, 1997).

Gascoigne, Bamber, *Encyclopedia of Britain* (Basingstoke: Macmillan, 1993).

Gaskill, Malcolm, *Crime and Mentalities in Early Modern England* (Cambridge: CUP, 2000).

Gatrell, V. A. C. and others, *Crime and the Law: A Social History of Crime in Western Europe since 1500* (London: Europa, 1980).

Gatrell, V. A. C., *The Hanging Tree: Execution and the English People 1770–1868* (Oxford: OUP Paperbacks, 1996).

Gee, Tony, *Up to Scratch: Bareknuckle Fighting and Heroes of the Prize-ring* (Harpenden: Queen Anne's Press, 1998).

Gillet, Henry, *Guide to the Archives of the Bank of England*, 2nd edn (London: Bank of England, 2001).

Glover, E. H., *The English Police: Its Origins and Development* (London: Police Chronicle, 1934).

Goddard, Henry, *Memoirs of a Bow Street Runner*, intro. and ed., Patrick Pringle (London: Museum Press, 1956).

Godfrey, B. and others (eds), *Comparative Histories of Crime* (Cullompton: Willan, 2003).

Godfrey, Barry and Paul Lawrence (eds), *Crime and Justice 1750–1950* (Cullompton: Willan, 2005).

Gough, Adi, *Pros and Cons: A History of Pre-policing and Early Policing Based on the Alford District of Lincolnshire*, 3 vols (Mablethorpe: SBK Books, 1996–98).

Grant, Douglas, *The Thin Blue Line* (London: John Long, 1973).

Green, Thomas Andrew, *Verdict According to Conscience: Perspectives of the English Criminal Trial Jury 1200–1800* (Chicago: University of Chicago Press, 1985).

Greenslade, M., *Victoria County History of Staffordshire*, vol. XX (London: University of London Institute of Historical Research, 1984).

Greenwood, Colin, *Firearms Control: A Study of Armed Crime and Firearms Control in England and Wales* (London: Routledge & Kegan Paul, 1972).

Gregory, Jeremy and John Stevenson, *The Longman Companion to Britain in the Eighteenth Century* (London: Longman, 2000).

Griffith, George, *Reminiscences and Records of the Midlands Counties during Ten Years Residence from 1869–1880* (Bewdley: George Griffith, 1880).

Griffiths, Arthur, *The Chronicles of Newgate* (London: Bracken Books, 1987 [facsimile reprint of 1883 original]).

Gurr, Ted Robert and others, *The Politics of Crime and Conflict: A Comparative History of Four Cities* (Beverley Hills, CA: Sage, 1977).

Guy, Kenneth (ed.), *New Letters of Robert Southey Vol. 2 1811–38* (New York and London: Columbia University Press, 1965).

Haden, H. Jack, *Street Names of Stourbridge and Its Vicinity*, vol. 1 (Kingswinford: Dulston Press, 1988).

Haden, H. Jack, *Street Names of Stourbridge and Its Vicinity*, vol. 2 (Kingswinford: Dulston Press, 1999).

Haining, Peter, *The English Highwayman: A Legend Unmasked* (London: Robert Hale, 1991).

Hall, Stuart and Gregor McClennan, *Custom and Law: Law and Crime as Historical Processes* (Milton Keynes: Open University Press, 1981).

Hammond, J. L. and Barbara Hammond, *The Village Labourer 1760–1832: A Study in the Government of England before the Reform Bill*, 4th edn, 2 vols (London: Guild Books, 1948).

Hammond, J. L. and Barbara Hammond, *The Town Labourer 1760–1832: The New Civilisation*, 2nd edn, 2 vols (London: Guild Books, 1949).

Hammond, J. L. and Barbara Hammond, *The Skilled Labourer 1760–1832*, revised edn (London: Longman, 1979).

Harper, Charles G., *Smugglers – Picturesque Chapters in the Story of an Ancient Craft* (Newcastle: Frank Cass, 1966).

Hart, Gwen, *A History of Cheltenham* (Leicester: Leicester University Press, 1965).

Hawkings, David T., *Criminal Ancestors: A Guide to Historical Criminal Records in England and Wales* (Stroud: Sutton, 1996).

Hawkings, David T., *Fire Insurance Records for Family and Local Historians 1696 to 1920* (London: Francis Boutle, 2003).

Hay, D. and F. Snyder (eds), *Policing and Prosecution in Britain, 1750–1850* (Oxford: OUP, 1989).

Hay, Douglas and others, *Albion's Fatal Tree: Crime and Society in Eighteenth-Century England* (London: Allen Lane, 1975).

Hewitt, Eric J., *A History of Policing in Manchester* (Manchester: E. J. Morton, 1979).

Hill, Brian, *The Early Parties and Politics in Britain, 1688–1832* (Basingstoke: Macmillan, 1996).

Hippisley Coxe, Antony D., *A Book about Smuggling in the West Country 1700–1850* (Padstow: Tabb House, 1984).

Hitchcock, Tim, *Down and Out in Eighteenth-Century London* (London: Hambledon, 2004).

Hobsbawm, Eric and George Rudé, *Captain Swing*, 2nd edn (London: Phoenix Press, 2001).

Holdsworth, William, *The History of English Law*, 16 vols (London: Methuen, 1903–66).

Holmes, T. W., *The Story of the Admiralty-to-Portsmouth Shutter Telegraph and Semaphore Lines, 1796–1847* (Ilfracombe: Stockwell, 1983).

Hopkins, Harry, *The Long Affray: The Poaching Wars 1760–1914* (London: Secker & Warburg, 1985).

Hostettler, J., *The Politics of Criminal Law Reform in the Nineteenth Century* (Chichester: Barry Rose Law Publishers, 1992).

Howard, D. L., *The English Prisons: The Past and Their Future* (London: Methuen, 1960).

Howard, George, *Guardians of the Queen's Peace: The Development and Work of Britain's Police* (London: Odhams, 1953).

Howe, Ronald, *The Story of Scotland Yard: A History of the CID from the Earliest Times to the Present Day* (London: Arthur Barker, 1965).

Hoyle, William, *Crime in England and Wales: An Historical and Critical Retrospect* (London: Effingham, Wilson & Co., 1876).

Hutchinson, John R., *The Press-Gang Afloat and Ashore* (1914; reprinted Whitefish, MA: Kessinger, 2004).

Ingleton, Roy D., *Mission Incomprehensible: The Linguistic Barrier to Effective Police Co-operation in Europe* (Clevedon: Multilingual Matters, 1994).

Inwood, Stephen, *A History of London* (London: Macmillan, 1998).

Jackson, Ian, *The Provincial Press and the Community* (Manchester: Manchester University Press, 1971).

James, P. D. and T. Critchley, *The Maul and the Pear Tree: The Ratcliff Highway Murders 1811* (London: Faber & Faber, 2000).

Jenkins, David and Takau Yoneyama (eds), *The History of Insurance*, 8 vols (London: Pickering & Chatto, 2000).

Jenkins, Philip, *A History of Modern Wales 1536–1990* (London: Longman, 1992).

Johnson, W. H., *Previous Offences: Sussex Crimes and Punishments in the Past* (Seaford: S. B. Publications, 1997).

Johnston, Leo, *The Rebirth of Private Policing* (London: Routledge, 1992).

Jones, David J. V., *Before Rebecca: Popular Protests in Wales 1793–1835* (London: Allen Lane, 1973).

Jones, David J. V., *Crime, Protest, Community and Police in Nineteenth-Century Britain* (London: Routledge & Kegan Paul, 1982).

Jones, David J. V., *Rebecca's Children: A Study of Rural Society, Crime, and Protest* (Oxford: Clarendon Press, 1989).

Jones, David J. V., *Crime in Nineteenth-Century Wales* (Cardiff: University of Wales Press, 1992).

Jones, Trevor and Tim Newburn, *Private Security and Public Policing* (Oxford: Clarendon Press, 1998).

Kayman, Martin A., *From Bow Street to Baker Street: Mystery, Detection and Narrative* (Basingstoke: Macmillan, 1992).

Killinger, George G. and Paul F. Cromwell (eds), *Issues in Law Enforcement* (Boston: Holbrook Press, 1975).

King, Peter, *Crime, Justice, and Discretion in England 1740–1820* (Oxford: OUP, 2000).

Klockars, Carl B., *The Idea of Police* (Beverly Hills, CA: Sage, 1985).

Knapp, Andrew and William Baldwin, *The Newgate Calendar*, vol. IV (London: J. Robins & Co., 1828).

Landau, Norma (ed.), *Law, Crime and English Society 1660–1830* (Cambridge: CUP, 2002).

Larn, Richard and Bridget Larn, *Shipwreck Index of the British Isles*, vol. II (London: Lloyd's Register of Shipping, 1995).

Leslie-Melville, A. R., *The Life and Works of Sir John Fielding* (London: Lincoln & Williams, 1935).

Lethbridge, J., *Murder in the Midlands: Notable Trials of the Nineteenth Century* (London: Robert Hale, 1989).

Lewis, R., *Police in Staffordshire* (Stafford: Stafford County Council, 1974).

Lieck, A., *Bow Street World* (London: Robert Hale, 1938).

Linebaugh, Peter, *The London Hanged* (London: Allen Lane, 1991).

Linnane, Fergus, *London's Underworld: Three Centuries of Vice and Crime* (London: Robson Books, 2003).

Lock, Joan, *Marlborough Street: The Story of a London Court* (London: Robert Hale, 1980).

Lock, Joan, *Tales from Bow Street* (London: Hale, 1982).

Lock, Joan, *Dreadful Deeds and Awful Murders – Scotland Yard's First Detectives 1829–1878* (Taunton: Barn Owl Books, 1990).

Lockwood, Martyn, *'A Policeman's Lot': Policing in Victorian Essex*, History Note Book No. 39 (Chelmsford: Essex Police, 2001).

McCalman, Iain, *An Oxford Companion to the Romantic Age: British Culture 1776–1832* (Oxford: OUP, 2001).

McConville, Sean, *A History of English Prison Administration*, vol. 1 (London: Routledge & Kegan Paul, 1981).

MacDonald, Alan, *Champions by Acclaim* (Auckland: David Hines, 1994).

McDowell, W. H., *Historical Research, A Guide* (London: Longman, 2002).

McKenzie, Ian K. and G. Patrick Gallagher, *Behind the Uniform: Policing in Britain and America* (Hemel Hempstead: Harvester Wheatsheaf, 1989).

McLynn, Frank, *Crime and Punishment in Eighteenth-Century England* (London: Routledge, 1989).

McMahon, Richard (ed.), *Crime, Law and Popular Culture in Europe, 1500–1900* (Cullompton: Willan, 2008).

Maguire, M. and others (eds), *The Oxford Handbook of Criminology*, 2nd edn (Oxford: Clarendon Press, 1997).

Manchester, A. H., *Sources of English Legal History: Law, History and Society in England and Wales, 1750–1950* (London: Butterworth, 1984).

Mayhew, Henry and John Binny, *The Criminal Prisons of London and Scenes of Prison Life* (London: Frank Cass, 1971).

Melville Lee, W., *A History of Police in England* (London: Methuen, 1901).

Miles, Henry Downes, *Pugilistica*, 3 vols (Edinburgh: John Grant, 1906).

Mitchell, B. R. and H. G. Jones, *Second Abstract of British Historical Statistics* (Cambridge: CUP, 1971).

Mitchell, R. J. and M. D. R. Leys, *A History of London Life* (Harmondsworth: Penguin, 1963).

Morgan, Gwenda and Peter Rushton, *Rogues, Thieves and the Rule of Law: The Problem of Law Enforcement in North-East England, 1718–1800* (London: UCL Press, 1998).

Morson, Maurice, *A Force Remembered: The Illustrated History of the Norwich City Police 1836–1967* (Derby: Breedon Books, 2000).

Morton, James, *Bent Coppers: A Survey of Police Corruption* (London: Little, Brown, 1993).

Mosse, George (ed.), *Police Forces in History* (London: Sage, 1975).

Munsche, P. B., *Gentlemen and Poachers: The English Game Laws 1671–1831* (Cambridge: CUP, 1981).

Murphy, Brian, *A History of the British Economy 1740–1970* (London: Longman, 1973).

Neale, Kenneth (ed.), *Essex 'Full of Profitable Thinges': Essays Presented to Sir John Ruggles Brise* (Oxford: Leopard's Head Press, 1996).

Nelson, R. R., *The Home Office 1782–1801* (Durham, NC: Duke University Press, 1969).

Newburn, T. and P. Neyroud (eds), *Dictionary of Policing* (Cullompton: Willan, 2008).

Newman, Gerald (ed.), *Britain in the Hanoverian Age 1714–1837* (New York and London: Garland, 1997).

Onions, C. T. (ed.), *The Shorter Oxford English Dictionary on Historical Principles*, 2 vols (Oxford: OUP, 1973).

Osborne, Bertram, *Justices of the Peace 1361–1848: A History of the Justices of the Peace for the Counties of England* (Shaftesbury: Sedgehill Press, 1960).

Paley, Ruth (ed.), *Justice in Eighteenth-Century Hackney: The Justicing Note Book of Henry Norris and the Hackney Petty Sessions Book* (London: London Record Society, 1991).

Palk, Deirdre, *Gender, Crime and Judicial Discretion 1780–1830* (Woodbridge: Boydell/RHS, 2006).

Palmer, Stanley H., *Police and Protest in England and Ireland 1780–1850* (London: Longman, 1992).

Paulson, Ronald, *The Life of Henry Fielding: A Critical Biography* (Oxford: Blackwell, 2000).

Philips, David, *Crime and Authority in Victorian England: The Black Country, 1835–60* (London: Croom Helm, 1977).

Philips, David and Robert Storch, *Policing Provincial England 1829–1856: The Politics of Reform* (London: Leicester University Press, 1999).

Phillipson, David, *Smuggling: A History 1700–1970* (Newton Abbot: David & Charles, 1973).

Philp, Roy, *The Coast Blockade: The Royal Navy's War on Smuggling*, 2nd edn (Horsham: Compton Press, 2002).

Platt, Richard, *The Ordnance Survey Guide to Smugglers' Britain* (London: Cassell, 1991).

Porter, Roy (ed.), *Myths of the English* (Cambridge: Polity Press, 1992).

Posner, Michael, *Midland Murders* (Wolverhampton: Star Publications, 1973).

Pringle, Patrick, *Hue & Cry: The Birth of the British Police* (London: Museum Press, 1956).

Pringle, Patrick, *The Thief Takers* (London: Museum Press, 1958).

Procter, Richard Wright, *Memorials of Bygone Manchester* (Manchester: Palmer Howe, 1880).

Quinault, R. and J. Stevenson (eds), *Popular Protest and Public Order: Six Studies in British History 1790–1920* (London: Allen & Unwin, 1974).

Radford, Peter, *The Celebrated Captain Barclay: Sport, Money and Fame in Regency Britain* (London: Headline, 2001).

Radzinowicz, L., *A History of English Criminal Law and Its Administration from 1750*, vol. 2 (London: Stevens & Sons, 1956).

Radzinowicz, L., *A History of English Criminal Law and Its Administration from 1750*, vol. 3 (London: Stevens & Sons, 1956).

Rawlings, Philip, *Crime and Power: A History of Criminal Justice* (London: Longman, 1999).

Rawlings, Philip, *Policing: A Short History* (Cullompton: Willan, 2002).

Reed, Mick and Roger Wells (eds), *Class, Conflict and Protest in the English Countryside* (London: Frank Cass, 1990).

Reilly, John W., *Policing Birmingham: An Account of 150 Years of Police in Birmingham* (Birmingham: West Midlands Police, 1990).

Reiner, Robert, *The Politics of the Police*, 3rd edn (Oxford: OUP, 2000).

Reith, Charles, *British Police and the Democratic Ideal* (Oxford: OUP, 1943).

Reith, Charles, *A Short History of the British Police* (Oxford: OUP, 1948).

Reith, Charles, *A New Study of Police History* (Edinburgh and London: Oliver & Boyd, 1956).

Reynolds, Elaine A., *Before the Bobbies: The Night Watch and Police Reform in Metropolitan London: 1720–1830* (Basingstoke: Macmillan, 1998).

Richardson, Ruth, *Death, Dissection and the Destitute* (London: Routledge & Kegan Paul, 1987).

Roberts, Richard and David Kynaston (eds), *The Bank of England: Money, Power and Influence 1694–1994* (Oxford: Clarendon Press, 1995).

Rudé, George, *Criminal and Victim: Crime and Society in Early Nineteenth-Century England* (Oxford: Clarendon Press, 1985).

Rudé, George, *The Crowd in History: A Study of Popular Disturbances in France and England 1730–1848* (London: Serif, 1995).

Rule, J., *Albion's People: English Society, 1714–1815* (London: Macmillan, 1992).

Rule, John and Roger Wells, *Crime, Protest and Popular Politics in Southern England 1740–1850* (London: Hambledon Press, 1997).

Rumbelow, Donald, *I Spy Blue: The Police and Crime in the City of London from Elizabeth I to Victoria* (London and Basingstoke: Macmillan/St. Martin's Press, 1971).

Sainty, J. C., *Office Holders in Modern Britain Volume V: Home Office Officials 1782–1870* (London: University of London Institute of Historical Research/Athlone Press, 1975).

Scott, Harold (ed.), *The Concise Encyclopedia of Crime and Criminals* (London: André Deutsch, 1961).

Scraton, Phil, *The State of the Police* (London: Pluto Press, 1985).

Senior, Hereward, *Constabulary: The Rise of Police Institutions in Britain, the Commonwealth and the United States* (Toronto: Dundurn Press, 1997).

Shakesheff, Timothy, *Rural Conflict, Crime and Protest: Herefordshire, 1800 to 1860* (Woodbridge: Boydell Press, 2003).

Sharpe, J. A., *Crime in Early Modern England 1550–1750* (London: Longman, 1984).

Sharpe, J. A., *Crime and the Law in English Satirical Prints* (Cambridge: Chadwyck-Healey, 1986).

Shaw, A. G. L., *Convicts and Colonies: A Study of Penal Transportation from Great Britain and Ireland to Australia and Other Parts of the British Empire*, 2nd edn (London: Faber, 1971).

Shearing, Clifford D. and Philip C. Stenning (eds), *Private Policing* (London: Sage, 1987).

Sheppard, Francis, *London 1808–1870: The Infernal Wen* (London: Secker & Warburg, 1971).

Shoemaker, Robert, *The London Mob: Violence and Disorder in Eighteenth-Century England* (London: Hambledon & London, 2004).

Shore, Heather, *Artful Dodgers: Youth and Crime in Early Nineteenth-Century London* (London: Royal Historical Society/Boydell Press, 1999).

Shpayer-Makov, Haia, *The Making of a Policeman: A Social History of a Labour Force in Metropolitan London, 1829–1914* (Aldershot: Ashgate, 2002).

Skyrme, Thomas, *History of the Justices of the Peace*, 2nd edn (Chichester: Barry Rose, 1994).

Slugg, Joseph Thomas, *Reminiscences of Manchester Fifty Years Ago* (Shannon: IUP, 1971 [reprint of 1881 original]).

Smith, Phillip Thurmond, *Political Policing, Public Order and the London Metropolitan Police* (Westport, CT: Greenwood Press, 1985).

Solmes, Alwyn, *The English Policeman 871–1935* (London: Allen & Unwin, 1935).

Spragg, Gillian, *Outlaws and Highwaymen: The Cult of the Robber in England from the Middle Ages to the Nineteenth Century* (London: Pimlico, 2001).

Stallion, Martin and David S. Wall, *The British Police: Police Forces and Chief Officers 1829–2000* (Bramshill: Police History Society, 1999).

Standley, A. J., *Stafford Gaol: The Chronological Story* (no publication details).

Stapleton, Barry (ed.), *Conflict and Community in Southern England* (Stroud: Alan Sutton, 1992).

Stead, Philip John (ed.), *Pioneers in Policing* (Maidenhead: Paterson Smith/McGraw Hill, 1977).

Stead, Philip John, *The Police of Britain* (London: Macmillan, 1985).

Steer, David, *Uncovering Crime – The Police Role*, Royal Commission on Criminal Procedure Research Study No. 7 (London: HMSO, 1980).

Stephen, J. F., *A History of the Criminal Law of England*, 3 vols (London: Macmillan, 1883).

Stevenson, John, *Popular Disturbances in England 1700–1832*, 2nd edn (London: Longman, 1992).

Summerville, Christopher (ed.), *Regency Recollections: Captain Gronow's Guide to Life in London and Paris* (Welwyn Garden City: Ravenhall, 2006).

Thirlby, Malcolm, *Life and Death in Prison: With Particular Reference to the Gaol at Stafford from 1777–1877* (Dudley: Dudley Teachers' Centre, 1979).

Thomis, Malcolm I. and Peter Holt, *Threats of Revolution in Britain 1789–1848* (London: Macmillan, 1977).

Thompson, E. P., *Customs in Conflict* (London: Merlin Press, 1991).

Thompson, E. P., *The Making of the English Working Class* (London: Penguin, 1991).

Thompson, F. M. L., *Social Agencies and Institutions*, Vol. 3, *The Cambridge Social History of Britain 1750–1950* (Cambridge: CUP, 1996).

Tilly, Charles (ed.), *The Formation of National States in Western Europe* (Princeton, NJ: Princeton University Press, 1975).

Tobias, J. J., *Crime and Industrial Society in the 19th Century* (London: Batsford, 1967).

Tobias, J. J., *Nineteenth-Century Crime: Prevention and Punishment* (Newton Abbot: David & Charles, 1972).

Tobias, J. J., *Prince of Fences: The Life and Crimes of Ikey Solomons* (London: Valentine Mitchell, 1974).

Tobias, J. J., *Crime and Police in England 1700–1900* (Dublin: Gill & Macmillan, 1979).

Torrington, F. William (ed.), *House of Lords Sessional Papers – Sessions 1770–81* (New York: Oceana Publications, 1976).

Trench, Charles Chenevix, *The Poacher and the Squire: A History of Poaching and Game Preservation in England* (London: Longmans, 1967).

Turner, Michael J., *The Age of Unease: Government and Reform in Britain, 1782–1832* (Thrupp: Sutton, 2000).

Van Thal, Herbert (ed.), *The Prime Ministers* (London: Allen & Unwin, 1974).
Viner, Christine, *Police in Britain: A Short History* (Ripon: Ripon Museum Trust, 1984).
Vogler, Richard, *Reading the Riot Act: The Magistracy, the Police and the Army in Civil Disorder* (Milton Keynes: Open University Press, 1991).

Wagner, E. J., *The Science of Sherlock Holmes: From Baskerville Hall to the Valley of Fear, the Real Forensics Behind the Great Detective's Greatest Cases* (Hoboken, NJ: Wiley, 2007).
Wall, David S., *The Chief Constables of England and Wales: The Socio-legal History of a Criminal Justice Elite* (Aldershot: Ashgate, 1998).
Ward, John, *'Blood Money': An Incident in Wolverhampton with National Consequences* (Wolverhampton: Wolverhampton MBC, 1988).
Watkins, Tracey J., *Newsplan: Report on the Newsplan Project in the West Midlands Sep. 1988 – Sep. 1989* (London: British Library, 1990).
Waugh, Mary, *Smuggling in Kent and Sussex 1700–1840* (Newbury: Countryside Books, 1985).
Webb, Sidney and Beatrice Webb, *English Local Government Vol. 1: The Parish and the County* (London: Frank Cass, 1963).
Weiss, Robert P. (ed.), *Social History of Crime, Policing and Punishment* (Aldershot: Ashgate, 1999).
Wells, Roger A. E., *Riot and Political Disaffection in Nottinghamshire in the Age of Revolutions, 1776–1803* (Nottingham: University of Nottingham, 1983).
Wells, Roger, *Insurrection: The British Experience 1795–1803* (Gloucester: Alan Sutton, 1983).
Wheeler-Holohan, V., *The History of the King's Messengers* (London: E. P. Dutton, 1935).
White, Peter (ed.), *Crime Scene to Court – The Essentials of Forensic Science* (Cambridge: Royal Society of Chemistry, 1998).
Wiener, Martin, *Men of Blood: Violence, Manliness and Criminal Justice in Victorian England* (Cambridge: CUP, 2004).
Willcocks, R. M., *England's Postal History to 1840* (Willcocks, 1975).
Williams, David Ricardo, *Call in Pinkerton's: American Detectives at Work for Canada* (Toronto: Dundurn Press, 1998).
Williams, Gwyn A., *The Merthyr Rising*, 2nd edn (Cardiff: Croom Helm, 1988).
Willis-Bund, J. W., (ed.), *Victoria County History of Worcestershire* vol. IV (London: St Catherine Press, 1924).
Wilsher, Peter, *The Pound in Your Pocket 1870–1970* (London: Cassell, 1970).
Wilson, Ben, *Decency and Disorder: The Age of Cant 1789–1837* (London: Faber & Faber, 2007).

Wilson, David and others, *What Everyone in Britain Should Know About the Police* (London: Blackstone Press, 2001).

Wise, Sarah, *The Italian Boy: Murder and Grave-Robbery in 1830s London* (London: Jonathan Cape, 2004).

Wright, Alan, *Policing: An Introduction to Concepts and Practice* (Cullompton: Willan, 2002).

Wright, Brian, *Insurance Fire Brigades 1680–1929: The Birth of the British Fire Service* (Stroud: Tempus, 2008).

Wyatt, Irene (ed.), *Calendar of Summary Convictions at Petty Sessions 1781– 1837*, Gloucestershire Record Series Vol. 22 (Gloucester: Bristol and Gloucestershire Archaeological Society, 2008).

Articles

Anderson, Jack, 'Pugilistic Prosecutions: Prize Fighting and the Courts in Nineteenth-Century Britain', published November 2001 on the Internet at: http://www2.umist.ac.uk/sport/SPORTS%20HISTORY/BSSH/ The%20Sports%20Historian/TSH%2021-2/Art3-Anderson.htm.

Beattie, John, 'Sir John Fielding and Public Justice: The Bow Street Magistrates' Court, 1754–1780', *Law and History Review*, vol. 25, no. 1 (Spring 2007), pp. 61–100.

Bertelsen, Lance, 'Committed by Justice Fielding: Judicial and Journalistic Representation in the Bow Street Magistrates Office, January 3–November 24, 1752', *Eighteenth Century Studies*, vol. 30 (1996–97).

Boyle, Kevin, 'Police in Ireland before the Union – Part I', *Irish Jurist*, VII (new series) (1972), pp. 115–37.

Boyle, Kevin, 'Police in Ireland before the Union – Part II', *Irish Jurist*, VIII (new series) (1973), pp. 90–116.

Boyle, Kevin, 'Police in Ireland before the Union – Part III', *Irish Jurist*, VIII (new series) (1973), pp. 323–48.

Brogden, Michael, 'The Emergence of the Police: The Colonial Dimension', *British Journal of Criminology*, vol. 27, no. 1 (1987), pp. 4–14.

Carson, W. G., 'Policing the Periphery: The Development of Scottish Policing 1795–1900 Part 1', *Australian and New Zealand Journal of Criminology*, vol. 17 (1984), pp. 207–32.

Carson, W. G., 'Policing the Periphery: The Development of Scottish Policing 1795–1900 Part 2', *Australian and New Zealand Journal of Criminology*, vol. 18 (1985), pp. 3–16.

Cowie, Leonard W., 'The Bow Street "Runners"', *British Heritage*, vol. 1, no. 4 (June/July 1980), pp. 46–57.

Cox, David J., 'Bow Street Runners in the Black Country: The Arrest, Trial and Execution of "Lord Howe"', *The Blackcountryman*, vol. 33, no. 1 (Winter 1999/2000), pp. 27–31.

Cox, David J., 'Damn her, if her won't go, chain her to the post – The Strange Case of Eliza Price', *Journal of the Police History Society*, no. 17 (2002), pp. 9–12.

Cox, David J., 'The Tipton Slasher and the American Giant', *The Blackcountryman*, vol. 36, no. 2 (Spring 2003), pp. 9–12.

Cox, David J., 'Civil Unrest in the Black Country 1766–1816', *Family and Local History Year Book*, 9th edn (Nether Poppleton: Robert Blatchford Publishing, 2005), pp. 30–3.

Dart, Gregory, 'Pierce Egan and Literary London, 1820–28', *History Workshop Journal*, vol. 51 (Spring 2001), pp. 181–205.

DeMotte, Charles, 'Policing Manchester in the Nineteenth Century', *Police Studies*, vol. 7, no. 3 (Fall 1984), pp. 155–74.

Dinsmor, Alastair, 'Glasgow Police Pioneers', *Journal of the Police History Society*, vol. 15 (2000), pp. 9–11.

Douglas Hay, 'Crime and Justice in Eighteenth and Nineteenth Century England', *Crime and Justice: An Annual Review of Research*, vol. 2 (1980), pp. 45–84.

Dunne, Laurence, 'Bow Street and the Police', *Police College Magazine*, vol. 2, no. 3 (September 1952), pp. 192–6.

Emsley, Clive, 'The Home Office and Its Sources of Information and Investigation 1791–1801', *English Historical Review*, XCIV (July 1979), pp. 532–61.

Emsley, Clive, 'An Aspect of Pitt's "Terror": Prosecutions for Sedition During the 1790s', *Social History*, vol. 6, no. 2 (May 1981), pp. 155–84.

Emsley, Clive, '"The Thump of Wood on a Swede Turnip?" Police Violence in Nineteenth-Century England', *Criminal Justice History*, vol. 6 (1985): pp. 125–50.

Emsley, Clive, 'Detection and Prevention: The Old English Police and the New (1750–1900)', *Historical Social Research*, vol. 37 (January 1986), pp. 69–88.

Emsley, Clive, 'A Typology of Nineteenth-Century Police', *Crime, Histoire et Sociétés*, vol. 3, no. 1 (1999), pp. 29–44.

Emsley, Clive, 'The Policeman as Worker: A Comparative Survey, c.1800–1940', *International Review of Social History*, vol. 45, part 1 (April 2000), pp. 89–110.

England, R. W., 'Investigating Homicides in Northern England, 1800–1824', *Criminal Justice History*, vol. 6 (1985), pp. 105–24.

Feather, Fred, 'The Slaying of Parish Constable Trigg', *Essex Police History Note Book No. 2* (undated).

Fonteyn, Chris, 'A History of Banking in Stourbridge', *The Blackcountryman*, vol. 29, no. 1 (Winter 1995/96), pp. 42–6.

Friedman, David, 'Making Sense of English Law Enforcement in the Eighteenth Century', *University of Chicago Law School Roundtable*, vol. 2, no. 2 (Spring/Summer 1995), pp. 475–505.

Gordon, Colin, 'Prison Talk: An Interview with Michel Foucault', *Radical Philosophy*, vol. 16 (Spring 1977), pp. 10–15.

Gray, Drew D., 'The Regulation of Violence in the Metropolis: The Prosecution of Assault in the Summary Courts, c.1780–1820', *London Journal*, vol. 32, no. 1 (March 2007), pp. 75–87.

Haem, Mark, 'La Repression du Banditisme en Grande-Bretagne aux XVIIème et XVIIIème siècles', *Revue Du Nord*, vol. 59, no. 234 (1977), pp. 365–75.

Hale, Donna C., 'Out of the Past … a New Police: Applied History and Police History', *Police Studies*, vol. 8, no. 4 (Winter 1985), pp. 214–19.

Hamby, James E., 'The History of Firearm and Toolmark Identification', *Association of Firearm and Tool Mark Examiners Journal*, vol. 31, no. 3 (Summer 1999) (reproduced on the Internet at http://www.firearmsid.com/A_historyoffirearmsID.htm).

Hart, Jennifer, 'Reform of the Borough Police 1835–1856', *EHR*, vol. 70 (1955), pp. 411–22.

Hastings, R. P., 'Private Law-Enforcement Associations', *Local Historian*, vol. 14, no. 4 (November 1980), pp. 226–31.

Hay, Douglas, 'War, Death and Theft in the Eighteenth Century: The Record of the English Courts', *Past and Present*, vol. 95 (1982), pp. 117–60.

Hay, Douglas, 'Manufacturers and the Criminal Law in the Later Eighteenth Century: Crime and "Police" in South Staffordshire', *Past and Present Colloquium: Police and Policing* (1983), unpaginated.

Henry, Brian, 'The First Modern Police in the British Isles', *Police Studies*, vol. 165, no. 4 (Winter 1993), pp. 167–79.

Hunt, Joseph, 'Bombelles in Britain: Extracts from the Diary Kept by a French Diplomat, the Marquis de Bombelles, During a Visit to the Midlands, 4 August–10 September 1784', *The Blackcountryman*, vol. 34, no. 4 (Autumn 2001), pp. 45–51.

Ignatieff, Michael, 'Police and People: The Birth of Mr Peel's "Blue Locusts"', *New Society*, no. 30 (August 1979), pp. 443–5.

Innes, J., 'Parliament and the Shaping of Eighteenth Century English Social Policy', *Transactions of the Royal Society*, 5th series XL (1990), pp. 63–92.

Innes, J. and J. Styles, 'The Crime Wave: Recent Writing on Crime and Criminal Justice in Eighteenth-Century England', *Journal of British Studies*, vol. 25 (1986), pp. 380–435.

Ireland, Richard, '"A Second Ireland"? Crime and Popular Culture in Nineteenth-Century Wales', in Richard McMahon (ed.), *Crime, Law and Popular Culture in Europe, 1500–1900* (Cullompton: Willan, 2008), pp. 239–61.

Jerrard, Brian, 'Early Policing Methods in Gloucestershire', *Transactions of the Bristol and Gloucestershire Archaeological Society for 1992*, vol. C (1993), pp. 221–40.

Johnson, D. A., 'Joshua Drewry and the First Staffordshire Newspapers', *Collections for a History of Staffordshire*, VI, Fourth Series (1970), pp. 186–208.

Jones, David J. V., 'The Poacher: A Study in Victorian Crime and Punishment', *Historical Journal*, Vol. XXII (1974), pp. 825–60.

Jones, David J. V., 'Life and Death in Eighteenth-Century Wales: A Note', *Welsh History Review* (1981), pp. 536–48.

Kelly, Martin A., 'Western Civilization's First Detectives', *Police Studies*, vol. 10, no. 1 (Spring 1987), pp. 36–41.

King, Peter, 'Decision Makers and Decision Making in the English Criminal Law 1750–1800', *Historical Journal*, Vol. XXVII (1984), pp. 25–58.

King, Peter, 'Newspaper Reporting, Prosecution Practice and Perceptions of Urban Crime: The Colchester Crime Wave of 1765', *Continuity and Change*, vol. 2, no. 3 (1987), pp. 423–54.

King, Peter, 'Locating Histories of Crime: A Bibliographic Study', *British Journal of Criminology*, vol. 39, no. 1 (January 1999), pp. 161–74.

King, Peter, 'Newspaper Reporting and Attitudes to Crime and Justice in Late-Eighteenth- and Early-Nineteenth-Century London', *Continuity and Change*, vol. 22, no. 1 (2007), pp. 73–112.

Kirchengast, Tyrone, *Victim Agency and the Development of Policing Power*, Social Science Research Network Macquarie Law Working Paper No. 2008-15 (April 2008).

Langbein, John, 'Criminal Trials before the Lawyers', *University of Chicago Law Review*, vol. 45, no. 2 (Winter 1978), pp. 263–316.

Langbein, John, '*Albion's* Fatal Flaws', *Past and Present*, vol. 98 (1983), pp. 96–120.

Langbein, John, 'Shaping the Eighteenth-Century Criminal Trial: A View from the Ryder Sources', *University of Chicago Law Review*, vol. 50, no. 1 (Winter 1983), pp. 1–136.

Lea, John, 'Social Crime Revisited', *Theoretical Criminology*, vol. 3, no. 3 (August 1999), pp. 307–25.

Little, Craig B. and Christopher P. Sheffield, 'Frontiers of Criminal Justice: English Private Prosecution Societies and American Vigilantism in the Eighteenth and Nineteenth Centuries', *American Sociological Review*, vol. 48 (February 1983), pp. 796–808.

Lyman, J. L., 'The Metropolitan Police Act of 1829: An Analysis of Certain Events Influencing the Passage and Character of the Metropolitan Police Act in England', *Journal of Criminal Law, Criminology and Police Science*, vol. 55 (1964), pp. 141–54.

McGowen, Randall, 'Revisiting The Hanging Tree: Gatrell on Emotion and History', *British Journal of Criminology*, vol. 40, no. 1 (January 2000), pp. 1–13.

McGowen, Randall, 'The Bank of England and the Policing of Forgery 1797–1821', *Past and Present*, no. 186 (2005), pp. 81–116.

McGowen, Randall, 'Managing the Gallows: The Bank of England and the Death Penalty, 1797–1821', *Law and History Review*, vol. 25, no. 2 (Summer 2007), pp. 241–82.

MacKay, Peter, 'The Foundation of a Professional Police Force was Historically Inevitable', *Police Studies*, vol. 10, no. 2 (Summer 1987), pp. 85–9.

MacKay, Peter, 'Class Relationships, Social Order and the Law in Eighteenth-Century England', *Police Studies*, vol. 11, no. 2 (Summer 1988), pp. 92–7.

McMullan, John L., 'The Political Economy of Thief-taking', *Crime, Law and Social Change*, vol. 23, no. 2 (June 1995), pp. 121–46.

McMullan, John L., 'The New Improved Monied Police: Reform, Crime Control, and the Commodification of Policing in London', *British Journal of Criminology*, vol. 36, no. 1 (Winter 1996), pp. 85–108.

Mander, G. P., 'The Wolverhampton "Association"', *Wolverhampton Antiquary*, vol. 2, no. 1 (July 1934), pp. 60–3.

Mander, G. P., 'The Wolverhampton Pitt Club', *Wolverhampton Antiquary*, vol. 2, no. 1 (July 1934), pp. 10–25.

Mander, G. P., 'Constables', *Wolverhampton Antiquary*, vol. 2, no. 2 (June 1937), pp. 71–9.

Morgan, Gwenda and Peter Rushton, 'The Magistrate, the Community and the Maintenance of an Orderly Society in Eighteenth-Century England', *Historical Research*, vol. 76, no. 191 (February 2003), pp. 54–77.

Morris, Robert, M., '"Lies, Damned Lies and Criminal Statistics": Reinterpreting the Criminal Statistics in England and Wales', *Crime, Histoire & Sociétés*, vol. 5, no. 1 (2001), pp. 111–27.

Munsche, P. B., 'The Gamekeeper and English Rural Society', *Journal of British Studies*, vol. XX, no. 2 (Spring 1981), pp. 82–105.

Neocleous, Mark, *Policing and Pin-Making: Adam Smith and the State of Prosperity*, Brunel University Department of Government Paper No. 5/97 (August 1997), pp. 1–24.

Notes and Queries: A Medium of Intercommunication for Literary Men, General Readers, etc., Sixth Series, vol. 5 (London: J. Francis, 1882).

Notes and Queries: A Medium of Intercommunication for Literary Men, General Readers, etc., Seventh Series, vol. 3 (London: J. Francis, 1887).

Notes and Queries: A Medium of Intercommunication for Literary Men, General Readers, etc., Seventh Series, vol. 4 (London: J. Francis, 1888).

Paley, Ruth, '"An Imperfect, Inadequate and Wretched System"? Policing London Before Peel', *Criminal Justice History*, vol. X (1989), pp. 95–130.

Pearsall, Ronald, 'The First Metropolitan Detectives: The Beginnings of the Bow Street "Runners" and Their Place in the History of the British Police', *Police Review*, no. 4208 (7 September 1973), pp. 1238–40.

Philips, David, 'The Black Country Magistracy, 1835–1860: A Changing Elite and the Exercise of Its Power', *Midland History*, vol. III, no. 3 (Spring 1976), pp. 161–90.

Philips, David and Robert D. Storch, 'Whigs and Coppers: The Grey Ministry's National Police Scheme, 1832', *Historical Research*, vol. LXVII (1994), pp. 75–90.

Pike, Alan R., 'A Brief History of the C.I.D. of the London Metropolitan Police', *Police Studies*, vol. 1, no. 2 (June 1978), pp. 22–30.

Porter, J. H., *Common Crime, Law and Policing in the English Countryside 1600–1800*, Brookfield Papers No. 2 (Exeter: University of Exeter, 1989).

Reddaway, T. F., 'The Origins of the Metropolitan Police', *The Nineteenth Century and After*, vol. CXLVII, no. 876 (January–June 1950), pp. 104–18.

Roberts, Randy, 'Eighteenth-Century Boxing', *Journal of Sport History*, vol. 4, no. 3 (Fall 1977), pp. 246–59.

Robinson, Cyril D., 'Ideology as History: A Look at the Way Some English Police Historians Look at the Police', *Police Studies*, vol. 2, no. 2 (Summer 1979), pp. 35–49.

Rumbelow, Donald A., 'Raw Lobsters, Blue Devils', *British Heritage*, vol. 1, no. 3 (April/May 1980), pp. 10–19.

Schwartz, Richard D. and James C. Miller, 'Legal Evolution and Societal Complexity', *American Journal of Sociology*, vol. LXX, no. 1 (July 1964), pp. 159–69.

Sharpe, J. A., 'Policing the Parish in Early Modern England', *Past and Present Colloquium: Police and Policing* (1983), unpaginated.

Shoemaker, Robert B., 'The "Crime Wave" Revisited: Crime, Law Enforcement and Punishment in Britain, 1650–1900', *Historical Journal*, vol. 34, no. 3 (September 1991), pp. 763–8.

Shoemaker, Robert B., 'The Taming of the Duel: Masculinity, Honour and Ritual Violence in London, 1660–1800', *Historical Journal*, vol. 45, no. 3 (September 2002), pp. 525–45.

Shoemaker, Robert B., 'The Decline of Male Honour and Public Violence in Eighteenth-Century London', *Social History*, vol. 26, no. 2 (May 2001), pp. 190–208.

Smith, Bruce P., 'English Criminal Justice Administration, 1650–1850: A Historiographic Essay', *Law and History Review*, vol. 25, no. 1 (Fall 2007), pp. 593–634.

Smith, Simon, 'The Irish Revenue Police', *Journal of the Police History Society*, no. 18 (2003), pp. 24–6.

Storch, Robert D., 'The Plague of Blue Locusts. Police Reform and Popular Resistance in Northern England, 1848–57', *International Review of Social History*, vol. XX (1975), pp. 61–90.

Storch, Robert D., 'Policing Rural Southern England Before the Police: Opinion and Practice 1830–1856', in D. Hay and F. Snyder (eds), *Policy and Prosecution in Britain, 1750–1850* (Oxford: OUP, 1989), pp. 211–66.

Styles, John, 'An Eighteenth-Century Magistrate as Detective: Samuel Lister of Little Horton', *Bradford Antiquary*, New Series, Part XLVII (October 1982), pp. 98–117.

Styles, John, 'Sir John Fielding and the Problem of Criminal Investigation in Eighteenth-Century England', *Transactions of the Royal Historical Society*, vol. 33, Fifth Series (1983), pp. 127–49.

Styles, John, 'The Emergence of the Police: Explaining Police Reform in Eighteenth- and Nineteenth-Century England', *British Journal of Criminology*, vol. 27, no. 1 (1987), pp. 15–22.

Sutton, James, 'The Staffordshire Society for the Apprehension of Felons', *Staffordshire Studies*, vol. 14 (2002), pp. 32–52.

Swift, Roger E., 'The English Urban Magistracy and the Administration of Justice During the Early Nineteenth Century: Wolverhampton, 1815–60', *Midland History*, Vol. XVII (1992), pp. 75–93.

Taylor, Howard, 'Rationing Crime: The Political Economy of Criminal Statistics since the 1850s', *Economic History Review*, vol. 51, no. 3 (1998), pp. 569–90.

Waters, Les, 'Paper Pursuit: A Brief Account of the History of the Police Gazette', *Journal of the Police History Society*, no. 1 (1986), pp. 30–41.

Williams, Chris, 'Counting Crimes or Counting People: Some Implications of Mid-Nineteenth Century British Police Returns', *Crime, Histoire & Sociétés*, vol. 4, no. 2 (2000), pp. 77–93.

Williams, J. Robert, 'The 1831 Riots in the Black Country – Part One', *The Blackcountryman*, vol. 7, no. 3 (Summer 1974), pp. 17–25.

Williams, J. Robert, 'The 1831 Riots in the Black Country – Part Two', *The Blackcountryman*, vol. 7, no. 4 (Autumn 1974), pp. 23–30.

Williams, J. Robert, 'The 1831 Riots in the Black Country – Part Three, *The Blackcountryman*, vol. 8, no. 1 (Winter 1975), pp. 40–6.

Zangerl, Carl H. E., 'The Social Composition of the County Magistracy in England and Wales, 1831–1887', *Journal of British Studies*, vol. XI (November 1971), pp. 113–25.

Other material

Anon., *Miscellaneous Documents on Law (including pre-Met), Punishment etc. (by various unknown authors* (London: Metropolitan Police Museum, undated).

Anon., *The Judge's Lodgings: Guide and Notes for Visitors* (Presteigne: Presteigne Shire Hall Museum, undated).

Beattie, J. M., 'Early Detection: The Bow Street Runners in Late Eighteenth-Century London' (unpublished essay).

Cockton, Peter, *Subject Catalogue of the House of Commons Parliamentary Papers 1801–1900*, 5 vols (Cambridge: Chadwyck-Healey, 1988).

Finnane, Mark, OU MA in Humanities Course, Unit A822, Block 3, 'Perceptions of the Offender'.

Palmers Index to The Times *Newspaper (London)*, 1792–1839 (Vaduz: Kraus Reprints, 1965).

Parker, Keith, *A 'Provincial Tragedy': The Story of Mary Morgan* (Presteigne: Shire Hall Museum, undated).

The Police and Constabulary List 1844, Police History Society Monograph No. 3 (1991).

Waters, Les, 'The Bow Street Runners: A Hand book of Police in London Working for Bow Street and the other Middlesex Justices Act Offices 1750–1839' (Huntingdon: unpublished work for Police History Society, undated c.1992).

Wheeler's Scrap Book No. 1 (Brierley Hill Library, West Midlands, undated).

Conference and seminar papers

Beattie, John, *English Detectives in the Late Eighteenth Century*, paper presented at the European Social Science History Conference, The Hague, March 2002.

Beattie, John, *John Fielding and the Bow Street Magistrates' Court*, paper presented at the European Centre for Policing Studies, Open University, Milton Keynes, March 2005.

Behre, Rainer, *Shipwrecks and the Body: 18th and 19th Century Encounters with Death and Survival at Sea*, paper presented at the Controlling Bodies – The Regulation of Conduct 1650–2000 Conference, University of Glamorgan, July 2002.

Cox, David J., *Copper-Bottomed Cases for Coppers to Get to the Bottom of – The Plundering of the* Adamant *and the* Earl of Wemyss, paper presented at the *Public Speaker Series*, Keele University, March 2007.

Dinsmor, Alastair, *Glasgow Police: The First Fifty Years*, paper presented at the Police History Society Conference, Ripon, September 2001.

Gray, Drew, 'A Well-Constructed and Efficient System of Police'? Constables, Substitutes and the Watching Systems in the City of London c.1750–1839, paper presented at the European Centre for Policing Studies, Open University, July 2002.

McGowen, Randall, *The Bank of England and the Policing of Forgery, 1797– 1821*, paper presented at the European Centre for Policing Studies, Open University, Milton Keynes, November 2003.

Snell, Esther, *Representations of Crime in the Eighteenth-Century Newspaper: The Construction of Crime Reportage in the Kentish Post*, paper presented at the European Centre for Policing Studies, Open University, Milton Keynes, March 2005.

Tennant, Maryse, *An Honourable Failure? A Reassessment of the Police of the First Cheshire Constabulary Force within the Wider Context of 19th Century Police Reform*, paper presented at the European Centre for Policing Studies, Open University, Milton Keynes, October 2008.

Theses and dissertations

Clements, Fewtrell, 'The Development and Aims of the Denbighshire Constabulary in the Nineteenth Century' (unpublished PhD thesis, Open University, 2004).

Eason-Swift, Roger, 'Crime, Law and Order During the Early Nineteenth Century: Exeter and Wolverhampton 1815–58' (unpublished PhD thesis, University of Birmingham, 1981).

Gray, Drew D., 'Summary Proceedings and Social Relations in the City of London, *c*.1750–1820' (unpublished PhD thesis, University of Northampton, 2007).

Harris, Andrew Todd, 'Policing the City, 1785–1838: Local Knowledge and Central Authority in the City of London (England)' (unpublished PhD thesis, Stanford University, 1997).

McGowan, John, 'The Emergence of Modern Civil Police in Scotland: A Case Study of the Police and Systems of Policing in Edinburghshire 1800–1833' (unpublished PhD thesis, Open University, 1996).
Macnab, Kenneth K., 'Aspects of the History of Crime in England and Wales 1805–60' (unpublished PhD thesis, Sussex University, 1965).

Paley, Ruth, 'The Middlesex Justices Act of 1792: Its Origins and Effects' (unpublished PhD thesis, Reading, 1983).

Reynolds, Elaine A., 'The Night Watch and Police Reform in Metropolitan London' (unpublished PhD thesis, Cornell University, 1991).

Sopenoff, R. C., 'The Police of London: The Early History of the Metropolitan Police 1829–1856' (unpublished PhD thesis, Temple University, 1978).

Index

Acts of Parliament:
1693 4 & 5 William and Mary c.8 (Highwaymen Act) 68
1751 25 Geo II c.37 (Murder Act 1752) 178
1752 25 Geo II c.36 68
1753 26 Geo II c.19 (Stealing Shipwrecked Goods Act) 188–9
1791 32 Geo III c.53 Middlesex Justices' Act (Police Act) 31–2, 66
1801 39 and 40 Geo III c.67 (Acts of Union) 5
1802 42 Geo III c.76 34
1803 43 Geo.3 c.58 (Ellenborough's Act) 193
1814 54 Geo III c.37 34
1821 2 Geo IV c.118 34
1825 6 Geo IV c.21 34
1826 7 Geo IV c.64 (Criminal Law Act) 183
1829 10 Geo IV c.44 (Metropolitan Police Act) 122, 218–19
1835 5 & 6 William IV c.76 (Municipal Corporations Act) 72, 138, 220–1
1839 2 &3 Vict. c.93 (Rural Constabulary Act) 138, 221
1839 2 Vict c.47 (Metropolitan Police Act) 224
1839 2 Vict c.71 (Metropolitan Police Courts Act) 224–5
1856 19 & 20 Vict c.69 (County and Borough Police Act) 138, 221

Addington, Sir William (Bow Street Chief Magistrate) 28, 83
Adkins, Harry (Bow Street Principal Officer) 37, 44, 49, 67, 106, 169–70, 172, 175, 177–83
Adkins, Joseph 171
Adkins, William (Bow Street Principal Officer 44, 49
Aldington, Sussex 90–1
Alfreston, Derbyshire 139
Alison, Sir Archibald 103
Allen, John 193
Allen, L. B. 71
Angelo, Henry 171
Annual Register, The 150, 193
Anthony, William (Bow Street Principal Officer) 43, 129
Antwerp 198
Archer, John 109
Armitage, Gilbert 15

Halls, Thomas 51, 173
Hanslope, Northamptonshire 201
Hart, Jennifer 72
Harvey, Lady 172
Hatton Garden Police Office 27
Haverfordwest 155
Hawkesbury, Lord (later 2nd Earl of
    Liverpool) 45
Hay, Douglas 72
Hellard, Lieutenant Samuel 90
Hereford 83
Heysham Hall, Lancashire 86–7
Higham Ferrers, Northamptonshire
    111
Hind, Thomas 107
Hobsbawm, Eric 189
Holyland, Francis 193
Home Department (Home Office)
    11, 27–8, 32, 35, 43, 45–6, 74–5,
    80, 82–3, 87–8, 90–3, 105–6, 109,
    114, 118, 121–2, 128–9, 149, 155–6,
    171, 182, 219–20, 229
Hone, Nathaniel 2
Horsham, Sussex 170
Howard, George 1
Howe, William 177–85
Huddersfield, Yorkshire 92, 106, 222
Hue & Cry (later The *Police Gazette*)
    10–15, 68, 175, 178–9, 186–7, 232
Hull, Yorkshire 220–1
Husband's Bosworth, Leicestershire
    78

Ingram, John 46
Ingram, William 192
Inwood, Stephen 48, 50
Ireland 5–6, 120

Jackson's Oxford Journal 33
James, George Payne Rainsford 41
Jealous, Charles 172
Jenkins, Philip 154
Jenner, Richard 168, 170
Jerrard, Bryan 77
Jonathan Wild 29

Jones, Constable Robert 121, 140–1
Jones, Constable, of Stourbridge 180
Jones, David J. V. 153–4, 155, 193

Kennedy, Christopher (Bow Street
    Principal Officer) 172
Kentish Post, The 8
Keys, Francis (Bow Street Principal
    Officer) 50, 107, 172, 203
Kidderminster, Worcestershire 180
King, Peter 77, 118, 158, 195
Kinver, Staffordshire 176, 180

Lambeth Street Police Office 31, 221
Langan, John 203
Lansdowne, Lord 46
Laurie, Sir Peter 117–18
Lavender, Edward 38
Lavender, John Nelson 38, 39
Lavender, Stephen (Bow Street
    Principal Officer) 36, 37, 38, 47,
    70, 71, 113, 119, 171, 181
Lawrence, Thomas 36
Lea, James 31, 221
Lea, John 189
Leadbitter, George (Bow Street
    Principal Officer) 42, 67, 201–3,
    205
Leeds Mercury, The 43
Leicester 89
Leipzig Bank 114
Leith, Edinburgh 91
Lines, Thomas 180
Lister, Samuel, JP 82
Little, Craig B. 142
Liverpool 149
Llandovery 155–6
Lloyd's of London 185–8
London:
    Aldywch 106
    Bethnal Green 204
    Bishopsgate 181
    Bridge Row, Pimlico 49
    Charing Cross 6
    Covent Garden 26, 111, 128